GALATIANS

Joseph A. Pipa, Jr

'Here is a clear, succinct, and powerful exposition of a key Pauline letter. Pipa writes *pastorally*, an apt reflection of Paul's own desire to inform and edify. He writes *learnedly*, aware of challenges to Paul's gospel from Federal Vision and New Perspective quarters. He writes *plainly*, laying bare and applying the apostolic insistence that Christ's work is finished: justification is through faith alone. Readers seeking a faithful Reformed exposition of Galatians will find stimulation to faith, devotion, and practical living on every page.'

Robert W. Yarbrough,
Professor of New Testament,
Covenant Theological Seminary, St. Louis, Missouri

'Martin Luther once called the Epistle to the Galatians "my Katie von Bora" – this letter was as dear to the Reformer as his own wife. In *Galatians: God's Proclamation of Liberty*, Joseph Pipa has given the church a clear, stirring, and accessible exposition of this beloved letter. Pipa's commentary is an admirable combination of expository care, theological clarity, and pastoral sensitivity. Any believer interested in learning more about Galatians needs to have this book on his shelf.'

Guy Prentiss Waters
Associate Professor of New Testament,
Reformed Theological Seminary, Jackson, Mississippi

GALATIANS

God's Proclamation of Liberty

Joseph A. Pipa, Jr

CHRISTIAN
FOCUS

Joseph A. Pipa Jr. is President and Professor of Historical and Systematic Theology at Greenville Presbyterian Theological Seminary, Greenville, South Carolina. He hold degrees from Belhaven College (B.A.), Reformed Theological Seminary (M. Div) and Westminster Theological Seminary (Ph. D) and has previously taught at Westminster Theological Seminary Philadelphia and Westminster Theological Seminary in California. His previous books include *The Lord's Day* (ISBN 978-1-85792-201-1) and the *The Westminster Confession of Faith Study Book* (ISBN 978-1-84550-030-6).

ISBN 978-1-84550-558-5

10 9 8 7 6 5 4 3 2 1

This edition published in 2010
by
Christian Focus Publications Ltd.,
Geanies House, Fearn, Ross-shire,
IV20 1TW, Scotland, UK.

www.christianfocus.com

Cover design by Alister MacInnes

Printed and bound by
Bell & Bain, Glasgow

FSC
Mixed Sources
Product group from well-managed forests and other controlled sources
www.fsc.org Cert no. TT-COC-002769
© 1996 Forest Stewardship Council

Contents

Dedication

I dedicate this book to my son, Joseph A. Pipa III, who by God's grace completed a B.S degree in business and was elected to the office of deacon.

Introduction

Throughout the history of the world, there have been great charters of freedom and liberty. Think of the *Magna Carta,* which was adopted in England in 1215, in which King John granted certain liberties to the English nobility, or the *Declaration of Independence,* in which the colonists declared liberty against the British in 1776 and formed the United States of America. The letter of Galatians is the Bible's great Magna Carta; it is God's Declaration of Liberty to every Christian man and woman. In Galatians, the Apostle Paul explains the glorious doctrine of justification (which I prefer to call 'free justification'), received by grace alone, based solely upon the grace of God. Galatians remains a very important book for the church to consider, because the issues connected to the letter are always with it in every age. We may divide the book into four sections: 1. Introduction with salutation and warning (1:1-9); 2. The defence of Paul's apostolic authority (1:10–2:21); 3. The explanation of justification by faith (3:1–5:1); and 4. Some practical exhortations that grow out of that and the relationship of justification to obedience in Christian living (5:1–6:18).

The Recipients

Paul addresses the letter to the churches of Galatia (1:2). There are two views concerning the recipients of this letter: the Northern Galatian Theory and the Southern Galatian Theory. The name Galatia was derived from the inhabitants of Northern Galatia; namely, the Celts that settled in the northern parts of the region. These Celts immigrated there in about 278 B.C. from Greece, Macedonia, and Thrace into what is now Northern Turkey. They were divided into three tribes:

Trochmis, Tectosages, and Tolisbogii. They established three cities: Tavium, Ancyra, and Pessinus. They were called Galli (Gauls, warriors) and Galatae (Galatians, nobility).

The Galatians established dominion over the Phrygians and were constantly making war with those who lived on their boundaries. Eventually, the Romans forced them to live within established borders. By 52 B.C. they were allied with Rome and were considered to be a kingdom. Their last king Amyntas extended the kingdom southward. When he died in 25 B.C., Rome took over and made the whole region a province, including parts of Phrygia, Lycaonia, Pisidia, and Isauria. The northern region which was known as Galatia gave its name to the entire province. By time of the New Testament the name Galatia had two-fold designation: the geographical region, Galatia proper; and the Roman province of Galatia.

If Paul was addressing those people living in the geographical region, he was writing to people living in the cities of Tavium, Ancyra, and Pessinus. If he was writing to people living in the province, he was writing to the churches he established in Acts 13 and 14. Internal evidence shows that he could not be addressing both groups. He speaks of details of his visit and makes allusion to his reception by them (4:12-16).

According to the Northern Galatian theory, on his second missionary journey Paul travelled from the southern area of the Galatian province (Acts 16:1-5) through the geographical region of Phrygia into the northern geographical region of Galatia (Acts 16:6). He would have established churches in the northern cities of Tavium, Ancyra, and Pessinus. This visit would have been his first trip to this area. In Acts 18:22, 23 Paul returned to this area on the beginning of his third missionary journey. What then are the arguments for the North Galatian theory? There are four in number.

First, Galatia is the proper name of the tribes that lived in the north. As Luke describes other geographical regions within the Galatian Province (Phrygia), it makes sense that when he refers to Galatia he is referring to the geographical region. Luke does not use the provincial name to describe the churches in Antioch of Pisidia, Derbe, and Lystra.

Second, Luke describes Paul's second missionary journey as passing through the Phrygian and the Galatian region

(Acts 16:6). Advocates of the northern theory interpret this to mean that when Paul left the southern area of the Galatian province (Derbe, Lystra, and Iconium) he went north through the region of Phrygia into the geographical region of Galatia before turning westward to Mysia. In Acts 18:23, Luke says that Paul left Antioch and passed successively through the Galatian region and Phrygia, strengthening all the disciples. Since Phrygia is a geographical area, Galatia must be as well.

Third, in Galatians 4:13, Paul refers to a physical infirmity he had while ministering to them. Luke gives no record of any physical infirmity in Acts 13 and 14. Therefore, Paul must be describing another group of churches.

Fourth, the tradition of the early church fathers was that the Galatian letter was written to the churches in the northern Galatian region.

The Southern Galatian theory maintains that Paul was writing to the churches he established in the Galatian province (Acts 13 and 14); namely, Antioch of Pisidia, Iconium, Lycaonia, Lystra, and Derbe. There are at least six arguments in favour of this theory.

The first argument is that Luke gives a lengthy detailed record of the establishment of these churches and Paul's second visit to them. He gives no record of any churches being established in northern Galatia. In fact, there is no record in Acts that Paul ever established churches in the northern province, though we figure that when he was in Ephesus the gospel surely spread into that territory. But it is clear from the evidence of Galatians itself that Paul had personally established the churches to whom he was writing.

Second, when Paul refers to churches in his letters, he uses provincial names (1 Cor. 16:5, 15; 2 Cor. 1:16). Note his use of Galatia in 1 Corinthians 16:1. It is true that in Galatians 1:22 he refers to the churches in Judea, which really was a part of the province of Syria. He does so to emphasize that he did not minister in the early Jewish churches. The other references though in this letter are to provinces: Syria and Cilicia (1:21) and Arabia (4:25).

Third, he mentions Barnabas three times, assuming they would have been familiar with him. Barnabas did not accompany Paul on his second and third missionary journeys; therefore, if Paul were writing to churches in the north, they would not have had any great familiarity with Barnabas.

Fourth, Paul assumes that there would be some in the congregation with knowledge of Judaism and of the Old Testament. We know that there were some Jewish Christians in the churches of south Galatia, but it is not likely that Jews were living in the northern geographical region.

Fifth, the provincial term Galatians was the only way to refer to cities in culturally diverse areas of the southern area of the Galatian province. They were from a diverse racial and linguistic background, and belonging to the Province of Galatia was the only cultural unifying factor.

Sixth, it would be remarkable that in a letter dealing with Gentiles and circumcision that Paul would have omitted reference to the decree of the Jerusalem council (Acts 15) if the council had already occurred. The council took place after Paul's first missionary journey and before his second missionary journey. The failure to refer to the decree in his letter would suggest that it was written before the council of Jerusalem had met.

Moreover, the answers to the arguments of the North Galatian theory are consistent with the South Galatian theory. When one looks at Acts 16:6, one sees that Paul would have had to go far to the northeast to visit the cities of Tavium, Ancyra, and Pessinus. His route, however, was to Mysia from where he attempted to go north into Bithynia. Thus the more logical way to understand Luke's description in Acts 16:6 is that Paul left Antioch of Pisidia, went north through Phrygia and the Galatian province, and turned west. Since Luke mentions Mysia, where Paul was not allowed by the Spirit to minister, it would be all the more remarkable that he would not mention Pessinus, the southwestern city of the geographical region, if Paul had ministered there. A similar explanation holds true for the third missionary journey. Since Paul is travelling to Ephesus, the reference to the Galatian region and Phrygia (in that order, Acts 8:23) makes most sense to be the churches in the south; south Galatia and Phrygia are on a direct route to Ephesus.

With respect to Paul's reference to physical infirmity, if he were ill, he would not likely have gone to the northern region.

It was a fairly destitute and harsh area. Moreover, Luke in Acts does not cover all of Paul's physical difficulties, as we see from 2 Corintians 4:7-12 and 11:23-27. In fact the malady he mentions could have been a result of the stoning he received in Lystra (Acts 14:19, 20).

With respect to the tradition of the early church, they were unaware that the churches in the south were in the Galatian Province when Paul ministered there. Thus they would not have considered the Southern Galatian theory.

The weight of evidence, therefore, is for the south Galatian theory.

The Date

If one holds to the Northern Galatian theory, then Paul would have written the letter on his third missionary journey in around A.D. 60.

There are two possible dates for the Southern Galatian theory. First, some maintain that Paul wrote the letter after the Jerusalem council. They believe that the visit to Jerusalem mentioned by Paul in Galatians 2:1-10 was the Jerusalem council. Moreover, the second visit implied in Galatians 4:13 describes the journey from Acts 16:1-5. Therefore, he would have written the letter after his second visit from Corinth about A.D. 51/52. They say that the account in Galatians 2:1-10 does not really fit the famine relief visit and Paul makes reference to a second visit to the Galatian churches: 'but you know that it was because of a bodily illness that I preached the gospel to you the first time' (Gal. 4:13).

The second possible date is that Paul wrote the letter after his first missionary journey and before the Jerusalem council met. The evidences for this view are fourfold: First, Paul does not mention the Jerusalem council, and if the church had settled the issue of the Judaizers, surely he would have made reference to that decree. Second, Paul unquestionably would have mentioned their native son, Timothy, if he had already joined Paul, which he did during the second missionary journey. Third, the second visit implied in Galatians 4:13 is the return trip described in Acts 14:19-25. Fourth, Peter would not have broken table fellowship after the Jerusalem council. Thus the preferable date is about A.D. 46, making this Paul's first epistle.

The occasion

Paul established these congregations during his first missionary journey (Acts 13 and 14). They would have consisted primarily of Gentiles, with a few Jewish members; therefore they would have been typical of subsequent congregations established by Paul. Of course the question would have been, what is the standard of membership in the church? Paul's answer was those who professed faith in Christ and were baptized, along with their children.

This answer created difficulties for some Jewish Christians. They were convinced that Paul was undermining the Old Covenant and that Gentiles needed to receive circumcision and keep the Jewish law if they were to be in the church. A group of these Jewish professing Christians began to follow Paul's footsteps and sought to undermine his work. They were called Judaizers. They attacked Paul's authority and his message. Apparently many in the Galatian congregations were tempted to submit to the teaching of the Judaizers. Paul wrote this letter to defend the gospel of the Lord Jesus Christ. In order to do so he also had to defend his apostleship.

The letter is foundational for understanding Paul's theology. He introduces here the majority of the themes of his ministry. In particular, he addresses the issues of how a person may be right with God and what is the Christian's relationship to the law.

The outline:

I. Introduction and Salutation with Warning, 1:1-9.
   A. Salutation, 1:1-5.
   B. Occasion, 1:6-9.

II. Biographical Argument, 1:10–2:21 (Defence of Apostleship).
   A. Independent of human teachers, 1:10-17.
   B. Independent of Jerusalem church, 1:18–2:10.
   C. Independent of Apostolic pressure, 2:11-21 (includes transition to theological argument).

III. Theological Argument, 3:1–5:1.
   A. The reality of conversion, 3:1-5.
   B. The Old Testament argument, 3:6-14.

- C. The relation of the covenants, 3:15-22.
- D. The role of faith, 3:23-4:7.
- E. The danger of apostasy, 4:8-11.
- F. The contrast of motives, 4:12-20.
- G. The contrast of bondage with liberty, 4:21–5:1.

IV. The Practical Results, 5:2–6:18.

- A. The danger of legalism, 5:2-12.
- B. The consequence of liberty, 5:13-15.
- C. The practice of liberty, 5:16–6:10.
- D. The motive of liberty, 6:11-16.
- E. The conclusion of the letter, 6:17, 18.

1

Salutations

(Galatians 1:1-5)

One of the difficulties with being President of a seminary is writing 'thank you' letters. It is not that I am ungrateful; I am. But I write scores of 'thank you' letters each month and I want to write in a way that genuinely expresses my gratitude without being trite or insincere. So I am sympathetic with the Apostle Paul, who also wrote many letters. At least thirteen of his letters are included in the Bible, and he began each letter according to the letter writing form of his day. He begins with a description of himself, next he mentions those to whom he is writing, and finally he declares a blessing for them. We are tempted to think that Paul used this form mindlessly, much as we often greet a stranger by asking 'How are you?' Often we do not really want to know how the person is doing; it is simply a formal greeting. When we read Paul's greetings, we tend to skip over them, thinking that there is nothing important in them. If we look carefully, however, at the salutations, we will discover that in each case he personalizes the salutation to fit the needs of the church and to lay the foundation for what he intends to write.

1. Apostolic Authority (1:1)

In verse 1 Paul begins by highlighting the uniqueness of his call: **Paul, an apostle (not sent from men or through the agency of man, but through Jesus Christ, and God the**

Father, who raised Him from the dead). In nine of his thirteen epistles, Paul begins by referring to himself as an apostle, a simple designation that points to the unique authority with which he wrote. The apostles were the spokesmen for the Lord Jesus Christ; those through whom Christ revealed his will to the church; those who by inspiration wrote much of the New Testament. The apostles – and others such as Luke and Mark who wrote under their authority – wrote with Christ's authority. Therefore, Paul uses this title to demonstrate his divine authority to write scripture.

The term 'apostle' means 'sent one' or 'messenger'. Occasionally the term is used for an ordinary messenger or emissary. Interestingly, in each of those cases in the New Testament the term always refers to 'a messenger of the church'. For example, Paul writes in Philippians 2:25 of Epaphroditis, 'who is also your messenger (apostle).' When biblical writers, however, use the term absolutely, calling such 'an apostle' or relate the person to Jesus Christ and call him 'the apostle of Christ,' they refer to one of the thirteen men (the twelve plus Paul), whom Christ appointed to the office of being his inspired spokesmen and writers, the foundation stones on which he would build his church (Eph. 2:20).

Notice how Paul expands the title by giving an elaborate description of his call. False teachers (I call them shadow apostles, since they followed Paul around) were claiming that Paul was not a true apostle. Therefore, as he begins his letter, he must carefully defend his apostolic office. He expands on his call both negatively and positively. Negatively, with respect to this call, he says he was 'not *sent* from men, nor through the agency of man.'

First, he asserts that his call is not from men. Every legitimate gospel minister must be able to say with the apostle Paul that he is not called or sent from men. A true minister does not thrust himself into the office; he does not run without being sent. God alone calls into the ministry. And so Paul's first negation applies to all ministers as well to the apostles.

Second, Paul expands his remarks with respect to his call in a way that applies exclusively to apostles: 'nor through the agency of man.' With these words, he describes his call to the apostleship. Paul points out that with respect to this call there was no human agency. In other words, the call was of a supernatural origin. In Paul's case, he received his call on the road to Damascus when God saved him.

The second part of the negation leads to the positive assertion that his call was 'through Jesus Christ, and God the Father, who raised him from the dead.' Here Paul asserts the supernatural origin of his call. Note, in passing, how he joins the Father and the Son grammatically; both the Son and the Father are the objects of the one preposition 'from'. (He uses a similar structure in verse 3.) By combining them in this manner, he expresses the unity of the divine Godhead; he asserts that Jesus Christ is the eternal Son of God, equal with the Father. Observe as well the contrast between the agency of man and the agency of Christ Jesus. If Paul was not called through the agency of man, but through Jesus Christ, then Jesus Christ is not merely a man; He is the God-man. By these simple expressions, Paul lays the foundation for the doctrine of the Trinity: these divine persons are the same in substance, equal in power and glory. So Paul joins the two persons together to emphasize the divine nature of his call. His call on the road to Damascus was a call from the triune God.

Furthermore, notice how Paul emphasizes the resurrection of Christ. An apostle must have been an eyewitness of the resurrection of Christ (Acts 1:22). Although he was not a disciple during Christ's earthly ministry, Paul could bear witness to the fact of the resurrection because he had been called to be an apostle by the risen Christ when he appeared to Paul in resurrection glory on the road to Damascus.

Paul, therefore, demonstrates that he was called by Christ and not by men. True, Ananias laid hands on Paul (Acts 9:10-19), but he simply repeated what God had already told Paul and done in him on the Damascus road. It is also true the church at Antioch commissioned Paul (Acts 13:1-3), but it was the Spirit of the Father and the Son who instructed them to do so. Hence Paul asserts that he was as uniquely an apostle as the twelve, since his call came directly from God.

Paul further demonstrates the unique nature of his office by contrasting himself with fellow pastors. He includes them in the greeting in verse 2: **And all the brethren who are with me**. By these words Paul shows his true humility. Paul often referred to those around him as fellow workers, fellow soldiers, and fellow labourers in the gospel. He was not on an ego trip. He had no need to lord it over his companions in order to guard his authority. Moreover, often in his letters, he included the names of those who laboured with him. In doing so he is saying, 'I have consulted with my fellow ministers, and they have heard my doctrine and are in perfect agreement with me.' Here he uses them as witnesses against the Judaizers.

Note, however, that Paul consciously distinguishes himself with respect to office. Although he treated them as co-workers, they did not share in his apostolic authority. His was the apostolic office; he was the inspired writer, not they.

Therefore, with a few strokes of a pen Paul asserts his apostolic authority. Because of this authority, we are studying the book of Galatians almost two thousand years later. The book of Galatians was written by an apostle, by inspiration of the Holy Spirit. That is why this book, along with the other sixty-five books, is in the Bible. They are not in the Bible because a man or a church council decided they should be included. No! They are self-attesting words of God. They bear the imprint of divine authority. From this very simple apostolic defence, we learn about the authority of the Bible and the confidence that we should have as we study it.

2. The Galatian Problem (1:2)

The recipients of this letter were **the churches of Galatia** (v. 2). Galatia was a Roman province which covered most of modern Turkey (see the Introduction). The province received its name from a group of Celtic invaders who came across from Europe and settled in the northern part of what is now Turkey, around the city of Ankara. Later those cities, in alliance with Rome, subdued the southern portion of that area and the whole territory became known as the 'Galatian Province.' Hence Paul is writing to churches located in Antioch, Lystra, Derbe, and Iconium. Note, that although he addresses them in the plural, 'the *churches* of Galatia,' he writes to them as a unit and deals with them as one church. The New Testament often uses the word, *ecclesia*, to describe the church located in a geographical area, which some call the regional church. Paul could as easily have written 'the church of Galatia.' In fact, in Galatians 1:13, he uses the term, *ecclesia,* in this way: 'For you have heard of my former manner of life in Judaism, how I used to persecute the church of God beyond measure and try to destroy it.' Paul attacked many different congregations, but he refers to them as the 'church of God.' This language reminds us of one of the biblical foundation stones for the Presbyterian system of church government; namely, the Bible uses the term 'church' for both an individual congregation and for a collection of congregations.

Paul's manner of addressing the churches in Galatia alerts them and us to the urgency with which he wrote. When Paul addressed the recipients of a letter, he would add some descriptive phrase. For example in addressing 'the church of God which is at Corinth' (1 Cor. 1:2), he goes on to address them as 'those who have been sanctified in Christ Jesus, saints by calling, with all who in every place call upon the name of our Lord Jesus Christ, their Lord and ours.' In fact, in almost every salutation, whether he was writing to a church or to an individual, Paul added certain specific details that personally distinguished the recipient. Yet with respect to the Galatians, he simply writes 'to the churches of Galatia'. Why does Paul alter his style in this one instance? His abruptness expresses the urgency of the letter and the great danger facing the congregation.

The sense of urgency is further expressed by the absence of any prayer or word of commendation. In his letters to all the other churches, Paul, after the words of blessing, would either express thanksgiving, a word of commendation or comfort, or a prayer. However, to the Galatian congregations, after the words of blessing, he immediately issues a warning (v. 6): 'I am amazed that you are so quickly deserting Him who called you by the grace of Christ, for a different gospel.' His amazement at their backsliding, his fear of their desertion for a different gospel, explains the brevity of the greeting. The very manner in which Paul addresses the Galatians is a blaring siren and a flashing red light. Paul is shouting with his pen, 'Look out! You are in great danger.' The Galatian Church was in serious peril.

The Galatian threat came from those whom I call shadow apostles. They were Jewish Christians from Jerusalem, who followed (shadowed) Paul around and taught his Gentile converts that they must become Jews in order to enjoy the full privileges of the church and the full remission of their sins. I also call them shadow apostles because they claimed a unique relationship with the church in Jerusalem. They alleged they were acting under the authority of the church in Jerusalem, with the authority of the apostles there. In order to discredit Paul's doctrine, they attacked his authority. These false teachers are called Judaizers. They taught that Jewish ceremonies, particularly circumcision, were necessary for a full standing in the church. As we will see later, Paul calls their message a different gospel.

Before we leave this section, let us note as well the subtlety of Satan. This church that was in danger of losing the gospel was founded by the apostle Paul. He was their first teacher. How can it be that an apostolic church could fall so quickly? This defection reminds us of the subtle ways of Satan and it alerts us to be watchful. We tend to think that because we trust Christ and are members of sound churches, both we and our churches are free from the danger of error. Do not forget that Satan never lets up. Paul warned the Ephesians elders in Acts 20:29, 30: 'I know that after my departure savage wolves will come in among you, not sparing the flock; and from among your own selves men will arise, speaking perverse things, to draw away the disciples after them.' We must always be on our guard.

3. The Benefits Of The Gospel (1:3-5)

In verse 3, Paul declares the benefits of the gospel: **Grace to you and peace from God our Father, and the Lord Jesus Christ**. These two terms, grace and peace, summarize these great provisions. Grace is God's attribute of benevolence and kindness by which He shows favour to some sinners, who deserved damnation, and delivers them from their sins.

Flowing from God's gracious character are His gracious acts on behalf of His people. It is the grace of God that regenerates them, justifies them, adopts them, and sanctifies them. Furthermore, the grace of God is the strength and the nurture that He freely gives them for Christ's sake so that they grow in grace and become strong in the Lord. So Paul reminds his readers of the rich benefits which God gave them and of the mercy of God which sustains them and causes them to become increasingly Christ-like. The phrase 'grace to you' is at the heart of the gospel. God in Christ gives to His people everything they need to live well the Christian life and then to live with Him in heaven for evermore.

In the gospel, the grace of God is accompanied with the declaration of God's peace. This peace is an objective peace. Christians once were God's enemies, and He looked upon them with a just wrath. Now God's wrath is turned away and He is reconciled to them. In this objective act of reconciliation, God first enables them to turn to Him in repentance, faith and love and then accepts them as His children.

The first fruit of this reconciliation is peace of conscience. Paul says in Romans 5:1: 'Therefore having been justified by faith, we have peace with God through our Lord Jesus Christ.' Without Christ our consciences condemn us and remind us of the judgment to come. In reconciliation God quiets the conscience through cleansing it by the blood of Christ (1 Tim. 1:5; Heb. 10:22). With this peace of conscience comes a wholeness of life. We understand that God, having given us His Son, will, in Him, freely give us all things. We have contentment and even joy in all circumstances and trials.

Therefore, these two words, grace and peace, summarize the benefits of the gospel. Note that this is a declaration and not a wish. Christians have good wishes for other people. We pray for one another that God will bless us. I often sign my letters 'God bless you' and I really mean that; it is my desire and prayer for that person. Yet Paul here means more than good wishes. In pronouncing grace and peace, Paul states that God is communicating these things to His people.

The Source of the Benefits (v. 3)

We see the surety of the declaration by its source: 'Grace and peace to you **from God our Father and the Lord Jesus Christ**.' Paul connects under the one preposition 'from' the first and second Persons of the Godhead and in joining the two names together he shows the full certainty of the declaration of grace and peace. It comes from God, who is reconciled to us as Father and who bestows this blessing upon us and it comes to us on the basis of the mediatorial work of Christ. Paul uses all three of the names of our Saviour, 'the Lord Jesus Christ,' to teach the sufficiency of His work. The title 'Christ' teaches that our Saviour was anointed by God as our prophet, priest, and king. While He was on earth He exercised these offices and, now in heaven, He is exercising them on our behalf (see Shorter Catechism questions 23–26). As prophet He reveals to us God's will for our salvation; as priest He has atoned for our sins and continues to pray for us; as king He rules over us and protects us. The personal name 'Jesus' reminds us that He is the God-man who alone can save us: 'You shall call His name Jesus, for it is He who will save His people from their sins' (Matt. 1:21). The title 'Lord' establishes that He is Jehovah God, who is now exalted in heaven and before whom every knee shall bow.

The Foundation of the Gospel Benefits (v. 4)

Paul has already anticipated what he would say in verse 4 by declaring in verse 3 that 'grace and peace is from God our Father and the Lord Jesus Christ'. In verse 4, he spells out the foundation of salvation: **(Christ) who gave Himself for our sins, that He might deliver us out of this present evil age, according to the will of our God and Father**.

Salvation, purposed for His people by God, has been purchased for them by Christ. The phrase 'gave Himself for our sins' refers to Christ's death on the cross. Paul is teaching the doctrine of substitutionary atonement and reminds his readers that the Lord Jesus Christ became their substitute: God 'made Him who knew no sin to be sin on our behalf, that we might become the righteousness of God in Him' (2 Cor. 5:21). As high-priest, He offered His perfect life as the propitiatory sacrifice for their sins. 'Propitiatory' means that Jesus Christ, the pure and spotless Son of God, bore the wrath of God in the place of His people. He interposed Himself between God's just wrath and them. On Calvary's cross He paid the penalty of sin by suffering in His body and soul the eternal punishment due to sinners. God punished His Son so He could justly look with favour on those whose place the Son took and give them grace and peace. In other words, grace and peace are ours because Christ offered Himself up as a sacrifice.

Note that the purpose of this sacrifice is further explained, 'in that' or 'in order that'; namely, 'for the purpose of delivering us out of this present evil age' (v. 4). The Bible speaks of two ages: the present age that stretches from the fall of Adam to the return of the Lord Jesus Christ and the age to come when God's people shall live with Him in the glorified eternal state. The present age is an evil age. Some Bible versions translate the word 'age' as 'world'. This translation is acceptable as long as we think of the 'world' in terms of the immoral world system. The physical, created world is not evil. Rocks and trees or food and drink in and of themselves are not evil. The world system is evil because it is under the dominion of Satan (2 Cor. 4:4).

This age is under the prince of darkness and we are in it in the bondage of our sins, the lust of our flesh, indulging the desires of the flesh and of the mind, children of wrath. But Christ, by His perfect sacrifice, has delivered His people from this evil age. He makes them sons and daughters of God. So not only does God forgive their sins, but also He makes them kings and priests unto God (Rev. 1:6; 5:10). Therefore, Christ in His perfect work has delivered them not only from the guilt and curse of sin, but also from the bondage and dominion of sin. God saved His people not simply to rescue them from hell, but also to conform them to the image of Jesus Christ.

The word 'deliver' or 'rescue' is a very strong word. It means to rescue from bondage and slavery (Acts 7:10, 34). It implies that Christ is a strong Saviour, who has done everything to deliver His people from the clutches of Satan and the power of his dominion. Yet their deliverance, although complete, is not fully realized in this life. In His wisdom, God did not free them completely from sin in this present evil age. He has left in each of them a remnant of sin so that they might work out their salvation with fear and trembling, knowing that it is God at work in them both to will and to do His good pleasure (Phil. 2:12, 13). Christians live in two worlds – in the already and in the not yet. They have begun to participate in heavenly realities; their citizenship is there and it cannot be lost. But they are also here in the midst of this present evil age, although no longer of the world; they have been delivered from it, but still live in it and struggle with the remnants of indwelling sin.

At the end of verse 4, Paul joins the purpose of God the Father to the work of Christ –'according to the will of our God and Father.' Some imagine a conflict exists between the Father and the Son with respect to our salvation. They view God the Father as stern and full of wrath and God the Son as gracious and forgiving. Paul reminds us that Christ has acted according to the eternal will of the Father. In other words, God has eternally planned our salvation. As Paul teaches in Ephesians 1:4, God chose His people in Christ before the foundation of the world. Perhaps Paul mentioned God's unified plan of salvation to demonstrate that the Judaizers were wrong when they taught that the Jews (the old covenant people) were saved in any way other than by the grace of God in Christ Jesus.

The Purpose of the Gospel (v. 5)

In verse 5, Paul concludes the salutation by pointing to the purpose of the gospel – **to whom be the glory forevermore. Amen**. This phase is so typical of Paul. He cannot write about salvation without praising God. He begins his discussion of election in the same manner in Ephesians 1:3: 'Blessed be the God and Father of our Lord Jesus Christ.' With the words of verse 5, Paul states the important truth that it was God's purpose, from all eternity, to save a people by sovereign grace, so that He might be glorified in them (Eph. 1:6; Rom. 11:36).

The Galatians needed to be reminded of this truth, because the system of the Judaizers promoted self-congratulation: 'I have done something to contribute to my salvation; I have been circumcised; I keep the Mosaic Law.' The moment we add some aspect of works to our acceptance with God, ceremonial or moral – walking an aisle or answering an invitation, being baptized, and being covenantally faithful – we introduce the element of self-congratulation. Such boasting is contrary to God's purpose in salvation. God saves by grace so that His people might boast in Him and in Him alone (1 Cor. 1:31).

The ultimate purpose of the gospel is that saved sinners should give all glory and honour to the triune God, the Father, the Son, and the Holy Spirit. The Westminster Shorter Catechism teaches that man's chief end is to glorify God and to enjoy Him forever. All of life needs to revolve around this centre. The desire for God's glory is the fountain of all true obedience. The grace of the gospel and the free grace of salvation do not make the redeemed passive. If Jesus Christ has died to deliver us from this present evil age, our concern should be to live in the power of that deliverance. We express our gratitude and we glorify God by seeking to walk carefully according to His law.

Study Questions

1. How does Paul begin his letters?
2. What are the three parts of the salutation?
3. Why is the salutation important?
4. Give a definition of an Apostle?
5. Why was it important that Paul defends his apostolic authority?
6. What two things does Paul say negatively about his call?
7. What does he assert positively about his call?
8. What does the salutation teach about Paul's view of church government?
9. What was the problem that Paul was addressing in the Galatian congregations?
10. What are some manifestations of this problem today?
11. What are the great benefits of the gospel?
12. What is the basis of these benefits?
13. How does the salutation prove the doctrine of the trinity?

2

Gospel Defection

(Galatians 1:6-10)

Our age places a high premium on toleration. Because of political correctness, often the only real sin in many circles is to be negative or critical. This attitude is carried over into the church and we often hear statements such as, 'Do not be negative! Do not preach on sin! Affirm us! Tell us how good we are! Do not deal with error and do not expose others who teach that error!' Because of this cult of toleration, many Protestants today are quite uncomfortable with the language used at times by men like Luther, Calvin and Knox; men who were not sparing in their denunciations when they dealt with those who opposed the gospel of the Lord Jesus Christ. The writers of Scripture give us ample warrant for the use of severe language in dealing with error and those promoting it, and Galatians 1:6-10 is an example of Paul's use of harsh language in exposing false teachers. Here he shows the serious danger of defecting from the true gospel by exchanging it for a counterfeit gospel.

A Counterfeit Gospel (1:6, 7)

In verse six, Paul abruptly addresses the problem: **I am amazed that you are so quickly deserting Him who called you by the grace of Christ, for a different gospel**. Normally at this point in his letters, Paul expressed thanksgiving for or offered a prayer on behalf of his readers. Therefore his abruptness in verse 6 should alert us to his concern over the pernicious error with which he is dealing as he writes to the churches of Galatia. He begins with an expression of incredulity: 'I am amazed.' He is astonished that they are willing to substitute a counterfeit gospel for the true one. He wonders aloud how those who had received the apostolic gospel could so quickly turn away.

The word 'deserting' in verse 6 expresses the treachery of a traitor. Like a soldier who deserts his regiment, the Galatians were in the process of turning aside from the true gospel to take hold of a counterfeit one. Paul uses the present tense of the verb, 'you are right now deserting,' to show that they were actually in the process of abandoning the gospel. The seriousness of their desertion is evident both in regard from whom they were deserting and for what they were deserting.

First, their defection was serious, even deadly, in that they were turning away from God, 'deserting Him who called you.' This language reminds us that it is God who speaks in the gospel. The gospel purposed by God and purchased by Christ is the means by which God speaks to sinners and calls them to faith in the Lord Jesus Christ, offering them both full remission from their sins and the privileges of sons and daughters. Therefore, to depart from the gospel is to turn aside from God. The Judaizers claimed to be God's spokesmen; after all they claimed that they were only applying the principles of the old covenant. Paul asserts that God proclaims a different message.

Paul reminds the Galatians that God called them effectually through the gospel, emphasizing its gracious character. The gospel is a message of salvation by grace alone, and through it God graciously bestows salvation. He not only calls sinners to Christ, but also 'by the grace of Christ'; namely, on the basis of what Christ has done. By this phrase (by the grace of Christ), he refers to the work of Christ delineated in verse 4. The gospel is the manifestation of God's grace because its benefits were fully accomplished by Christ, its benefits are received by faith alone, and it is God who applies the benefits to sinners as He calls them in the gospel.

Furthermore, Paul highlights the seriousness of the defection by highlighting that to which they were turning. They were rejecting God 'for a different gospel'. They were embracing a 'gospel' that was a competing message, an alternative to the gospel Paul preached. Paul, however, quickly points out that it is not another gospel; rather he calls it **which is really not another** (v. 7). In reality, there is no other gospel. They were being duped by a counterfeit, **only there are some who are disturbing you, and want to distort the gospel of Christ**.

In saying that the counterfeit distorts the true gospel of Christ, Paul reminds us of the close connection of his gospel with the completed work of the Lord Jesus Christ. His gospel is about Christ; his is the gospel of atonement; his gospel declares the full remission of sin and divine justification of sinners based on the atonement. The counterfeit gospel preached by the Judaizers was based upon the work of Christ plus human endeavour, such as circumcision and Jewish ceremonies. We are reminded of the seriousness of gospel defection. To add to the gospel – whether works, sacraments, baptism, or anything else – is to detract from the gospel.

Obviously, the success of counterfeiting depends upon the similarity of the forgery to the real thing. We are not deceived by monopoly money, so there is no risk of someone's accepting payment with it. When someone, however, pays you with a counterfeit $20 bill, and you believe you are receiving real money, it is serious. You have been defrauded of $20. The idea of counterfeit is what Paul means by 'different'. The gospel taught by the Judaizers was a counterfeit and, because it was a counterfeit, it was deadly; it was soul-damning.

The Danger of Gospel Defection (1:8-10)

In verses 8-10, Paul discusses the eternal consequences of the counterfeit: **But even though we, or an angel from heaven, should preach to you a gospel contrary to that which we have preached to you, let him be accursed. As we have said before, so I say again now, if any man is preaching to you a gospel contrary to that which you received, let him be accursed. For am I now seeking the favour of men, or of God? Or am I striving to please men? If I were still trying to please men, I would not be a bond-servant of Christ**. Paul uses very strong language – 'let him be accursed' – to emphasize the dangers of the counterfeit gospel. The word translated 'accursed' is 'anathematized' (*anathema*). This term is used in the Greek translation of the Old Testament for the word 'ban.' Items that were devoted to the ban were to be destroyed (Josh. 7:1). In Acts 23:12, the term refers to the oath of self-destruction taken by the enemies of Paul who vowed that they would not eat or drink until they had killed him. In 1 Corinthians 16:22, Paul uses this term for eternal damnation: 'If anyone does not love the Lord, let him be accursed (anathematized).' Paul was not issuing a mild reprimand, saying, 'Now you really ought not to talk that way.' He was pronouncing, 'Let everyone who teaches another gospel be eternally damned.'

In verse 8, Paul applies the anathema even to himself: 'Even though we should preach to you a gospel contrary to that which we have preached to you, let us be accursed.' Paul begins with himself, because the false teachers accused him of having different gospels – one for the Jews and another for the Gentiles. Hence he begins by pronouncing this anathema on himself in order to assert that the gospel he preached was the one that he had received directly from the Lord Jesus Christ. It is the apostolic, authoritative gospel, and Paul has not tampered with it. He has not held back anything of it, nor has he adjusted it to suit his hearers.

Next Paul uses the angels to establish his argument: 'But even though we, or an angel from heaven, should preach to you a gospel contrary to that which we have preached to you, let him be accursed.' Just as we know that Paul would not have preached another gospel, we recognize that a pure angel from heaven, who is a servant of God, could not preach another gospel. By introducing angels into the discussion, Paul makes the point that no one in all of the creation has the authority to change the gospel.

Perhaps Paul had in mind the account in 1 Kings 13 of the prophet that went up from Judah to prophesy to Jeroboam at Bethel. God had revealed to the prophet that he was to return by a different way and by no means was he to stay or eat in the area. But an old prophet from the northern kingdom, who wanted some fellowship, went after him and said, 'An angel spoke to me by the word of the Lord, saying, "Bring him back with you to your house"' (1 Kings 13:18). The prophet from Judah returned, and God put him to death. Why did He slay him rather than the prophet who lied? He should have seen through the deception. An angel cannot change the message that had been infallibly received from God. Paul establishes the principle that no matter how important the person, if he changes the gospel, he will be accursed. The false teachers probably claimed the support of Peter and James, but Paul implies that even if someone such as Peter or James changed the gospel, God would curse him.

In verse 9, Paul applies the principle to the false teachers. 'As we have said before, so I say again now, if any man is preaching to you a gospel contrary to that which you have received, let him be accursed.' Paul warns them that it matters not who a man is, from whom he claims authority, or what credentials he offers; if his gospel differs from Paul's, let him be accursed. The apostolic gospel bears its own imprint; it carries its own authority, and we may not add to or take away from it.

Paul enforces his commitment to the true gospel in verse 10 by speaking of his own motives: 'For am I now seeking the favour of men, or of God?' We could translate this, 'Am I seeking to persuade in order to please men or to please God?' The false teachers accused Paul of adjusting the gospel. If that were so, whom was he trying to please? Was he trying to please men? Was that his motive? He answers, 'If I were still trying to please men, I would not be a bond-servant of Christ.' Paul thought of himself as a steward of the gospel that he had received. He was not his own man. He was compelled to preach the gospel; he must be a faithful steward of the gospel. Therefore, he could only preach the gospel that he received from God. Since he was not preaching for the favour of men, he would not adopt the methods of men. He sought God's approval, and so he preached the whole counsel of God with respect to the gospel.

Paul states the issue clearly for all Christian ministers. He raises the question that we must constantly be asking: 'Are we trying to please men or are we trying to please God?' We will remain faithful only by reminding ourselves that we are bondservants of God. We have received this gospel from Him and, at the end of the day, we want to look up and ask, 'Father, do You approve?' A minister motivated by this truth will have a tremendous resolve and resistance against temptations of compromise and pleasing men.

Of course, if God condemns the false preacher of the counterfeit gospel, He also condemns those who believe this counterfeit gospel. Not to believe the gospel in its entirety, with its clear presentation of the perfect work of Christ, its demands of repentance and faith, and its response of obedience that flows out of justification by faith alone, is to be cursed.

This passage calls to mind the importance of knowing right doctrine and being well grounded in the truths of the gospel. To depart from the true gospel for another gospel is to turn from God to a counterfeit that exposes one's soul to eternal damnation.

What are some of the modern counterfeits with which we should be concerned? We can divide them into three categories. First, there is the liberal gospel that says that Christ is a good example and we are to follow Him. As long as our good works outweigh our bad works, all is well between us and God. Those who believe this counterfeit gospel remain dead in their sins and trespasses. Even though it is a liberal gospel, many might be shocked to realize how often people in conservative, evangelical churches express a similar delusion when asked about their hope of eternal life. They say, 'I am trying to live a Christian life.' Sometimes such an answer is not a true reflection of their heart or faith, but if it is they are lost. Many wrongly think that in addition to trusting in Christ they must do something else in order to be justified. They have added to the gospel. Many people today in conservative churches do not really understand the gospel of free justification.

The second modern counterfeit is the sacramental gospel. The sacramental gospel is the gospel of the Roman Catholic and Greek Orthodox Churches. To the work of Christ these churches add works and penance, prayers and sacraments, the intercession of Mary and the saints, and purgatory and the mass as ways to atone for sin. Such a gospel is another gospel, a soul-damning gospel. There is a modern, Protestant perversion of the gospel that comes perilously close to the sacramentalism of Rome and teaches that baptism unites us to Christ, and as long we are covenantally faithful we remain in Christ. This teaching replaces regeneration and conversion with baptismal union. It too is deadly.

The third modern counterfeit gospel is not necessarily soul-damning, but its consequences are soul-damaging. That is the gospel of Arminianism that asserts human autonomy in coming to Christ; the sinner is free to choose for or against Christ and may choose to apostatize after he is converted. This free will gospel ultimately is an expression of the gospel that diminishes the full gracious provision of God in Christ and adds to it works of faith and perseverance. In the biblical gospel, faith is a gift of God, not something that earns favour. Perseverance is a grace Christ has purchased, not an act of my will by which I put myself under the gospel and must keep myself there.

Study Questions

1. What problem does Paul address in verse 6?
2. Why is Paul amazed?
3. For what two reasons is their defection serious?
4. From what and whom were they defecting?
5. To what were they defecting?
6. Why are counterfeits so dangerous?
7. What does 'anathema' mean? Why does Paul apply the 'anathema' to himself?
8. What Old Testament account might he have had in mind when he speaks of an angel bringing another gospel?
9. What was the sin of the prophet from Judah in 1 Kings 13?
10. What does Paul say about his motives in verse 10?
11. What does this passage teach about the importance of knowing right doctrine?
12. List and discuss the three types of gospel counterfeits.

3

A Supernatural Gospel

(Galatians 1:11-17)

In Galatians 1:11–2:21, an autobiographical section, Paul begins by using his experience to counter the accusations of the false teachers. In 1:8, Paul has made the astonishing claim that any gospel that differed from his was a counterfeit. Such a bold claim has been and still is considered by many to be arrogant. Paul was aware that he must defend this claim, particularly against the false teachers who claimed equal authority with Paul and accused him of tampering with the gospel. They averred, as noted above, that he proclaimed one message for the Gentiles and another for the Jews. Moreover, they asserted that he was at odds with the apostles in Jerusalem. In response Paul argues from his own experience to defend both his apostleship and his message. In verses 11-12 he boldly asserts the supernatural origin of his gospel message, and in verses 13-17 he proves the supernatural origin of the gospel.

The Origin of Paul's Gospel (1:11, 12)

In these verses Paul asserts the heavenly origin of his gospel message: **For I would have you know, brethren, that the gospel which was preached by me is not according to man. For I neither received it from man, nor was I taught it, but I received it through a revelation of Jesus Christ**. Verse 11 demonstrates how important this issue was to Paul. He says, 'I would have you know.' In other words, he did not want them to be ignorant of the fact that his gospel was of a supernatural origin. The false teachers had accused Paul of tampering with the gospel. He says that he would not tamper with it or change it because he received it directly from Christ.

Paul defends himself because the integrity of his apostolic authority (and consequently the New Testament) has been called into question. Therefore, he begins with an emphatic assertion that the gospel preached by him was not according to man. To emphasize this point he states it both negatively and positively. Negatively, he says, 'I neither received it from man nor was I taught it' (v. 11).

Paul is not denying that he had learned facts about the life of Christ from those who were eyewitnesses of it. He had heard about the miracles and the teaching of Christ, about the events pertaining to the crucifixion and the resurrection. He had heard Stephen's sermon (Acts 7). However he claims that, although he received information about Christ from others, he had received supernaturally the gospel message that he preached. His message included, among other things, his interpretation of the Old Testament, his theological explanation of the events of Christ's life, his doctrine of the atonement, his doctrine of free grace, his doctrine of justification, and his doctrine that the Jews and the Gentiles are now one in the church of the Lord Jesus Christ through the perfect work of His redemption. These things, says Paul, he had not received from any man – not from Ananias, not from the apostles in Jerusalem, and not from James, the brother of Christ. He declares, 'No man was his teacher.'

Positively, he asserts, at the end of verse 12, that he 'received it through a revelation of Jesus Christ'. In other words, he received his gospel message directly from Jesus. By this claim, Paul asserts divine authority for his letters and message. He asserts the same thing for the rest of Scripture: 'For all Scripture is inspired by God and profitable for teaching, for reproof, for correction, for training in righteousness; that the man of God may be adequate, equipped for every good work' (2 Tim. 3:16, 17). The gospel, the Scriptures and our religion are of supernatural origin and have come to us by divine revelation. It arose not from the doctrines of men; nor was it derived from the traditions of the church. God has given us a supernaturally inspired Bible, and the Spirit of Christ opens our minds and hearts to understand its truth.

The Manner of Paul's Conversion (1:13-16a)

Having asserted in verses 11 and 12 the supernatural character of his message, Paul sets out to prove this assertion from his experience. In verses 13-16, he demonstrates the unique origin of his gospel message from the manner of his conversion.

Observe that Paul makes his point both negatively and positively. Negatively, he reminds the Galatians of what he was like before his conversion (vv. 13, 14): **For you have heard of my former manner of life in Judaism, how I used to persecute the church of God beyond measure, and tried to destroy it; and I was advancing in Judaism beyond many of my contemporaries among my countrymen, being more extremely zealous for my ancestral traditions**.

Paul had been fanatically committed to the traditions of the Pharisees. By 'ancestral traditions' he specifies the Pharisaic system with its humanly invented laws and rituals and its rigid scheme of works righteousness. He was zealous for these things, advancing in Judaism beyond many of his contemporaries (note Philippians 3:6 where Paul writes that he was blameless with respect to the righteousness found in the law, that is, he was guiltless of violating the Pharisees' rigid standards of external obedience). He surpassed most of his contemporaries in his pursuit of self-righteousness. He was committed to pursuing right standing with God through works, and because of his zeal for Judaism he hated the gospel: 'You have heard of my former manner of life in Judaism, how I used to persecute the church of God beyond measure and tried to destroy it' (v. 13).

Why was this so? The church preached a message of salvation through Christ alone. Nothing in the church's message exalted man or Judaism. The message called for self-denial and repentance: it denied all self worth regarding one's ability to contribute to salvation and the continuing uniqueness of a Jewish kingdom; it required the denial of oneself in order to receive Jesus Christ, who was crucified and raised from the dead as the Saviour. Paul hated this message, and his hatred expressed itself in his zealous persecution of the church. How might we summarize Paul's argument here? He asks, in essence, 'Why would I ever return to that which I have rejected? Yes, I once loved Pharisaism; I once was committed to these things, but no longer.' What had happened? Paul was radically transformed by the gospel of grace. Therefore he could not countenance teaching that God saves by faith plus works. God had saved him from that erroneous belief.

In verses 15 and 16 Paul describes his transformation positively: **But when He who had set me apart, even from my mother's womb, and called me through His grace, was pleased to reveal His Son in me, that I might preach Him among the Gentiles, I did not immediately consult with flesh and blood**. Verses 15 and 16a are dependent clauses leading up to the main clause in verse 16b, 'I did not...' In this clause Paul relates his conversion to his ministry and states that, after his conversion, he did not seek the counsel of men before he began to preach.

Paul points out four aspects of his conversion. First, he was converted by *sovereign grace*. He emphasizes that it was God who set him apart and who was pleased to reveal His Son to him. Paul did not contribute to his conversion. On the contrary, he had hated this gospel. Yet although he hated Christ, it was God's good pleasure to save him; it was God's electing choice that determined Paul would come to Christ.

Second, Paul shows that his conversion was by *sovereign preparation*. God set him apart even from his mother's womb. With this language Paul boldly compares himself to the Old Testament prophet, Jeremiah (Jer. 1:5). As God had prepared that prophet from the womb according to His divine choice, so He prepared Paul. Neither Paul nor the prophets were chosen because they had great potential. Rather, God who chose them to salvation and service also equipped them with their gifts. Paul asserts that God gave him his gifts; He gave him his personality; He gave him his zeal. God prepares us not only for salvation, but also for whatever service He would have us to do in His church.

Third, Paul says that God saved him by a *sovereign call*. Paul refers to his call on the road to Damascus, the effectual call of the gospel. Under the general command to repent and believe, the Holy Spirit works secretly and supernaturally, giving a new heart to a sinner, so that he or she responds to the gospel invitation (John 6:44). Paul had been 'kicking against the pricks'. He had been under the conviction of his own covetousness (Rom. 7:7, 8) and desire for acclamation. Because he was under conviction, he hated Christ all the more. But suddenly Christ subdued Paul by effectually calling him to Himself. In Paul's case, his calling to salvation in Christ included his calling to office, his commissioning as an apostle.

Fourth, Paul points out that his conversion was by a *sovereign means*, 'when God was pleased to reveal His Son in me' (v. 16). This sovereign means was God's opening Paul's heart in order to show him Christ in such an extraordinary way that he was transformed by that sight. Christ was revealed *in* him, not just *to* him. Christ seized Paul for Himself and immediately began the great process of sanctification so that Paul might preach the gospel to the Gentiles.

Hence with this argument from his experience, Paul demonstrates the absurdity of the accusation that he was adding to the gospel or still taught to the Jews a gospel of works plus faith. Why would he add anything to this gospel of grace by which God had saved him in such a free and sovereign manner? How could anyone think that he who had been saved from his hatred of the gospel of grace and his addiction to the self-righteousness of Pharisaism would begin to add one element of human worth or endeavour to the gospel message?

The Independence of Paul's Message (1:16b-17)

Paul continues to prove the supernatural nature of his ministry by demonstrating that he received his message independently of the apostles. When and where did Paul receive his message? When he says at the end of verse 16, **I did not immediately consult with flesh and blood**, he is reiterating that he did not receive his message from man nor was he taught it by other men. This assertion is his way of pointing out that his message had no human derivation. Perhaps his use of the phrase 'flesh and blood' alludes to Christ's statement concerning apostolic revelation in Matthew 16:17. When Peter, speaking on behalf of the apostolic band, said, 'Thou art the Christ, the Son of the living God,' Jesus answered, 'Blessed are you, Simon bar

Jonah, because flesh and blood did not reveal this to you, but my Father who is in heaven.' Paul asserts that he received his message in the same way that the other apostles received theirs: not from men, but from God in heaven.

In verse 17 Paul adds: **I did not go up to Jerusalem to those who were apostles before me; but I went away to Arabia and returned once more to Damascus**. He points out that he began his ministry independently of the Jerusalem Church. He was so confident of his call that he did not rush off to get the confirmation of the apostles there. Because the Lord Jesus Christ had appeared to him and called him to be an apostle to the Gentiles, Paul needed no other confirmation. Therefore he immediately began his ministry in Damascus, a ministry independent of the Jerusalem apostles.

Paul did not receive his message in Jerusalem, but in the desert of Arabia. It seems that soon after his conversion and after spending a brief period in Damascus, he was led by the Spirit into the desert of Arabia, where he spent three years. Luke in Acts omits this episode, telescoping the events that Paul describes here (Acts 9:17-25). It would appear that Paul returned to Damascus to preach after the three years in Arabia, for it was after the return that he was forced to flee over the city wall of Damascus in a basket. By Arabia, Paul probably meant the desert south of Damascus, possibly in present day Jordan. This area was under the rule of Aretas, the king of the Nabateans, whose capital was Petra. Under the Romans, the kingdom of the Nabateans became the province of Arabia.

During this time in the desert Paul received the further revelation that Christ promised him at his conversion on the Damascus road. For three years, as the apostle Paul prayed and meditated on the Old Testament, the Spirit of Christ revealed the fullness of the gospel to him: his understanding of the Old Testament (how Christ fulfilled the Old Testament); his doctrine of the cross; and his grasp of the mystery of the gospel, that Gentiles as well as Jews have free and equal standing in the church of the Lord Jesus Christ, and upon the same basis.

Before leaving this section, I would like to expand two points. First, Paul's experience is in part a paradigm for conversion. The question is not, 'Did Paul exercise faith?' Certainly he believed. But he believed because he was called by God, who gave him faith as a free gift. Paul's conversion is a magnificent example of what takes place in the effectual call of the gospel.

Of course there were aspects of Paul's conversion that are not normative. Christ visibly and aurally manifested Himself, and the call to believe in Christ included a call to the apostleship. The Bible teaches, however, that the Christ who revealed Himself to Paul on the road to Damascus reveals Himself to us in the Sacred Scriptures by the Spirit.

Furthermore, conversion exactly follows the paradigm in terms of the inner and secret workings of God. God comes at His appointed time and regenerates a sinner. When God regenerates, there is no longer the question, 'Do I want to believe?', but the affirmation, 'I do believe.' Whether conversion takes place in infancy, in childhood, or in adulthood, it matters not. Regeneration is work of sovereign grace.

Second, when God converts, He effects a transformation. Conversion is not merely a human response; rather it is the exercise of supernaturally-granted repentance and faith that comes from a heart that is born again, from a new heart with new affections and a will that is now inclined unto good. A new heart will always express itself in marks of transformation. Although there remains a wrestling with sin and there may be times of declension, a clear and unmistakable transformation begins at conversion. Justification is always accompanied by sanctification.

Study Questions

1. What is Paul's purpose in Galatians 1:11-16? What does he mean by 'gospel'?
2. What does Paul deny about the origin of his gospel (v. 12a)?
3. What does he assert is the origin of his gospel (v. 12b)?
4. How does Paul's conversion illustrate the supernatural character of his gospel (vv. 13, 14)?

5. What four things does Paul point out about the sovereign character of his conversion (vv. 15, 16a)?
6. How does Paul's testimony demonstrate the absurdity of the accusation that he had one message for Jews and another for Gentiles?
7. What is Paul proving in verses 16b-17?
8. When and where did Paul receive his message?
9. What did Christ teach him in the Arabian Desert?
10. How does Paul's testimony refute the 'free-will' theology of modern evangelicalism?
11. What is the true mark of conversion?

4

An Independent Message

(Galatians 1:18-24)

Political candidates often use popular topics to win votes. They look at particular concerns and interests in a region and adapt their campaign to issues that would strike a chord there. Similarly, throughout the history of the church, false teachers have used important issues in order to alienate the people of God from the true revealed faith of Scriptures.

One of the primary strategies of liberalism has been to create a wedge between the religion of Jesus of Nazareth and that of the apostle Paul. Liberal theologians claim that the religion of Christ is a moral religion requiring only that we follow Him in gentleness, peace, and good works. It is a very inclusive religion, embracing all varieties of people and ideas. They summarize their view of Christ's religion by the Golden Rule, 'Do unto others as you would have them do to you.' By contrast, they say that Paul's religion is strict and narrow, excluding those who do not embrace his theology of the cross. The Christian church, according to these teachers, originated from Paul, not Christ. According to them, mankind's greatest religious need is to get back to the 'historical' Christ and his teaching. There have been any number of attempts to discover the historic Jesus in the writings of the New Testament, the latest being the Jesus Symposium, which meets annually to sift the Gospel accounts in order to discern the 'real' Jesus.

Unfortunately, liberals are not the only ones guilty of creating a division between Christ and Paul. Some evangelicals do so as well. There are numerous conservative churches in which people complain, 'The pastor preaches Paul's theology; he preaches too much from the epistles. He ought to teach simply what Christ taught from the Gospels.' In these congregations, people who call themselves Christians and profess to believe the Bible drive this wedge between the revealed religion of Paul and the religion of the Lord Jesus Christ. This issue is to some degree created, and further evidenced by, the popularity of the red-letter editions of the Bible. By highlighting the words of Christ, we tacitly affirm that Christ's words are more important than those of Paul or Peter.

In the book of Galatians Paul deals with this supposed tension between his teaching and that of Christ. As we have seen, the Judaizers were claiming that Paul's message altered the gospel taught by Christ. Paul's message, they said, was not that of the Jerusalem apostles: he had tinkered with the gospel. In the first chapter of Galatians, Paul attacks head-on the issue of the integrity of his gospel, by establishing its supernatural character and origin. He maintains that his alone is the true gospel and the measure of all others. If other versions do not conform to the gospel that he preached, they were to be regarded as counterfeits.

In the previous section (vv. 11-17), Paul began to establish the supernatural nature of his gospel, demonstrating that he did not receive it from men. In this section he asserts his independence of the Jerusalem church: **Then three years later I went up to Jerusalem to become acquainted with Cephas and stayed with him fifteen days. But I did not see any other of the apostles except James, the Lord's brother. (Now in what I am writing you, I assure you before God that I am not lying.) Then I went into the regions of Syria and Cilicia. And I was still unknown by sight to the churches of Judea which were in Christ; but only they kept hearing, 'He who once persecuted us is now preaching the faith which he once tried to destroy.' And they were glorifying God because of me** (vv. 18-24).

In these verses, Paul offers two more biographical arguments to prove the integrity of his office and message: (1) his ministry was exercised independently of the Jerusalem church; and (2) his ministry had the hearty approval of the Jewish church.

His Ministry was Exercised Independently of the Jerusalem Church (1:18-20)

In verses 18-20, Paul further confirms the divine character of his call and gospel by the fact that he was not dependent on the Jerusalem Church for his office or message. Before looking at Paul's biographical account in Galatians, we should coordinate the events Paul lists here with Luke's account in Acts 9:19-30. Luke relates that after Paul's conversion he spent several days with the disciples in Damascus and 'immediately he began to proclaim Jesus in the synagogues, saying, "He is the Son of God"' (v. 20). In Galatians 1:17, Paul relates that shortly after his conversion he went to Arabia. Luke omits this section and picks up with Paul's return to Damascus in Acts 9:23-25 (cf. Gal. 1:17), concluding with Paul's dramatic escape over the city wall in a basket. Luke then gives a more detailed account of Paul's first visit to Jerusalem (9:26-30). Paul uses this visit in Galatians 1:18-20 to prove his independence of the Jerusalem Church and the apostles.

With this background in mind, let us pick up Paul's biographical argument. 'Then three years later I went up to Jerusalem' (18-20, cf. Acts 9:26-30). His theology by this time was fully developed. He did not make the trip to Jerusalem to learn the gospel, but to become acquainted with the other apostles. We see this as well from the short amount of time he stayed: he could not possibly have developed his detailed theology in two weeks.

Even though he went up to meet the apostles, initially they feared him, apparently not knowing of his conversion. Barnabas took him under his care and introduced him to the apostles. For some unexplained reason he spent time with only Cephas (Cephas is the Aramaic for Peter) and James, the brother of the Lord. The older writers say that James is the apostle James (the son of Alphaeus), a relative of Jesus, while most later writers teach that this James is the half-brother of Jesus. If the second interpretation, which I prefer, is correct, in what way was James an apostle? Some suggest that Paul includes James under the term 'apostle' and uses the term in the broader sense of one commissioned by the Church or who had apostolic authority (perhaps appointed by Jesus during his post-resurrection appearance to James recorded in 1 Corinthians 15:7). In other words, in addition to the apostle Peter, Paul met with James who, although not one of the twelve apostles, had great authority in the Jerusalem church, an authority seen later when he moderated the Jerusalem council (Acts 15).

Paul spent fifteen days with Cephas. We can try to imagine what occurred as they were together. Paul would have related the message he had received from Christ, and Peter would have related the message he preached. As they compared notes they would have been in perfect agreement, for Peter clearly believed there was no difference in their message. Years later he testified that Paul's letters are Scripture: 'And regard the patience of our Lord to be salvation; just as also our beloved brother Paul, according to the wisdom given him, wrote to you, as also in all of his letters, speaking in them of these things, in which are some things hard to understand, which the untaught and unstable distort, as they do also the rest of the Scriptures to their own destruction' (2 Pet. 3:15-16). Paul's assertion of independence would not exclude his learning from Peter many details about the earthly ministry of the Lord Jesus Christ.

Therefore, Paul proves that his appointment to the apostolic ministry was a divine appointment and that his message was a divinely revealed message by the fact that his call and message were independent of the Jerusalem Church. He seals this claim parenthetically with an oath: 'Now in what I am writing to you, I assure you before God that I am not lying' (v. 20). This oath demonstrates how crucial this matter is to him. He also uses such a strong assertion later, in 1 Timothy 2:7: 'For this I was appointed a preacher and an apostle (I am telling the truth, I am not lying) as a teacher of the Gentiles in faith and truth.' With this oath in Galatians 1:20, he calls on God as his witness to the independence of his office and his divinely-appointed mission to the Gentiles.

Paul's independence does not imply an independent spirit. Today it would be highly improper and presumptuous for a minister to go out independently of the authority of the Church.

There were aspects of Paul's call that were unique. A call to apostleship had to come directly from Christ the Lord, never through human agency. In this respect, Paul's call is clearly different from a minister's call at the present time. Although ministers today must be called by Christ, their call is always through the Church and must be confirmed by the Church. And so we may not take this page out of Paul's book to argue for a ministry independent of the Church's confirmation. However, because Christ Himself commissioned Paul to go directly to the Gentiles, he laboured independently of the Jerusalem Church.

His Ministry Had the Hearty Approval of the Jewish Church (1:21-24)

Having proven that his ministry and message are directly from the Lord, Paul affirms next that the church enthusiastically accepted his apostolic ministry. In verses 21-24, he demonstrates that his ministry had the full approval of the Jewish Church. According to God's purpose, his ministry was primarily among Gentiles: 'Then I went into the regions of Syria and Cilicia' (v. 21). According to Acts 9:28, 29, he spent the two weeks in Jerusalem teaching and preaching. However, apart from those two weeks he did not minister in Judea, during that time he was 'with them moving about freely in Jerusalem, speaking out boldly in the name of the Lord. And he was talking and arguing with the Hellenistic Jews; but they were attempting to put him to death. But when the brethren learned of it, they brought him down to Caesarea and sent him away to Tarsus.' We see here that the scope of his ministry from the very beginning was different from that of the other apostles. He ministered in Syria, the province where Damascus and Antioch were located, and in Cilicia, the province where Tarsus was located. We learn from Acts 11 that Paul first ministered in Tarsus in Cilicia. When the Jerusalem Church heard that Gentiles in Antioch had believed, they sent Barnabas to Antioch in Syria to inspect the work. Recognizing the work of the Spirit in what was happening in there, he went to Tarsus in order to bring Paul to Antioch. They ministered together for an entire year (Acts 11:21-26). So according to apostolic strategy, while the twelve were to minister among the Jews, Paul was to labour in Gentile regions. And although he did minister to Jews in those regions, his primary focus was Gentiles.

In verses 22-24, he argues that the church knew and approved of his work: 'And I was still unknown by sight to the churches of Judea which were in Christ; but only, they kept hearing, "He who once persecuted us is now preaching the faith which he once tried to destroy." And they were glorifying God because of me.' Paul demonstrates that from the beginning he had the approbation of the Judean churches and leaders; implicitly the apostles gave their approval when he left Jerusalem to go to Gentile ministry. Peter knew what Paul was teaching, and he left Jerusalem in good fellowship with the church. Furthermore, they sent no letter after him contradicting what he was teaching, nor did they send other teachers after him, as the Judaizers would do later, to counteract his ministry. Paul had the implicit approval of the apostles.

Moreover, in verses 22-24, Paul asserts that he had the full approval of the Jewish church.[1] Even though he was still unknown by sight to them, when they heard about his ministry they praised God that this one who once persecuted them was now preaching the faith in Gentile regions. They glorified God for His gracious work in Paul and to the church. They knew what Paul was doing and fully approved. So Paul demonstrates that his independence of the Jerusalem church was not a problem. There was no tension between Paul and the apostles, and no division existed between the message of the Lord Jesus Christ and that of Paul.

Study Questions

1. What has been and is the division that some people seek to make between Paul and Jesus?
2. How does this manifest itself in evangelical congregations?

1 Paul refers to these Jewish congregations as 'the churches of Judea which were in Christ' to clarify that, although their members were Jewish, they were Christian churches because of union with Christ. Similarly, the predominately Gentile churches were Christian churches because of union with Christ.

3. Have you ever thought that Christ's words were superior to the rest of the Bible?
4. What biographical argument does Paul use in verses 18-24 to prove the integrity of his office and message?
5. Relate the time line in Galatians 1:16-21 to the events described by Luke in Acts 9:19-30?
6. Why did Paul go up to Jerusalem?
7. What is the significance of the oath in verse 20?
8. What is Paul proving in verses 21-24?
9. How do we know that the church in Judea approved of Paul's gospel?
10. What does this section teach us about the authority of the Bible in general?
11. What does it teach about Paul's letters?

5

Progress Report

(Galatians 2:1-10)

Regardless of the project, it is important that we evaluate our progress. We set goals and check our work by them to determine what kind of progress we have made. Progress evaluation is one of the major reasons teachers in schools give tests and grades. Many of us make New Year's resolutions, but if these resolutions are to be effective, we must assess how we are doing. In Galatians 2:1-10, Paul explains how he evaluated his progress – he went up to Jerusalem and laid his gospel on the table that he might measure whether or not he had run in vain during the years since he had been previously in Jerusalem. This does not mean that Paul was concerned that there might be error in his gospel or that he had omitted some important truth. He did not doubt that he was correct, but he wanted to be sure that the other apostles and he were still working in harmony, that they all were going in the same direction. The Judaizers (the false teachers) claimed that they were working under the authority of James, Peter, and John. Paul, however, shows the absurdity of their claim by showing that before he began his first missionary journey, he went up to Jerusalem to verify that he and the Jerusalem apostles were teaching the same message.

The Confirmatory Mission (2:1-5)

First, Paul expresses the purpose of this mission; namely, it was confirmatory: **Then after an interval of fourteen years I went up again to Jerusalem with Barnabas, taking Titus along also. And it was because of a revelation that I went up; and I submitted to them the gospel which I preach among the Gentiles, but I did so in private to those who were of reputation, for fear that I might be running, or had run, in vain. But not even Titus who was with me, though he was a Greek, was compelled to be circumcised. But it was because of the false brethren who had sneaked in to spy out our liberty which we have in Christ Jesus, in order to bring us into bondage. But we did not yield in subjection to them for even an hour, so that the truth of the gospel might remain with you**.

This visit to Jerusalem was Paul's second after his conversion (Acts 11:27–12:25). The beginning of the interval of fourteen years probably goes back to Paul's conversion (around A.D. 33). He says that he went up to Jerusalem on this second occasion as a result of a divine revelation, most likely with respect to the famine relief that the church was told to send to Jerusalem in about the year 46 (Acts 11:27-30). Paul took advantage of the trip to consult with the Jerusalem apostles in order to affirm the unity of their message and mission. The meeting described by Paul is not the Church Council recorded in Acts 15 (see Introduction). Rather, it is a private meeting, 'I did so in private' (v. 2). He met with Peter, John, and James, the brother of the Lord. It was during this period that James, the brother of John, was put to death and Peter temporarily placed in prison. The church was in no position to have a public meeting.

Paul went up to Jerusalem in order to establish that he had not been running pointlessly –'for fear that I might be running, or had run, in vain' (v. 2). He wanted to be sure that they and he were not at cross purposes; therefore, he laid out before them his gospel – 'I submitted to them the gospel which I preach.' He asked, 'Are you teaching the same thing I am?' The unity of the church was at stake here. Paul wanted to know whether they were in agreement. Were they going to allow these false teachers to disrupt the unity of the church? Were they going to insist on another standard for membership in the church? Paul did not want the churches he had planted among the Gentiles constantly attacked by those claiming authority from Jerusalem. Moreover, the Judaizers could grievously infect the faith of Gentile Christians. Some of them might fall away from the standards of the gospel – exactly what was happening in the Galatian churches. Therefore, he went up to Jerusalem to consult with the apostles.

Paul states in verses 3-4 that Titus, a Gentile Christian, was not compelled to be circumcised. If the Judaizers were correct, surely the Jerusalem apostles would have required Titus to be circumcised. Paul would later circumcise Timothy (Acts 16:1-3). He did so as part of his missionary strategy; since Timothy was half Jewish, unconverted Jews would have been offended by his being uncircumcised. In Titus' case, the liberty of the gospel was at stake. Is it Christ alone that saves? Is it by Christ alone that sinners are justified? Is it in Christ that they have liberty? Or is it Christ plus circumcision? Did Titus need to be circumcised to be saved and accepted by God? Paul would not compromise on this point. He was willing to be all things to all men on any issue that did not involve the integrity of the Scripture and the liberty of the gospel, but he would not budge an inch on any principle that affected the free grace of the gospel.

In verse 4, Paul says his meeting with the apostles was prompted by the treachery of the false teachers 'who had sneaked in to spy out our liberty which we have in Christ Jesus, in order to bring us into bondage.' For Paul, the liberty of free justification and adoption was at the very heart of the gospel. He proclaimed full pardon on the basis of the completed work of Christ to all that repent and believe. Any violation of free justification would bring people under the bondage of legalism (trying to earn salvation by human effort).

Notice as well, the strategy of the false teachers. Paul says they 'sneaked in to spy out our liberty'. By this language, Paul describes something of the strategy of a heretic. Because they are convinced they are right in their doctrinal interpretation, false teachers believe they can use any kind of stratagem to insinuate themselves into the church in order to entice people to follow them. Invariably, they resort to subterfuge and trickery to capture the minds and hearts of God's people. They will even lie and take false vows to conceal their true beliefs. They do not come in openly, but sneak in. They do not come in and say, 'I disagree with you in points A, B and C.' No! They hide their beliefs in order to worm themselves into the confidence of God's people. This activity has gone on throughout the history of the Church and continues to this day. The leadership of the church must be vigilant and constantly on guard against false teachers. For this reason, confessional integrity is important. Denominations and congregations that have confessional standards need to require faithful adherence to those statements of faith.

Paul reports to the Galatians that he 'did not yield in subjection to them for even an hour' (v. 5). By 'them' he refers not to the apostles, but to the false teachers. He refused to accommodate his message to their demands because the integrity of the gospel was at stake – 'So that the truth of the gospel might remain with you' (v. 5). In other words, for the sake of the Gentile churches, Paul held fast to the gospel of free grace.

The Common Message (2:6, 7)

Paul declares that the Jerusalem apostles and he preached the same message (see 1 Cor. 15:1-11). Furthermore, he says that message was the same for both Jew and Gentile. They agreed on one message, the gospel of liberty, the gospel of grace.

Paul's words here can be wrongly interpreted: **But from those who were of high reputation (what they were makes no difference to me; God shows no partiality) – well those who were of reputation contributed nothing to me** (v. 6). Some think that Paul speaks of the apostles disparagingly, when he refers to them as those 'who were of high reputation (what they were makes no difference to me; God shows no partiality)'; 'who were of reputation' (v. 6); and 'who were reputed to be pillars' (v. 9). Why does Paul speak in these terms of the Jerusalem apostles? Is he putting them down? No! Paul is using sanctified sarcasm or irony. The Judaizers (as they sought to undermine Paul's ministry) probably referred to the Jewish apostles as pillars in the church, men of great reputation. They told the Galatians that those of high reputation, the pillars of the church in Jerusalem, the Jerusalem apostles, did not agree with Paul. Paul uses their terminology as he refutes their claim. In doing so, he also refutes their self-righteous pride, by asserting that God is not a respecter of persons. Paul has already said that even if an angel from heaven were to preach a different gospel, let him be accursed. In the next section we can read how Paul confronted Peter over the issue of the liberty of the gospel. Paul, therefore, uses this language to emphasize that false teachers may not hide behind titles. He reminds us that regardless how highly a man is esteemed, we may not follow him if he departs from the truth. Paul asserts, even if it is an apostle, if a man departs from the truth, he is of no repute in the church of God. Paul did not look down on the Jerusalem apostles, but uses this language to establish again that there is only one gospel.

Note that Paul states both negatively and positively that they had a common message. Negatively he says at the end of verse 6, they 'contributed nothing to me.' In other words, his message was not influenced or changed by them. He went to Jerusalem, sat down with Peter, John and James, and explained what he believed the gospel was, the message that Christ had given to him by revelation. They had nothing to add to his message.

Positively, he points out that they agreed that their message was the same. He states in verse 7, **But on the contrary, seeing that I have been entrusted with the gospel to the uncircumcised, just as Peter had been to the circumcised**. Observe that Paul does not repeat the noun 'gospel.' By using the one word for both ministries, he emphasizes the unity of their message. The difference lay only in strategy. Peter was to minister primarily to Jews (the circumcised), and Paul to Gentiles (the uncircumcised).

So Paul and the Jerusalem apostles agreed that there was one faith, one common apostolic message. What Paul asserted in chapter 1 and proved through his own experience – namely, that he had received his message supernaturally from Christ Jesus – he now confirms, by asserting that the Jerusalem apostles and he agreed completely on the message of the gospel.

The Common Ministry (2:8-10)

Paul expresses the common nature of their ministry in verses 8-10: **(For he who effectually worked for Peter in his apostleship to the circumcised effectually worked for me also to the Gentiles), and recognizing the grace that had been given to me, James and Cephas and John who were reputed to be pillars, gave to me and Barnabas the right hand of fellowship, that we might go to the Gentiles and they to the circumcised. They only asked us to remember the poor – the very thing I also was eager to do**.

The mutual recognition of apostolic office was confirmed by the exercise of the apostolic gifts. Paul says parenthetically in verse 8: 'For he who effectually worked for Peter in his apostleship to the circumcised, effectually worked for me also to the Gentiles.' The effectual working of God is a reference to extraordinary apostolic gifts. How did God testify to the validity of the apostolic ministry of Peter (he here represents all the Jerusalem apostles)? He granted him the power to perform signs and wonders. The writer to the Hebrews states this clearly in Hebrews 2:3, 4: 'How shall we escape if we neglect so great a salvation? After it was first spoken through the Lord, it was confirmed to us by those [the apostles] who heard him, God also bearing witness with them, both by signs and wonders and by various miracles and by gifts of the Holy Spirit according to His own will.' So how did God confirm the Jerusalem twelve as apostles? By granting them power to perform extraordinary miracles ('worked effectually in them'). How did God confirm the apostleship of Paul? By granting him the power to do the same works ('effectually worked for me also'). Paul expands on this concept in 2 Corinthians 12:11, 12: 'I have become foolish; you yourselves compelled me. Actually I should have been commended by you, for in no respect was I inferior to the most eminent apostles, even though I am a nobody. The signs of a true apostle were performed among you with all perseverance, by signs and wonders and miracles.' Even though the false teachers in the church in Corinth were discrediting Paul's apostleship, he had performed the signs of a true apostle when he was there.

In what way were these signs proof of the apostolic office? God gave them directly only to the apostles, who in turn could bestow them on others. No one could receive these gifts except through an apostle. It was easy for Paul to prove to the Jerusalem apostles that he did not receive his gifts from them. He, like them, received them directly from the Lord. Paul's use of gifts here is important for understanding why the extraordinary gifts of apostolic times, such as speaking in tongues, have ceased. Since the Lord gave the gifts directly to the apostles and they bestowed them on others, when the apostles and those that received the gifts from the apostles died, these gifts ceased.

In verse 9, Paul demonstrates that they were committed to a common ministry. 'Recognizing the grace that had been given to me, James and Cephas and John ... gave to me and Barnabas the right hand of fellowship.' Note that, although the right hand of fellowship is extended to both Paul and Barnabas, Paul refers only to himself as the recipient of this grace. He is here talking about the grace of office. They recognized that Paul had the apostolic office.

Therefore, when Peter, John and James recognized that Paul was an apostle, they shook hands. This might be the most significant handshake in the history of the human race. It was much more important than world leaders shaking hands after an economic summit. In this handshake, the church united under one apostolic ministry. James, the moderator of the Jerusalem church, with Peter and John, representing the twelve, extended the right hand of fellowship to Paul and Barnabas. This handshake expressed that there was one message and one ministry.

The only difference would be that of strategy. The early missionary strategy was for Paul to minister primarily to Gentiles and Peter, with the other apostles, primarily to the Jews. The only thing they wanted Paul to do was to remember the poor. Paul was committed to this principle as part of his missionary strategy. He later states in Romans 15:26-27: 'For Macedonia and Achaia had been pleased to make a contribution for the poor among the saints in Jerusalem. Yes, they were pleased to do so, and they are indebted to them. For if the Gentiles have shared in their spiritual things, they are indebted to minister to them also in material things.' Such relief was a very concrete way to express the unity of the church.

Indeed, Paul and Barnabas were in Jerusalem on this occasion delivering famine relief to the church there (Acts 11:27-30). Later, in 6:6-10, Paul will address the Galatians concerning this important area of Christian service.

The progress report is in and there was no disagreement between Paul and the Jerusalem apostles. Paul confirms that there is one apostolic message and mission. Furthermore, our faith in the one great message of Scripture is strengthened. When you reflect on that handshake you realize that in that one handshake twenty-one of the twenty-seven New Testament Books are directly represented (Paul's Epistles, John's Gospel, Epistles, and Revelation, Peter's two epistles, and James' Epistle). Four more are represented indirectly, since Luke and probably the writer to the Hebrews (if not Paul) wrote under Paul's authority, and Mark under Peter's. That leaves only Matthew and Jude. Matthew, one of the twelve, was represented by Peter, while Jude, the brother of Jesus Christ, was represented by his brother James. So, that handshake represents the entirety of the New Testament, reminding us indeed that we have received one apostolic faith.

Study Questions

1. What trip to Jerusalem is Paul describing in Galatians 2:1-10?
2. What was Paul's purpose on that trip other than famine relief?
3. Why does Paul take Titus?
4. Why is Titus not circumcised? Why does Paul later circumcise Timothy?
5. What does Paul call the false teachers (v. 4)?
6. What was the strategy of the false teachers (v. 4)?
7. Why does Paul refer to the apostles as 'those of high reputation' and 'reputed to be pillars'.
8. What two things does Paul offer as proof that they had a common message (vv. 6 and 7)?

9. How did the Holy Spirit work effectually in Paul and the apostles?
10. What does this claim teach us about the cessation of extraordinary gifts?
11. What is important about the handshake (v. 9)?

6

Showdown at Antioch

(Galatians 2:11-14)

One of the great problems in today's culture is the inability of people to recognize that ideas and actions have consequences. A person buys something on credit without stopping to think if he can afford it. In the church, leaders make decisions to do certain things not recognizing that the consequence of their actions is opposed to the gospel or the doctrines of grace. The problem is that people often fail to think theologically. Today's church is often governed by pragmatism – if it works, do it – which means that it fails to a large extent to apply biblical principles to everything it does. The apostle Paul, however, always thought theologically. He had the ability to get to the root of an issue and understand not just its causes, but its presuppositions and conclusions. He could anticipate consequences involved in a particular theory or act. Galatians 2:11-14 is a good example of Paul's ability to anticipate the consequences of a specific thought or action.

The Public Rebuke (2:11-14)

In verse 11 Paul relates an occasion on which he had to rebuke Peter publicly: **But when Cephas came to Antioch, I opposed him to his face, because he stood condemned**. Paul refers to Peter by the Aramaic translation, Cephas. Does he do this deliberately to suggest that Peter was acting as a Jew and not as a Christian? Certainly his actions demanded visible censure. Literally Peter 'was one who was condemned.' In other words his actions were self-condemning.

Paul relates the background of the occasion in verses 12-13: **For prior to the coming of certain men from James, [Peter] used to eat with the Gentiles; but when they came, he began to withdraw and hold himself aloof, fearing the party of the circumcision. And the rest of the Jews joined him in hypocrisy, with the result that even Barnabas was carried away by their hypocrisy**. Peter had come to Antioch at some stage between Paul's second visit to Jerusalem and the Jerusalem Council (the Council is described in Acts 15). While in Antioch, Peter enjoyed table fellowship with the Gentiles. Previously he had learned from the Lord that all foods were clean and that it was not improper for Christian Jews to have social interaction with Christian Gentiles (Acts 10:1-29).

Yet when certain men came down from Jerusalem to Antioch Peter withdrew from having table fellowship with Gentile believers. Paul calls these men 'the party of the circumcision.' They were of the Judaizers, Christian Jews who taught that Gentiles needed to be circumcised and then observe all other Jewish customs in order to have full and equal standing in the Church. They claimed to represent James, the brother of the Lord and a leader of the Jerusalem church. When they arrived Peter began to distance himself from the Gentiles, because he was intimidated by the group from Jerusalem, 'fearing the party of the circumcision' (v. 12). Paul uses a verb form (began to withdraw) to show that Peter did not break immediately. Instead he wrestled with the temptation to break fellowship with the Gentiles. Eventually, intimidated by the circumcision party, he separated from the Gentiles and held himself aloof. Paul refers to Peter's act as 'hypocrisy' because he was acting against the revelation he had received earlier (Acts 10:1-29).

As a consequence of Peter's behaviour, the remainder of the Christian Jews followed his example. (Even Barnabas was led astray into this hypocrisy!) One ought not to be surprised at the others following Peter's example; after all, he was the most eminent of the apostles.

This is the situation in which Paul had to rebuke Peter: **But when I saw that they were not straightforward about**

the truth of the gospel, I said to Cephas in the presence of all, 'If you being a Jew live like the Gentiles and not like the Jews, how is it that you compel the Gentiles to live like Jews? (v. 14). In other words, because Peter had withdrawn from table fellowship, he had forced the Gentile Christians to become Jews in order to continue to have fellowship with him.

It was no small thing that Paul rebuked Peter before the local church in Antioch. Paul called to task one of the pillars of the whole church, one of the trio of prominent leaders in Jerusalem (with James and John). Paul admonished him because his actions were contrary to the gospel – 'they were not straightforward about the truth of the gospel.' The term 'straightforward' means 'to walk in a straight line or uprightly.' This rebuke was severe; a public humiliation of an apostle.

We can note two significant lessons from the confrontation. First, there is the importance of the ministry of Christian rebuke and exhortation, one that is greatly neglected in today's church. We would much rather talk to others *about* the one with the problem than *to* the one with the problem. Some Christians by temperament are condemnatory and self-righteous, willing to rebuke anybody at the drop of a hat. The great majority, however, hold back from giving any kind of biblical rebuke. This diffidence is exacerbated by living in a culture that places a premium on toleration, so that we dare not put ourselves in a position of saying that someone is wrong. Therefore, we have difficulty in admonishing a Christian brother or sister.

Keep three things in mind if you have difficulty in exhorting and encouraging others. First, admonition is a means that the Holy Spirit uses for the well-being of a Christian brother or sister. We do not rebuke to score points or to win an argument, but so that the Holy Spirit might bring repentance. Remember what Jesus says in Matthew 18:15: 'And if your brother sins, go and reprove him in private; if he listens to you, you have won your brother.'

Second, we are to admonish with love and gentleness. We ought not to come arrogantly, pointing a finger. Instead we come alongside and identify with our brother or sister in love and compassion. We approach an erring friend not self-righteously, but rather as a fellow-traveller, openly owning our own weaknesses and struggles, while expressing genuine concern. Moreover, we always ought to approach our friend prayerfully, praying for him and the matter about which we intend to confront him.

Third, we are to come humbly, seeking to determine the truth of the situation and to deal with the person according to the facts. Obviously, if the person's sin is grievous and public, we ought to deal with it immediately. But, if it is a rumour or a pattern that we think we recognize, we need to approach our friend cautiously and get his side of the story.

With these cautions in mind, we need to exercise this ministry of rebuke and admonition, recognizing that God has entrusted such a ministry to all of us. Paul writes in Romans 15:14: 'And concerning you, my brethren, I myself also am convinced that you yourselves are full of goodness, filled with all knowledge, and able also to admonish one another' (cf. 1 Thess. 5:14; Heb. 3:13).

The second lesson we learn here is that no individual, regardless of office, or stature, or reputation, is beyond error and so beyond the necessity of reproof. Peter was a great man, chief among the Jerusalem apostles. Twice, he boldly testified to Christ before the Sanhedrin; he was the first to take the gospel to the Gentiles; he was loved and recognized by all Christians that knew him or had heard of him. None of this, however, deterred the apostle Paul from rebuking him publicly.

As we know, the Roman Catholic Church claims that Peter was the first Bishop of Rome and the predecessor of the Popes. It considers the Pope to be above error, yet here we find the first Pope (by their tradition) severely rebuked by Paul. God reminds us to treat no one as if he were beyond error. We must not exalt men to a level with Scripture. Those of us who are pastors, church officers, and professors of theology need to understand we are not above mistake, error, and sin. When we err or sin, it is good for us to be rebuked.

The Serious Problem (2:14)

But why was Paul so severe? Why did he not call Peter aside and privately rebuke him? Paul gives the reason in verse 14: **But when I saw that they were not straightforward about the**

truth of the gospel. In other words, Peter by his action was perverting the gospel. You remember that Paul has only one measuring stick and that is the truth of his gospel. 'If an angel or an apostle preaches another gospel, let him be accursed.' If an apostle lives in such a way so as to deny the truth of the gospel, let him be rebuked. Peter's offence was ultimately a denial of the gospel. Paul says that 'the truth of the gospel' is on the line at this point. Note, he does not say the gospel, but 'the truth of the gospel.' Many hide behind the term 'gospel.' There is, however, only one gospel and that is what Paul means by the phrase 'the truth of the gospel.' Paul means the gospel of free grace, justification received by faith alone.

The Judaizers denied the truth of the gospel when they added to the gospel message the necessity of circumcision and Jewish observances in order to attain full standing in the Church. When Peter broke table fellowship with the Gentile Christians, he in effect was saying, 'You must do more than trust in Christ to have fellowship with me.' When they ate with Peter, they were experiencing the unity of the church of Christ in the gospel. No secondary standards were applied. Then Peter got up from their table and went into the next room to eat with the Jews. What did his action proclaim? In that one act, the Judaizers got everything they wanted without having to win one theological argument. By his action, Peter was saying that profession of union with Christ was not a sufficient basis for Gentile Christians to have fellowship with him. They had to be circumcised; they had to become Jews. This is what Paul means at the end of verse 14: **If you being a Jew live like the Gentiles and not like the Jews, how is it that you compel the Gentiles to live like Jews**?

We know that Peter did not intend to affirm the Christ-dishonouring doctrines of the Judaizers. He had not thought through to the consequences of his actions. Instead he acted out of fear; he was intimidated. He acted without thinking and his action caused other Jewish Christians, including even Barnabas, to follow his example. Paul understood the breach of the gospel involved in Peter's act. He saw the immediate consequences and held Peter accountable for his actions. We must hold ourselves accountable for the consequences of how we think and how we behave, and we must be willing to hold others accountable as well. We must be like Paul and ask the question, 'What will be the outcome of this action?'

For example, every time a well-meaning Christian makes up a list of man-made rules that go beyond the Bible to govern Christian behaviour (do not go to movies, do not use any alcohol), he in effect denies that the Bible is a sufficient standard to govern behaviour, the only rule of faith and practice. His sincere desire to help people become holy will lead them eventually to downplay the Word of God. Christ says in Mark 7:8, 9 that to follow man-made traditions and laws leads one to neglect and set aside the commandments of God. He adds in verse 13, 'thus invalidating the word of God by your tradition which you have handed down, and you do many things such as that.' We must never capitulate to a list of man-made rules or teachings. To do so is to deny the sufficiency of Scripture. Paul teaches us that such actions have consequences.

Paul does not tell us if Peter repented. He does not need to. His purpose is not to humiliate Peter further. We know from the remainder of Scripture that Peter immediately repented. If he had not done so, Paul would have informed us, since he is demonstrating his apostolic authority. He exercised his authority against another apostle who heeded the rebuke. We know from Peter's remarks about Paul in 2 Peter 3:16 that Peter highly esteemed him.

Therefore, the rebuke was successful, showing the truth of Paul's free gospel and his apostolic authority. Let us learn from Peter's example the necessity of humbling ourselves under rebuke. The Psalmist writes in Psalm 141:5: 'Let the righteous smite me in kindness and reprove me; It is oil upon the head. Do not let my head refuse it.' You and I, like Peter, are to humble ourselves under godly admonition. We must be willing to humble ourselves when someone rightly rebukes us. Husbands must be willing for their wives to admonish them. Their headship as husbands does not exempt them from receiving a rebuke from their wives. Parents must be willing to be rebuked by their children. Their authority over them is not threatened, when they humble themselves before their children. All of us must be open to any brother's or sister's admonition.

Sometimes you will be unconvinced by the admonition. Rather than respond defensively, thank the person for the rebuke and offer to pray about it. Other times, you will know the rebuke is deserved. Say, 'You are right. Thank you, forgive me.'

Study Questions

1. How does Paul demonstrate his apostolic authority in Galatians 2:11-14?
2. For what does Paul rebuke Peter?
3. Why does he refer to him as Cephas?
4. What does Paul mean in verse 14 when he says, 'If you being a Jew live like the Gentiles and not like the Jews, how is it that you compel the Gentiles to live like Jews?'
5. How was Peter's action contrary to the gospel?
6. What are the two lessons we learn here about the importance of admonition?
7. What three things should we keep in mind in exhorting someone?
8. Why did Paul rebuke Peter publicly and not in private?
9. What do we learn here about the consequences of actions?
10. What are the consequences of legalistic, extra biblical rules?
11. How does this rebuke establish Paul's apostolic authority?
12. How should we respond to a rebuke that we are not certain is valid?
13. How should we respond to a valid rebuke?

7

Justification by Faith Alone

(Galatians 2:15-16)

'It is appointed for men to die once and after this comes the judgment,' says the writer to the Hebrews (9:27). Because of this truth, one of the most important questions for a person to answer is, 'How can I be right with God?' Some suppress their conscience, when it testifies of judgment and prompts this question, by denying the existence of God; while others labour to convince themselves that there is no existence after death. Both of these attempts go against the grain of the testimony of the conscience,[1] which is like dragging fingernails across a chalkboard, because we possess immortal souls. Our whole being testifies that there is something more than this present life and thus the persistent questions, 'What do I do about the life to come?' or 'How can I be righteous before a holy God?'

Even though a few suppress the question, a greater number answer it incorrectly. Some say, 'As long as I sincerely seek God,

1 Conscience is that faculty placed by God between man and God in order to act as a referee of judgment. One writer states: 'A kind of silent reasoning of the mind whose definitive sentence is received by some affection of the heart, whereby those things which are judged to be good and right are approved of with delight, but those things which are evil and naught are disapproved with grief and sorrow. God hath placed this in all men, partly to be a judgment and testimony of that integrity to which man was at first created, and of that corruption that followed sin: partly that God may have a tribunal erected in the breast of men to accuse delinquents, and to excuse those who do what is good and right' (quoted in Samuel Annesley, 'How May We Be Universally And Exactly Conscientious? In *Puritan Sermons*, 6 vols. Wheaton: Richard Owen Roberts, Publishers, 1981, 1.3).

whoever He might be, then I know that all is well.' Others say, 'If I do good to my neighbour or if my good deeds outweigh my bad deeds, all is well between God and me.' Still others say, 'I am trusting in my church and the sacraments to make me acceptable to God.' Paul gives the correct answer in this letter to the Galatians. In fact, the primary reason he wrote it was to answer once and for all the question, 'How can a person be right with God?' Paul uses his confrontation with Peter in Antioch as a transition from the biographical defence of his ministry and message to his doctrinal defence of justification by faith alone.

Chapter 2:15, 16, may be interpreted in one of two ways. Some, like the translators of the New American Standard Version, include these remarks as part of Paul's statement to Peter. Others, like the translators of the English Standard Version, believe that Paul's remarks to Peter are concluded in verse 14 and that in verse 15 Paul, building on his remarks to Peter, begins discussing the doctrine of justification by faith alone. I prefer this second interpretation of the division of the text. In these verses Paul expounds free justification. It is free, because we receive it by faith alone and contribute nothing to it; it is by grace. The apostle proves the necessity of free justification, defines the nature of free justification, and confirms his doctrine by Scripture.

The Necessity of Free Justification (2:15, 16a)

In verse 15, 16a, Paul proves the necessity of free justification, by demonstrating that Jews could only be justified by faith: **We are Jews by nature, and not sinners from among the Gentiles: Nevertheless, knowing that a man is not justified by the works of the Law but through faith in Christ Jesus**. The premise on which this argument is based is that those within the covenant community have a special standing in the sight of God. He contrasts Jews, who are God's covenant people, with Gentiles, who were not part of the Old Testament covenant people (Eph. 2:11, 12). When he says that we are Jews by nature and not Gentile sinners, he is not claiming that Jews were not sinners. Rather, he is pointing out that within the covenant they were separated from the world of paganism and unbelief. Paul is simply asserting the special position of all those who are in covenant with God.

This concept of God's people being in the covenant explains what Paul means in 1 Corinthians 7:14, when he says that the children of a Christian are holy. There is a holy standing that belongs to those in the covenant. Christians and their children are not like the sinners of the world; they have been separated unto God and are under the covenant headship of the Lord Jesus Christ. Paul asserts the same thing here about the old covenant people. The question then is raised, 'How is one who is in covenant with God justified?' Paul says in answer, 'We Jews, who are in covenant with God, who possess His special revelation, and enjoy the manifestations of His glory, are not like the pagans. Nevertheless, we cannot be justified by our works.' Paul establishes a contrast with the word 'nevertheless.' He states negatively that no person can be justified by keeping the law. The term 'man' is a word that includes all people, men, women, boys, and girls.

Paul uses the term 'justified' in a judicial sense, to express acquittal. This meaning is the primary way the Bible uses the verb 'to justify.' It is the language of the courtroom that expresses freedom from guilt and condemnation. For example, we read in Proverbs 17:15, 'He who justifies the wicked and he who condemns the righteous both of them alike are an abomination to the Lord.' The antonym (opposite) of 'justify' is 'condemn.' To condemn is a judicial act by which a judge or a jury declares the accused to be guilty. The opposite of 'to condemn' is 'to declare innocent.' Another example of the term 'justify' is in Exodus 23:7, where God speaks of Himself as the judge: 'Keep far from a false charge. Do not kill the innocent or the righteous for I will not acquit (justify) the guilty.' God emphasizes that He will not justify (acquit) the person who breaks his law. Therefore, to justify is to declare righteous in a judicial sense. The Westminster Shorter Catechism 33 says that justification 'is an act of God's free grace.' In other words, it is a once and for all judicial action done by God. This judicial concept is the primary meaning of the verb 'to justify' throughout Scripture.

Paul is teaching that one's keeping of the law is not the basis of acquittal in the sight of God. He is dealing in the immediate context with the ceremonial law, and some contend that Paul is only referring to ceremonial requirements (such as circumcision, food laws, and Sabbaths) and argue that the Judaizers were teaching that one has to be circumcised and become a Jew in order to receive full remission of sins. In response to that teaching they interpret Paul as asserting that justification is not by ceremonies. Paul, however, uses the most comprehensive phrase possible to describe the works he has in view, 'works of the Law.' As he often does, he moves from a specific problem (the doctrine of the Judaizers) to a universal principle – that no sinful individual can be justified by God on the basis of obeying His law. Ultimately it matters not whether we are talking about ceremonial laws (circumcision, baptism, the Lord's Supper, church membership) or moral laws. There is no possible way for a sinful person to be justified by works or efforts.

Paul expands on this concept in Romans 3:19, 20: 'Now we know that whatever the Law says, it speaks to those who are under the Law, that every mouth may be closed, and all the world may become accountable to God; because by the works of the Law no flesh will be justified in His sight; for through the Law comes the knowledge of sin.' Obviously Paul has in view the moral law, since it is what God uses to bring the knowledge of sin. Therefore the phrase 'works of the law' refers to any effort to earn God's favour by obedience. None can be justified by 'works of the law.'

Therefore, Paul reminds us that no amount of human effort, no amount of law-keeping (moral or ceremonial), will enable anyone to be declared innocent in the sight of God. Why? God is a holy, perfect judge, who demands purity and holiness in all of those made in His image (Deut. 32:4). His law is perfect and absolutely exact in its demands. All of us, naturally descending from Adam, are born dead in sins and trespasses; we are born under the wrath and curse of God. God is a holy judge, who cannot look with favour on any sin; He declares in Exodus 23:7, 'I will not acquit the guilty.'

How foolish to think that we can satisfy God's justice with our ceremonies, our obedience, our human effort, or our suffering. Although some creditors will accept fifty cents on a dollar, God does not. He will not even accept ninety nine cents on a dollar. He demands perfection. Imagine a man that has been proven guilty of murder pleading at his sentencing: 'Your honour, I would remind you that I have never had a traffic ticket; I have never stolen anything from my neighbour; I have been a faithful husband.' Could such efforts at obedience ever atone for the guilt of murder? Of course not! A human judge, in that respect, cannot accept fifty cents on a dollar. Again, imagine that you are six months in arrears on your mortgage payment, and the bank has been very patient with you. They have done everything possible to bear with you, but you have paid nothing on your loan, not even the interest. When the bank comes to repossess your house, will it help for you to say, 'Remember in previous years I never missed a payment nor was I ever late in making a payment. In fact a few times I even paid extra principal'? Does your past performance satisfy the debt? No way!

This statement reminds us of the importance of using the law of God in preaching and evangelism. First, the law is the declaration of God's character. When faced with the perfect holiness of God, a sinner will become aware of his corruption. Second, the holy, perfect, searching demands of the law of God condemn us. The law will convict us of specific sins and of the sinfulness of our nature. Hence, the law teaches us that no one can be justified before God by the works of the law. The church today is negligent in its use of the law in evangelism. We must preach the law. People need to be exposed to the holy demands of God for it is the law of God that will break the heart of a sinner and drive him to Christ.

It is important to understand that baptism and covenant standing do not justify. When we profess Christ, we are brought into the covenant of grace with our children. We and they have a special standing before God. They with us are members of the church; however, that membership does not justify them. Every member of the covenant community is justified when he rests in Christ alone for salvation. Therefore, Paul proves from the covenant experience of the Jews that the Judaizers are wrong.

The Nature of Free Justification (2:16a)

How then were Jews accepted by God? How were their sins dealt with? How was David justified? How was Abraham justified? Paul answers the question, **Through faith in Christ Jesus, even we have believed in Christ Jesus that we may be justified by faith in Christ, and not by the works of the Law**.

Definition of Justification

By this answer Paul establishes the nature of justification. He teaches that we are justified by faith. The noun 'justification' refers to the state of the one whom God has justified. In justification, God does two things: He forgives all sin and He declares the person to be righteous in His sight. Earlier we referred to the Westminster Shorter Catechism, 33: 'Justification is an act of God's free grace, wherein he pardoneth all our sins, and accepteth us as righteous in his sight, only for the righteousness of Christ imputed to us, and received by faith alone.' This statement is an excellent summary of what Paul is saying in Galatians 2:16. First, God forgives all of the sins of the one whom He justifies. Paul spells this out in Romans 4:6-8 (quoting Psalm 32:1, 2): 'Just as David also speaks of the blessings upon the man to whom God reckons righteousness apart from works: Blessed are those whose lawless deeds have been forgiven and whose sins have been covered. Blessed is the man whose sin the Lord will not take into account.' Second, God accepts the justified person as righteous. Judicially, God considers the justified person to be innocent: 'He made Him who knew no sin to be sin on our behalf that we might become the righteousness of God in Him' (2 Cor. 5:21).

The Ground of Justification

In this verse, Paul emphasizes the instrumentality of faith. But he is not saying that faith itself justifies. Instead he states that our faith is in Christ Jesus: 'faith in Christ Jesus' and 'believed in Christ Jesus.' Paul sets Christ before us as our only hope of salvation. To use a theological phrase Christ, not faith, is the ground or basis of our justification. Paul is saying that Jesus of Nazareth is the suitable and sufficient Saviour of sinners.

God in His holy covenant law demands two things from us: perfect obedience and eternal punishment for disobedience. Christ as our covenant head came to satisfy both of these demands. He obeyed the law of God perfectly and gave Himself as a sacrifice for the sins of His people. Hence God accepts them as righteous because of the righteous obedience of the Lord Jesus Christ. It is imputed to them so that they are reckoned righteous in God's sight (Rom. 5:19; 2 Cor. 5:21). The term 'impute' means to place to the account of. Our guilt was placed on Christ and His obedience was reckoned to us.

Jesus offered His sinless soul as a sacrifice for sinners. He was the propitiation for our sins, bearing God's wrath and satisfying God's justice (Rom. 3:25, 26). Christ and Christ alone has satisfied the demands of the law. God accepts His payment of the penalty of sin in the place of ours. God does not simply say, 'I will forget your sin.' No, God is holy and He cannot justify the wicked. How then does God justify us? He does so through His Son taking the place of the wicked and satisfying the justice of God. Therefore, God, for the sake of His Son, may justify the wicked.

The Role of Faith

How then do we receive this perfect obedience and suffering of Christ in our place? By faith. It is through faith in Christ Jesus that we are justified. The work of Christ becomes ours when we are brought into union with Him through faith. What is faith? The Shorter Catechism (Number 86) defines faith in this helpful way: 'Faith in Jesus Christ is a saving grace, whereby we receive and rest upon him alone for salvation, as he is offered to us in the gospel.' Faith not only believes the facts about Jesus Christ and the gospel, it also rests on Him alone for salvation.

When the Bible says that faith saves, it does not mean that faith contributes anything to earn salvation. As we have seen, the saving quality is in Christ; He is the ground of our salvation and the efficient means of our justification. Faith is the instrument by which we receive Christ and are brought into union with Him. It is the hand of the beggar receiving God's gift of justification; faith is the instrument by which one receives justification. This role of faith is what is meant in the phrase, 'justification by faith alone.'

Confirmation of the Doctrine (2:16b)

Paul continues by appealing to the Old Testament: **Since by the works of the law shall no flesh be justified** (v. 16). He quotes the Greek translation of Psalm 143:2. The Greek translation, called the Septuagint, uses the term 'to justify' to translate the Hebrew for 'is righteous.' Paul proves from

Scripture that 'shall no flesh be justified,' that our standing before God is solely on the basis of justification received by faith.

Further to confirm his doctrine, he changes the phrase of both the Hebrew and Greek, 'no one living' to 'no flesh.' By using the word 'flesh,' Paul makes a play on words. The term 'flesh' may mean a human being, but the Bible also uses it to refer to our sinful nature. In other words, the Bible teaches that every person born of a human father and mother is born with a sinful nature. As we observed earlier, all are born dead in sin and trespasses. Therefore, the use of the term 'flesh' signifies that no mortal man can be justified by his own works, because all mortals are born dead in their sins and trespasses. Therefore, Paul confirms the necessity of free justification. If we hold to the early date for the book of Galatians, this is the first occasion in Paul's ministry that he writes about the doctrine of justification and he could not be any clearer.

This doctrine is very humbling. In Luke 18 Christ tells the story of a Pharisee and a tax-collector. The Pharisee justified himself (paraded his works and worth before God), while the tax-collector humbly confessed his sin before God. Christ concludes, 'I tell you, this man [the tax-collector] went down to his house justified rather than the other; For everyone who exalts himself shall be humbled, but he who humbles himself shall be exalted' (Luke 18:14).

Excursus on Justification

The teaching of Paul in Galatians 2:15, 16 directly contradicts a number of positions on justification being taught in evangelical churches and denominations today; namely, the teachings of Norman Shepherd, N.T. Wright and the New Perspective on Paul, and the Federal Vision. The conflicts over both Shepherd and the Federal Vision are located mainly in American evangelical Presbyterianism, whereas the New Perspective on Paul is propagated and discussed worldwide.

Shepherd differs with my interpretation of these two verses on two very significant points. First, he teaches that God does not impute Christ's active obedience to us. According to Shepherd, in justification God imputes Christ's sufferings and death to us and in our justification God pardons all our sins.

He defines justification exclusively in terms of forgiveness of sins: 'For Paul in Romans 3:28, justification is the forgiveness of sins so that we are accepted by God as righteous and receive the gift of eternal life. Justification is the forgiveness of sins.'[2] He continues, 'Paul makes clear that justification is the forgiveness of sin grounded in the righteousness of Jesus Christ. That righteousness is his propitiatory sacrifice offered on the Cross in obedience to the will of his Father in heaven.'[3] Shepherd continues by denying the imputation of Christ's active obedience to us: 'Salvation comes ultimately through Jesus Christ who does two things: he deals definitively with the guilt of sin, and he deals definitively with the corruption of sin. By his death and resurrection he pays the penalty for sin and on this ground bestows the gift of forgiveness. This is justification. By his death and resurrection he destroys the corruption of sin so that we are recreated in righteousness and holiness. This is sanctification. Those who are justified and sanctified in union with Christ are the righteous who will inherit the kingdom and enter into eternal life.'[4] You will notice that the only righteousness a believer has in Shepherd's definition is the righteousness of sanctification. Shepherd's position has been popularized by a number of adherents of what is called the 'Federal Vision.'

Second, Shepherd teaches that repentance and believing works are part of the instrumental means of receiving justification. He introduces repentance and obedience into the instrumental role of justification.[5]

With respect to the first position: the Bible clearly asserts that Christ's active obedience was imputed to us: see 2 Corinthians 5:21; Romans 5:19. The obligation of perfect obedience is based upon the first covenant with Adam. Shepherd denies the covenant of works with Adam and so the need for any acceptance based upon perfection. The Bible clearly teaches that Adam was the first covenant head and Christ the last (Rom. 5:12ff; 1 Cor. 15:21, 45). If God only pardons our

2 P. Andrew Sandlin, ed., *Backbone of the Bible* (Nacogdoches, TX: Covenant Media Press, 2004), 87.

3 Ibid., 87.

4 Ibid., 118.

5 Ibid., 90-100.

sins and does not impute perfect righteousness to us, we are in no better position than Adam before the fall. Therefore, rather than justification being a completed status or standing (Rom. 5:2), it is a state that must be maintained.

Note how this relates to Shepherd's second error, the role of faithful works in justification. He clearly contradicts what Paul says in Galatians 2:15 and Romans 3:19, 20. But if God does not impute Christ's active obedience to us, then we must maintain an obedience of our own in order to be accepted by God.

The second position is that of the New Perspective on Paul. This theology has evolved and a number of adherents do not agree with each other on all points. Where they do agree is that second temple Judaism (the Jews of the days of Jesus and Paul) was not teaching a works religion and that Paul was not writing against salvation by works in Galatians and Romans. Rather, Paul is dealing with the issue of Gentile standing in the church; he teaches that Gentiles do not have to become Jews to be equal in the covenant community. More particularly, as N. T. Wright works out this theology, justification refers to covenant membership and as such is a declaration that a person's sins have been forgiven, but it involves no legal action on God's part: 'If we use the language of the law court, it makes no sense whatever to say that the judge imputes, imparts, bequeaths, conveys or otherwise transfers his righteousness to either the plaintiff or the defendant. Righteousness is not an object, a substance or gas which can be passed around the courtroom.'[6] Furthermore, justification means that sinners 'are declared in the present, to be what they will be seen to be in the future, namely the true people of God.'[7]

With respect to Paul's use of justification in Galatians, Wright argues that Paul is not dealing with forensic justification: 'how you define the people of God: are they to be defined by the badges of Jewish race, or in some other way?'[8] Paul employs justification in Galatians to argue that the way to tell who belongs to God's people is not by pointing to Jewish circumcision, dietary laws, or feast days, but by pointing to

6 N. T. Wright, *What Saint Paul Really Said*, 98, 99, 129, 131.
7 N. T. Wright, *Paul*, 121; Wright, *Romans*, 468.
8 N. T. Wright, *What Saint Paul Really Said*, 120..

faith – all those who have faith in Jesus belong to God's people and, hence, are justified.

Obviously, Paul and the rest of the Scripture counter these claims. When Paul says that covenant Jews could not be justified by works of the law, he is saying that even they needed to come to God by faith and not by works. He clearly bases justification on the work of Christ and in Romans 3:23ff explains that work in terms of a wrath-bearing, justice-satisfying death. As we have shown justification is a legal term and Paul is dealing with the pardon of sin and the gift of righteousness.

The third error I mentioned is that of the Federal Vision. Like the New Perspective on Paul, this group is not entirely cohesive, but the main outline of their theology is clear. Moreover, they bring together a number of strands of the first two erroneous positions on justification. The more radical of them maintain that baptism brings one into special union with Christ. The non-elect enjoy all the same privileges in this union as the elect with the exception they are not given persevering grace and so will fall away. Many in this position hold to Shepherd's view on the covenant of works, the non-imputation of Christ's active obedience, and a role of believing works in justification. But Paul shows clearly throughout the book of Galatians that the sacraments, or any other human activities, do not effect any union with Christ nor do they justify sinners before God.

Study Questions

1. What is one of the most important questions you need to answer?
2. What are the two ways of relating verses 15 and 16 to the previous verses?
3. How does Paul prove the necessity of justification from covenantal experience?
4. What does Paul mean by the term 'to justify'?
5. What does he say negatively about justification?
6. What does he mean by 'works of the law'?

7. Why can no one be justified by law keeping?
8. Why is it necessary to use the law in our preaching and evangelism?
9. What is justification?
10. What is the ground for justification?
11. How does one receive justification?
12. What is the role of faith?
13. Define faith.
14. Does baptism or being a church member justify?
15. How does he confirm necessity of justification?
16. What verse does he quote?
17. Why does he use the term ‘flesh’?

8

Justification and Obedience

(Galatians 2:17-21)

Many critics of the Protestant doctrine of justification claim that salvation by grace alone encourages people to continue in sin. The Roman Catholic Church maintains that the doctrine of justification received by faith alone is a legal fiction. A legal fiction is something acted on as fact in spite of its possible falsity. For example, when a couple marries for legal purpose, like immigration, but has no intention of living together in marriage, their marriage is a legal fiction. Since they do not intend to live together as husband and wife, their marriage is but a paper relationship. When Roman Catholic theologians accuse Protestants of practising a legal fiction with their doctrine of justification, they claim that the doctrine of free justification makes a person legally righteous, but leaves his character unaffected. Regardless what one says about the person, he remains a wicked sinner.

Paul answers this charge in 2:17-21 when he anticipates the age-long objection that his doctrine of free justification encourages sin. In verse 17, he asks, **But if, while seeking to be justified in Christ, we ourselves have also been found sinners, is Christ then a minister of sin?** In other words, if we are saved by grace and not by works, what will keep us from lawlessness? In Romans 6 Paul states the same objection in different terms, 'Do we sin that grace might abound?' We hear this same objection from those who teach a man-centred gospel. They claim that if you proclaim a full assurance of salvation, on the basis of God's free grace, people will have no motivation to serve God. Paul answers this objection by showing that salvation by works promotes sin, salvation by grace promotes holiness, and that salvation by works destroys grace.

Salvation by Works Promotes Sin (2:17-19)

Paul answers the anticipated objection by turning it around and demonstrating that a works approach to righteousness promotes sin. He says it makes a person transgress against the law and against the grace of the gospel. Paul frames the question in verse 17: **But if, while seeking to be justified in Christ, we ourselves have also been found sinners, is Christ then a minister of sin**? Paul is building on the story of the confrontation with Peter. He says in verses 15 and 16: 'We are Jews by nature, and not sinners from among the Gentiles; nevertheless knowing that a man is not justified by the works of the law but through faith in Christ, even we have believed in Christ Jesus, that we may be justified by faith in Christ, and not by works of the law.' In my comments on that passage I observed that Jews, although in a special relationship with God through the old covenant, still had to be saved by grace and not by works. But, if Jews are saved by grace and not by works, what happens to the importance of obedience? If law-keeping does not contribute to one's standing with God, why keep the law? Will not the law be useless? This is the objection Paul anticipates.

Observe, however, that he phrases the question in a way to prejudice the answer: 'Does this make Christ a minister of sin?' He cries out, 'May it never be!' Such a thought is inconceivable and of course the Judaizers would have said it was inconceivable, which is exactly why Paul phrases the question, 'Is Christ then a minister of sin?' Remember Paul's argument in chapter one. He had insisted that it was Christ who revealed to him the message of free grace. Consequently Paul taught the doctrine of Jesus Christ. Therefore, if free grace promoted sin, then Christ would be the minister of sin.

Furthermore, who is the object of Paul's gospel? It is Christ. Salvation is His work, not the work of the sinner; one is saved by Christ alone, not Christ and something else (ceremony or law). And so, if Paul's message encouraged sin, Christ would be the minister of sin. The very manner in which Paul phrases the objection alerts the Galatians and us to the foolishness of the objection. We know that Christ came to remove sin. He came to make us holy and righteous. His purpose was not simply to deliver us from hell, but to make us a holy people for God's possession (1 John 3:5). Therefore, if the objection were true, one must fault Jesus Christ; He would be a minister of sin. Paul responds, as any true believer would, with a firm denial, 'May it never be!' It is unthinkable that Christ should be a minister of sin or that the grace of the gospel would condone or promote sin. In fact, it is blasphemous to think of the holy and pure God-man as a minister of sin.

Having stated the objection in this way, Paul continues by proving that salvation by grace is not a licence to sin. He does so by showing that salvation by works actually causes one to transgress the law, because it works against the purpose of the law. The purpose of the law is not to help us earn God's favour, but to show us our need of Christ because we cannot keep the law. In verse 18, Paul states this point autobiographically: **For if I rebuild what I have once destroyed, I prove myself to be a transgressor**. Why does Paul slip into autobiographical mode? First, by referring to himself, he is lessening the severity of his rebuke of Peter. By his actions Peter was rebuilding what had been destroyed. As a consequence of his actions, Peter was communicating that man had to contribute something to his acceptance with God. Peter had in fact reversed the message of the gospel and was rebuilding what he and Paul had destroyed. Paul, having dealt with Peter, uses himself as the example, 'If I rebuild what I have destroyed then I am a transgressor.'

A second reason for the autobiographical expression is to establish a principle. Paul often establishes one in this way. By his ministry, Paul had destroyed salvation by works or self-righteousness. Before his conversion Paul himself had sought to earn God's acceptance by his behaviour. He could claim that with respect to the external righteousness of the law he was blameless (Phil. 3:4-6), but once Christ subdued him, his entire life had been spent in destroying any form of human worth or pretence or self-righteousness. He reasons here that, if he were to reverse the direction of his ministry, he would be a transgressor of the law. He would be transgressing the purpose of the law, because God had given no law or system of law-keeping that could save from sin.

The problem, of course, is not with the law; it is with the heart of the sinner. The law was given because of transgression (1 Tim. 1:8-10). We continue to need the law as Christians, because we each have within us the remnants of sin and our hearts are easily deceived; therefore, we need the law to direct our paths. The law is a restraint and a guide, but it is not able to save from the penalty for sin; it cannot deliver from the guilt or the power of sin. Therefore, Paul says that he would be a transgressor of the law if he taught that the law should do something contrary to what God designed it to do.

In verse 19, Paul expands on the use of the law for the unconverted: **For through the Law I died to the Law, that I might live to God**. The law is designed to convict us of sin and to shows us our need of Christ. By its commands, it irritates our sinful nature. We either strive to earn God's favour by it or we rebel against it. Paul illustrates the work of the law in Romans 7:7-8: 'What shall we say then? Is the law sin? May it never be! On the contrary, I would not have come to know sin except through the law; for I would not have known about coveting if the law had not said, "You shall not covet." But sin, taking an opportunity through the commandment, produced in me coveting of every kind; for apart from the Law sin is dead.' Sin lies slumbering in the heart until the law says, 'Thou shall not,' and suddenly there is a great war.

We see this reaction in our children. They have not thought twice about doing something until we tell them not to do it. Then they want nothing more than to do the thing forbidden them. We see it in ourselves. When the law says 'You shall not' or 'You shall,' we rebel. When our spouse cautions that we are driving in an unchristian manner, what is our first response? We step on the accelerator and go faster. Yes, even a regenerate person may respond in this way. Inevitably, in the unregenerate the law stirs up sin. As a result Paul says, 'If I started teaching works righteousness, I would not be promoting holiness; rather I would be promoting sin, because apart from Christ that is what law does.' The law is designed to be like salt on the wound of the sinful nature, like water on the oil fire of the sinful nature. It stirs up sin within us. Therefore, for Paul to teach contrary to the purpose of the law would make him a transgressor of the law.

We can now see how salvation by works actually produces sin. It makes us transgressors and turns us into hypocrites. We pretend to be what we are not. Any use of the law to earn acceptance with God invariably produces sin and hypocrisy. The law cannot put sin to death; therefore works righteousness makes one a transgressor against the law. A person might perform the law outwardly, while his heart remains unchanged.

Salvation by Grace Promotes Holiness (2:19-21)

Having established that works righteousness produces transgression, Paul now demonstrates that the gospel produces holiness. He introduces the doctrine of union with Christ because it is union with Christ that connects justification to sanctification.

By Grace We Die to Law (2:19, 20)

First, by the grace of the gospel we die to law: **For through the law I died to the law, that I might live to God** (v. 19). Paul teaches that the gospel works with the law. There is a gracious use of the law in our evangelism and in our approach to Christian living. We do not use the law as a means of attaining a right standing with God, but through the correct use of law God delivers us from the law. We read here one of those rather unique Pauline expressions, 'By law I died to law that I might live to God.'

It is very important in today's spiritual climate that we understand what it means to be dead to law. Every person is born under law. Paul uses the term 'law' to refer to the moral requirements of God, which are summarized in the Ten Commandments. We are under the law in two ways.

Perfect Obedience. The law demands perfect obedience. We are born under the covenant of works and God has not abrogated the demands of this covenant. His command to Adam, 'Do this and live,' remains in effect. Every person is born with the responsibility to obey God perfectly. This responsibility was further emphasized in God's covenant with the Jews: 'So you shall keep My statutes and My judgments, by which a man may live if he does them; I am the Lord' (Lev. 18:5). Paul reminds us of this responsibility in Romans 2:12: 'For not the hearers of the Law are just before God, but the doers of the Law will be justified.' Consequently, an obligation to perfect obedience remains and hypothetically if anyone kept the law perfectly (none but Christ did), he would obtain eternal life.

The Curse for Disobedience. The promise, though, implies the curse. We all are under the curse of the law. God says, 'Cursed is everyone that does not abide by all things in the law' (Gal. 3:10; Deut. 27:26). Not only are we born with the responsibility to meet the demands of the covenant of works, we also are born under its curse and condemnation because (1) we are born guilty of Adam's violation of the initial covenant and (2) we continue in the practice of sin. Our sin grows like a mighty mountain in the presence of God and it hangs over us as a constant curse. The law declares that we are guilty, condemned, and damned. And so we are under the law with respect to its obligation to perfect obedience and with respect to its curse.

The Law and Christ

But how does the law enable us to die to sin? When law is used lawfully, it drives us out of ourselves unto Christ. That is what the law did for Paul. That is what the law does for all people who believe in Jesus. Paul expands on this theme in 3:24-25: 'Therefore the Law has become our tutor to lead us to Christ, that we may be justified by faith. But now that faith has come, we are no longer under a tutor.' So the law drives us to Christ that we might receive the free grace of the gospel. Because it demands perfect obedience, the law teaches us that we can do nothing to commend ourselves to God. We cannot contribute in any way to a right standing before him. We fall short and are under condemnation. Therefore the law, by driving us out of ourselves, causes us to die to any attempt at righteousness by law-keeping.

As the law shows us our sin it leads us to Christ, who kept the law for us and died for us. The law puts the law to death, because the law put Christ to death. The law is like the

White Witch in *The Lion, the Witch, and the Wardrobe*. She justly demanded the death of Edmund, who had violated the law, but Aslan takes Edmund's place and satisfied the demands of the law by dying under its penalty. Christ was put to death in our place under the just demands of the law. He took upon Himself the demands of the covenant, 'Do this and live.' By His own perfect obedience, He fulfilled the covenant. He obeyed the law of God perfectly, earning life for us. Moreover, God imputed the guilt of our sins to Jesus so that He became liable to the curse of the law and suffered that curse, satisfying its penalty, on the cross. In this two-fold work, Jesus fulfilled the covenant of works. As a result, law, which condemns us, brings us to Christ who satisfied all its demands in our place. Therefore, at the end of verse 20 Paul writes, **the Son of God who loved me and delivered Himself up for me**, reminding us that Christ was the substitute for His people; He died in their place. The phrase 'delivered Himself' teaches that He freely offered Himself. Paul, of course, cannot talk about Christ's offering Himself without referring to His infinite love, 'who loved me.' The love of Jesus is the great fountain out of which this sacrifice flows. Therefore, as we take hold of Christ by faith we are reminded that it was His love that caused Him to offer Himself for us and satisfy the demands of the law.

But Christ was more than just a ransom for sinners. Paul says he died to law because he died with Christ: **I have been crucified with Christ; and it is no longer I who live, but Christ lives in me; and the life which I now live in the flesh I live by faith in the Son of God who loved me and delivered Himself up for me** (v. 20). Here Paul refers to his union with Christ. What happened to Christ also happened to His people. Paul uses the perfect tense which describes a completed act with ongoing consequences when he writes, 'I have been crucified with Christ.' Christ is the last Adam, our covenant head, and because of this union, what He did for us, we did in Him. Just as we sinned in the first Adam, so in the last Adam we died to the law, because the demands of the law were satisfied for us in our union with Christ.

The power of the law and sin is broken. Therefore, we are freed from the law, its curse and condemnation, and its provocation. We are under the headship of Christ who has died for us and lives. We now walk in the liberty that is in Christ, and not as toddlers and young children who need many rules in order to bring them to maturity. We are the mature sons and daughters of God. And what is it that frees us? It is free justification. Therefore, free justification promotes holiness, because in union with Christ we died to law. In fact, because the law and its claims have been satisfied, we are free to live unto God according to the standard of moral holiness.

By Grace we are Transformed in Holiness (2:20)

Secondly, not only does God free us by law from the law, but also the free grace of the gospel transforms us in holiness. When Paul asserts in verse 19 that we have died to the law, he is not teaching that we have died to the law as a moral standard. We have not died to the law in order to live selfishly and sinfully for ourselves. No, we died to the law that we might live unto God. Now we have a new power to walk according to the moral law of God, not to earn God's favour, but to please Him. This power also relates to the perfect work of Christ, because not only have we been crucified with Christ, we also live with Him. 'I have been crucified with Christ; and its is no longer I who live, but Christ lives in me; and the life which I now live in the flesh I live by faith in the Son of God' (v. 20). Although I live in this mortal body, with the visible vestiges of sin, corruption, and weakness, I am in union with Christ. He lives in me. I live by the power of His life.

Therefore, salvation by grace promotes holiness. When God converts a sinner, the same power that raised Christ from the dead regenerated that person. He now lives unto God and will not walk deliberately in sin. Therefore, this doctrine of free grace, this justification received by faith alone, this declaration that we do nothing to contribute to our standing before God, is no legal fiction. No one who has been crucified in Christ, no one who is in union with Him by faith through regeneration, will continue to live in sin.

In Christians, the law no longer irritates and provokes their natures and stirs them up to sin, but rather the law now comes to renewed hearts that love God. It says, 'Love God with heart, mind, soul and strength' and the renewed heart says, 'Yes indeed, that is what I want passionately to do.' When the law says, 'Love your neighbour as yourself,' the new heart says, 'Yes indeed, that is what I want to do in order to return thanks to God who has saved me by His grace.' And I recognize that as I do so, I do not do it in my own strength. Instead I live by faith in Christ; it is no longer I, who live, but Christ lives in me; and the life which I now live in the flesh I live by faith in the Son of God. It is Christ in me; it is resurrection power. Not only does justification not create a legal fiction, but also it is only the grace of free justification that will promote holiness in God's people.

Now this being dead to sin and alive to God is a very important mark for self-examination. There are many people that are living a lie. They know all the right doctrines; they know all about free justification, but their hearts remain untouched by the power of the gospel. Yet we know that we cannot separate justification and sanctification. On the other hand, look at the joy and the confidence that is here for those who struggle with their sins and know how far short they come. Because of the remnant of sin within us, we sin every day, but the glorious truth is that God's work is invincible and it shall not fail. He who began a good work in a sinner will bring it to completion. When you wrestle with your sin and cry out in your wretchedness like the apostle Paul, because the things that you should do you do not do, and the things that you should not do you do (Rom 7:19, 20), remember that Christ is in you.

Salvation by Works Sins against Grace (2:21)

Having demonstrated that it is not works righteousness, but the gospel of grace, that promotes holiness, Paul concludes this section by demonstrating that works righteousness actually causes us to transgress against the grace of the gospel: **I do not nullify the grace of God; for if righteousness comes through the Law, then Christ died needlessly** (v. 21). If we add to the gospel, we nullify the grace of God and become transgressors against the purpose of the gospel. As it is the purpose of the law to drive us outside of ourselves to Christ, so it is the purpose of the gospel to deliver us from sin by Christ. The gospel of free grace is God's remedy for sin on the basis of Christ's perfect work. Paul says that if he taught a qualified works righteousness, he was sinning against the gospel, because he was denying its God-ordained purpose. And he would be uttering the most blasphemous thing imaginable, for he would be saying that Christ died needlessly. Salvation by works asserts that either Christ did not do enough or that Christ really did not need to do anything at all.

And just as works righteousness makes the one who seeks righteousness by the law a hypocrite, it also makes the one who transgresses against the gospel proud and arrogant. After all, if I can do something to contribute to my salvation, salvation is not by Christ alone. If I am saved by Christ plus my works, I have reason to boast. The purpose of free and sovereign grace is to put the knife to the heart of pride.

It is the height of folly for a man who claims to understand the grace of God to be proud of his knowledge. The gospel teaches us that, although we deserve God's wrath and hell, He chose us from eternity without any good cause in us. Moreover, Christ has done everything as our covenant head in order to accomplish our salvation. These truths should humble us every day before God and in our relationships with one another.

Study Questions

1. Why do Roman Catholics call our doctrine of justification a legal fiction?
2. How does Paul anticipate this objection?
3. In what two ways does a works approach to righteousness promote sin?
4. How does the doctrine of salvation by works cause one to be a transgressor of the law?
5. Why does Paul use himself as an example in verse 18?
6. What is the purpose of the law with respect to the unconverted?
7. What is the practical effect of a non-Christian trying to live by the law?

8. In what two ways does free justification promote holiness?
9. How does law put to death law?
10. What are the demands of the law?
11. How has Christ satisfied these demands?
12. Does death to the law free us from living by the standards of the law?
13. In what way have we been raised with Christ?
14. If we are truly justified Christians will we continue to practice sin?
15. What is the confidence that belongs to us because of our union with Christ?
16. How does your baptism relate to your union with Christ?

9

Indictment of Spiritual Folly

(Galatians 3:1-5)

Chapter 3 begins a new section in Paul's attack against the doctrine of the Judaizers and his presentation of the gospel of grace. In the first two chapters, through a series of autobiographical arguments, the apostle defended his apostleship and the revelation that he had received from the Lord Jesus Christ. The climax of the autobiographical section is his confrontation with Peter.

Paul uses this last autobiographical argument to make the transition into his theological argument. In the concluding verses of chapter 2, he introduces the theme of justification by faith (vv. 14-21). Having made the transition, he begins in chapter 3 his doctrinal defence of the doctrine of salvation by free grace. In verses 1-5, the apostle indicts them for their spiritual folly and gives two arguments to prove his case.

The Indictment (3:1a)

Paul indicts the Galatians in verse 1 with a stringent rebuke: **You foolish Galatians, who has bewitched you?** He calls them to account for succumbing to the temptation to add to the gospel of the Lord Jesus Christ. Their consideration of the requirement of circumcision and observance of the ceremonial laws exposed their folly.

Does Paul here violate Christ's commandment in Matthew 5:22 ('And whoever shall say, You fool, shall be guilty enough to go into the fiery hell')? Christ condemns speaking with contempt, out of wrath and self-seeking anger. Throughout the Bible, however, God classifies people as fools. Paul is building on the theme of the fool found in the book of Proverbs. The fool, the naïve person and the simple one are the types of person whose thoughts and patterns of life are not shaped by Scripture. The foolish are those who think and act like the world. Paul is telling the Galatians that they are acting foolishly and not with biblical sense. He says, 'When you succumb to the doctrine of the Judaizers, you are acting spiritually foolish. You are forsaking the revealed way of God for the way of the world.'

Then Paul intensifies his rebuke by asking them, **Who has bewitched you?** They are acting as someone who has lost his rational senses, who acts contrary to biblical revelation. Perhaps he is even alluding to a superstitious idea that circumcision contained some magic by which spiritual benefits were communicated through the physical act. If this were the case, they were bewitched by superstitious promises. Of course, underlying his indictment is the role of Satan. All temptation is a 'bewitching', because in temptation Satan promises results that cause us to set aside the truth of Scripture with respect to doctrine and practice.

It is very important to understand Satan's strategies. Satan normally does not come directly to tempt us with some grievous error or sin. Rather, he will seek to bewitch us, to entice us. Every day, professing Christians are bewitched by the siren song of Satan, some times through suggestions of popularity, at other times by immoral relationships. None of us are exempt, because this is how temptation works. Whatever the sin, Satan is out to trick us. When we feel the beguiling power of temptation, we should remember these words of the apostle Paul, 'O foolish Galatians, who has bewitched you?' All temptation is a bewitchment and can bring us into spiritual folly. That is Paul's indictment of the Galatians.

The Evidence (3:1b-5)

Then Paul proves this indictment. He uses two arguments to show the spiritual folly of the Galatians. First, they were acting contrary to the gospel by which they were brought initially to Christ: **You foolish Galatians, who has bewitched you before**

whose eyes Jesus Christ was publicly portrayed as crucified? Paul reminds them of how God delivered them from the guilt of sin, from the burden of an accusing conscience, from all of the misery of trying to make themselves acceptable to God. God used the preaching of Christ in the gospel to deliver them from sin with its burden, guilt and bondage.

Notice the glorious description Paul gives of preaching. By such preaching 'Christ was publicly portrayed as crucified.' Paul describes his preaching as the painting of word pictures, as the placarding of truth. He reminded the Galatians what the preaching of the cross accomplished among them. Preaching should proclaim Christ crucified with such power and vividness that people see and feel the power of the cross. Paul is not talking about a spine-tingling, sensational description of the crucifixion. Neither is he talking about a dramatic presentation of the physical act of crucifixion. No! He is talking about preaching the doctrine of the cross, about preaching the reality and effect of the substitutionary atonement of Christ.

Paul's language suggests that preaching must be earnest and passionate. He himself preached with such a passion, as if Christ was crucified there in the midst of the congregation. As Paul was preaching, their hearts were seized with the beauty and glory of Christ, with the sufficiency of His atonement, with the only hope of deliverance being Christ. It was by that kind of preaching that God delivered them from their sins. Therefore, Paul reminds them, 'Remember what God did to save you! Remember how beautiful and glorious Christ was as I preached Him to you. Do you want to nullify that? Are you willing to say that what Christ did was not sufficient for you?' Yet they were now 'bewitched,' foolish, because in resorting to circumcision they had denounced the sufficiency of Christ. The most useful antidote against temptation is to think on the beauty and loveliness of the Lord Jesus Christ.

Second, Paul demonstrates that the doctrine of the Judaizers was contrary to the indwelling work of the Holy Spirit in the lives of the Galatian believers. In verse 2, Paul introduces a series of questions: **This is the only thing I want to find out from you**. To determine this one thing he probes their consciences with a series of four rhetorical questions with respect to their reception of the Holy Spirit. First, **Did you receive the Spirit by the works of the law, or by hearing with faith** (v. 2)? Notice that Paul has put this question in the context of preaching. 'Hearing with faith' is literally 'hearing in faith.' In other words, as they heard the gospel they responded in faith and repentance. The question implies the answer that they received the Spirit when they believed, not by works of the law. This question and answer are very important, because the Spirit was at the forefront of all apostolic ministry and the spread of the gospel. As Paul speaks about the Spirit, he is talking both about the gift of the Spirit and the gifts of the Spirit. The Spirit was given to them when they responded in faith to the gospel.

Moreover, the gospel was not preached merely in word; the apostolic gospel was accompanied by wonderful signs and seals. Consider Acts 14:3: 'Therefore they spent a long time there speaking boldly with reliance upon the Lord, who was bearing witness to the word of His grace, granting that signs and wonders be done by their hands.' Paul asks, 'Have you forgotten what happened when I preached the gospel of Christ?' God had attested the reality of that gospel by granting signs and wonders and miracles. When Calvin was taunted by a Romanist that he did not have any miracles to confirm his teaching, he responded that he did not need any. His message was from the Bible and had already been confirmed by the miracles recorded in the New Testament. Paul claims that the Spirit confirmed his message. He said, 'Do you remember how you have received the Spirit? Through the works of the law? No! Through the preaching of Christ, which you received by faith alone.'

Furthermore, the Spirit was granted to them under Paul's preaching to demonstrate that the gospel had come to Gentiles as well as to Jews. You remember that when Peter was preaching in Cornelius' house the Spirit fell upon that Gentile household. Later, in his defence of taking the gospel to these Gentiles (Acts 11:17), Peter informed the church leaders in Jerusalem that the Spirit came upon the Gentiles in the same way He came upon the early church in Jerusalem on the Day of Pentecost. This proof was sufficient grounds for Peter's baptizing these Gentiles. Paul reminds the Galatians that the Spirit sovereignly came upon them in order to manifest that they were hearing God's truth and that God indeed had made salvation available to Gentiles. They were baptized with the Spirit as they believed the gospel. Consequently, they did not receive the Spirit by the works of the law, but rather by believing the gospel.

Paul constructs his second argument with another question in verse 3: **Are you so foolish? Having begun by the Spirit, are you now being perfected by the flesh?** Here he demonstrates that when they received the Spirit, they received everything they needed for salvation. The Spirit of Christ, the Spirit of the triune God indwelling them, is the Spirit that brings and guarantees all the benefits of redemption: regeneration, adoption, justification, sanctification, perseverance, assurance, confidence, and glorification. They received all of these things in the Spirit, because He is the pledge and provider of them all. Paul, therefore, asks, 'Having begun by the Spirit are you going to perfect the work of God in the flesh?' By the term 'flesh' he is referring to the fleshly works of the circumcision and ceremonies. Were they able to perfect through a works righteousness what they received by faith? The answer is obvious; having begun by the Spirit, they should continue in the Spirit, because He who has begun a good work in them would bring it to fruition.

The third question is in verse 4, **Did you suffer so many things in vain – if indeed it was in vain?** The word 'suffer' may be translated 'experience.' Hence the question is, 'Did you experience so many things in vain?' Their experience testified to them of the Spirit's work in their lives. They had embraced the gospel experientially; their consciences bore witness to the reality of what Paul was preaching. If he is wrong, all is pointless. All the joy and peace they experienced in the gospel would be in vain; they would lose it all if they tried to continue by fleshly methods.

He concludes with his fourth question, **Does He then who provides you with the Spirit and works miracles among you, do it by the works of the Law, or by the hearing with faith** (v. 5)? The answer by now is obvious; they received the Spirit by faith; they continue in the Spirit by faith; their experience has testified to these things; all these things happened because they believed the gospel.

Paul leads them through this series of questions to demonstrate the folly of departing from the gospel of grace for a false gospel of works righteousness. By these arguments Paul reminds us of the importance of faith as the living and active principle throughout all of Christian experience. Sometimes we tend to state the doctrine of sanctification in a way that suggests a Christian, having begun by faith, completes his salvation by works.

Indeed, we have an important work to do in sanctification, but we must never pursue it apart from Christ who works in us. The Westminster Confession of Faith affirms with respect to faith: 'But the principal acts of saving faith are, accepting, receiving, and resting upon Christ alone for justification, sanctification, and eternal life, by virtue of the covenant of grace' (XIV:II). We believed in Christ not only for justification and adoption, but also for sanctification. We are to depend on Him and the Spirit that is in us for all growth in grace. The Spirit is working in us, applying to us the death of Christ and the resurrection of Christ in order that we might die to sin and become more Christlike. Therefore, faith acting on Christ is the instrument not only of justification, but also of sanctification. This role of faith, however, is not passive. We are to work out our salvation. We are to be diligent. Christ says, 'If you love me you will keep my commandments.' But faith responds by looking to Christ for all things.

In this section, moreover, we learn three distinguishing marks of preaching. First, it was *Christo-centric*. In verse 1, when Paul says, 'before whose eyes Jesus Christ was publicly portrayed as crucified,' the apostle is simply stating that he preached Christ and Him crucified (1 Cor. 1:2). We know that Paul preached the whole counsel of God, so when he talks about preaching Christ, he is not omitting any doctrines of the faith. He, however, reminds us that every doctrine is a road that leads to Christ. Our sermons need to be full of Christ. Whatever the doctrine or commandment preached, it should lead us to Christ and remind us that only in Christ do we have the power to obey.

Second, Paul's preaching was *intellectual*. His arguments are carefully constructed; the rhetorical questions are carefully worked out. Paul expected his audience to think. A true preacher must expect his listeners to consider what he says.

He must never forget that the Christian faith is propositional, rational truth, which must be communicated in such a way that people are required to think about it.

Third, Paul's preaching was *experiential*; namely, it was marked by Christian experience and passion. He himself experienced and loved the doctrines he proclaimed. He preached them with a passion and in such a way as to probe the consciences of his hearers. He also related the truth of the Spirit's work to their experience so that the whole person – mind and heart – was called on to respond to the truth of God. Contemporary preaching must deal with people in this manner as well.

Study Questions

1. What is Paul's indictment of the Galatians?
2. What does he means by calling them foolish?
3. What does he mean by the term 'bewitched' to describe the work of Satan?
4. What do we learn here about Satan's strategies?
5. What is Paul's first argument to prove his indictment?
6. How does works righteousness detract from the preaching of Christ?
7. What is Paul's second argument?
8. How does he construct this argument?
9. List and discuss each argument.
10. What do we learn here about the role of faith in our sanctification?
11. What three things do we learn here about preaching?

10

Children of Abraham

(Galatians 3:6-9)

Paul is demonstrating what it means to be declared righteous by God and to receive that righteousness by faith in Christ. The defence of this doctrine is the great theme of the book of Galatians. The apostle refutes the error of the Judaizers by contrasting justification by faith with their doctrine of salvation by faith and works.

In verses 1-5, Paul uses the experience of the Galatians to remind them that they had received Christ by faith through the preaching of the gospel and that by faith they received the Holy Spirit, who was given as the pledge of forgiveness of sins and adoption as the children of God.

Having laid that foundation, Paul begins in verse 6 to prove his doctrine from the Old Testament, beginning with the story of Abraham. We recognize the fittingness of this strategy. Since the Judaizers were saying that the Gentiles, in order to enjoy the full privileges of the church, had to become Jews, they adamantly claimed that the Gentiles, in order to be saved, had to become circumcised children of Abraham. Paul refutes this error from the Bible by teaching two things: first, one becomes a child of Abraham by faith and, second, one inherits the promises of Abraham by faith.

Children by Faith (3:6, 7)

A sinner becomes a child of Abraham by faith: **Even so Abraham believed God, and it was reckoned to him as righteousness. Therefore, be sure that it is those who are of faith who are the sons of Abraham** (vv. 6, 7). Notice Paul's use of logic. He expects people to think, to use their minds. He states a truth in verse 6 and then draws an inference in verse 7. In verse 6, he establishes that Abraham was saved by faith, receiving righteousness by faith. Paul quotes Genesis 15:6: 'Then he (Abraham) believed and the Lord reckoned it to him as righteousness.' Remember the context of that declaration. Abraham had just defeated the kings of the east. You can imagine how vulnerable he felt afterwards. Would that powerful coalition seek revenge? Since he had very few resources, would they destroy him? It is in that context that God says, 'Do not fear, Abraham, I am shield to you; and your reward shall be very great' (Gen. 15:1b). God reminded Abraham what he had promised earlier in Genesis 12.

In response, Abraham began to plead with God, 'O Lord God, what will you give me, since I am childless and the heir of my house is Eliezer of Damascus? … Because you have given me no offspring, and a member of my household will be my heir' (Gen. 15:2, 3). (The custom of the times dictated that, if one died without a natural heir, one's estate passed to his steward.) Abraham was saying that he could not receive what God has promised without a son. He was asking, 'Where is the promised seed?' God had promised Abraham an innumerable seed, yet he did not even have one son. God took him outside of his tent and renewed the promise with respect to his seed. God said to him, 'Now look towards the heavens, and count the stars, if you are able to count them…. So shall your descendants be' (Gen. 15:5). Therefore, when Abraham felt his weakness and inability to accomplish anything, God graciously renewed the promise of a great seed that would possess the nations of the earth.

In response to this promise, **Abraham believed in the Lord** (v. 6). Abraham's faith began with the recognition of his utter inability and poverty. He had to believe in the sufficiency of God; he was certain that God would do whatever He promised. Abraham confessed, 'I rest in God, not in my own strength.' Although later Abraham's faith would falter and he would attempt to procure an heir through Hagar (Gen. 16), yet at this moment he rested in God and in the promises of the Saviour to come.

In response to Abraham's faith, God declares him righteous, **and He reckoned it to him as righteousness** (v. 6). What does it mean that God reckoned Abraham as righteous? God imputed His righteousness to Abraham; He said that Abraham was righteous in His sight. This declaration is part of justification: God forgives our sin and declares us to be righteous in His sight for evermore. Abraham was already converted; he had followed God for many years. God, however, makes this declaration at this time in order to demonstrate how one is saved. God spells out the theological principle that a person receives righteousness through believing the promises of God and not through his own works and efforts. God also reminds us that whether it is the day we first come to Christ or many years later, we are justified by faith alone and by nothing else.

In verse 7 Paul draws the inference: **Therefore be sure that it is those who are of faith who are the sons of Abraham**. Although this declaration was made thousands of years ago, we may be certain of its validity today. Everyone who trusts in God by faith is a son of Abraham. Remember the Judaizers had been saying that salvation was by faith plus circumcision. One had to become a Jew to be saved. There was an element of truth in what the Judaizers were saying. They correctly understood that God had only one people. There is only one church and it consists of the spiritual descendants of Abraham. God will not have another people who are saved in another way.

The Judaizers' problem was their failure to understand how one became a part of the seed of Abraham. They said to the Gentiles who believed that they also must be circumcised. They had to become Jews in their flesh and not just in their hearts. In contrast Paul draws this very important inference that a person becomes a child of Abraham by faith. When he says, 'Be sure that it is those who are of faith who are the sons of Abraham' he is simply saying that one is in the church by faith.

In what way are Christians the sons of Abraham? First, we are sons by way of imitation; we enter the church in exactly the same way that Abraham entered the church, by faith. As with Abraham, our faith begins with a sense of bankruptcy, with a realization that we are sinners under God's wrath and condemnation. We are unable to do anything to save ourselves. We cannot atone for our sins or expiate the guilt which deserves eternal hell. Saving faith begins with this realization. Each one of us – whether born in a covenant household, not knowing a day that we were not resting in Christ, or whether coming to Christ later in life – must have this existential realization of sin and depravity.

Therefore our faith begins where Abraham's faith began, with the sense of our helplessness. Then it moves to an assurance that God is who He says He is and will do all that He promises. When God promises that He will receive sinners who come to Him in Christ, He is saying that He will pardon all their sins and declare them to be righteous in His sight for the sake of Christ. The believer assents to these promises and trusts in God to do what He has promised. He rests in Christ alone for salvation. As a result, he becomes a son of Abraham by imitation. We are saved in the same way as he was.

Second, we are also sons of Abraham by covenant unity. God has appointed Abraham as the covenant head of the visible family of God, and we enter into his household through faith. When we receive justification by faith, we enter into an organic link with Abraham. He is our father, and if Abraham is our father, God is our Father. And so it is by faith, and faith alone, that we enter into God's family.

Heirs by Faith (3:8, 9)

In verses 8 and 9, Paul goes a step further and shows that by faith we receive the blessings of Abraham: **And the Scripture, foreseeing that God would justify the Gentiles by faith, preached the gospel beforehand to Abraham, saying 'All the nations will be blessed in you. So then those who are of faith are blessed with Abraham, the believer.'**

In order to remind the Galatians what God promised Abraham when He called him, Paul quotes the conclusion of God's promise in Genesis 12:1-3. The promise reads, 'Now the

Lord said to Abram, "Go forth from your country, and from your relatives, and from your father's house, to the land which I will show you; and I will make you a great nation, and I will bless you, and make your name great; and so you shall be a blessing; and I will bless those who bless you, and the one who curses you I will curse. And in you all the families of the earth shall be blessed."' In verse 8, Paul draws our attention to the climax of the promise, 'all the nations of the earth will be blessed in you.'

Notice how Paul personifies the Scripture. He says that the Scripture, foreseeing that God would justify the Gentiles by faith, preached the gospel beforehand to Abraham saying, 'All the nations shall be blessed in you.' This statement gives an important insight into Paul's theology of Scripture. Paul is teaching that what God said to Abraham, and what Moses recorded hundreds of years later in the Book of Genesis, are to be treated in the same manner. In other words, God speaks in Scripture. It is His word. There is not an iota of difference in the word spoken by God to Abraham and that word recorded by Moses in Genesis 12. Paul could say that the Scriptures 'preached' to Abraham because the Scriptures are the divine, infallible, inerrant record of what God had said to Abraham.

Paul, by inference, also teaches that Abraham was justified long before he was circumcised. Later, in Romans 4, Paul will build on this argument; here he just implies it, when he says, 'foreseeing that God would justify the Gentiles by faith, he preached the gospel.' In other words, before Abraham was circumcised, he received the gospel. He believed God; his justification is declared in Genesis 15:6, but God does not command him to be circumcised until Genesis 17. Paul demonstrates that it was God's intention to save the Gentiles in exactly the same way that He saved Abraham, and that is by faith.

God had promised Abraham that the nations would be blessed in him. These nations would receive His blessings in exactly the same way Abraham had received them, by faith. By faith Abraham believed God; by faith he went out from Haran believing the promises of God. Therefore Paul reminds us that we receive the blessings of Abraham by faith alone.

In verse 9, Paul derives a conclusion from the preceding verse, **So then, those who are of faith are blessed with Abraham, the believer**. Because God promised him that all the nations would be blessed in him, all Christians are in Abraham's household and we receive the blessings in exactly the same way that he received them.

What are these blessings? Obviously they cannot be the temporal promises given to Abraham, because Paul says the promise belongs to all those in the church in all ages. He is reminding us that the blessings promised to Abraham were the blessings of the gospel that were first promised in Genesis 3:15 and repeated throughout the Bible; namely, the forgiveness of sins, the gift of the Holy Spirit, and eternal life.

The writer to the Hebrews clearly states that these were the blessings promised to Abraham. He says Abraham was looking for a heavenly city as his inheritance (Heb. 11:15, 16). Abraham recognized the spirituality of the blessings. They were packaged in the temporal blessings and the land promise, but those things were only the wrapping. Who would ever be content on Christmas morning or on his birthday with a beautiful package? You would not be content with the packaging; you want the gift that is inside the package. Neither was Abraham content with the package of the land promise and temporal blessings. He sought eternal life, God as his inheritance, and the forgiveness of sins. These are the things God gave to Abraham, and Paul reminds us that God gives the same to us if we are the sons of Abraham. It is by faith we become the sons of Abraham and by faith we receive these great promises of Abraham.

Two lessons are evident here. First, this Scripture passage teaches that God has but one people. By faith Gentiles enter into Abraham's family, which is the church. Consequently, God teaches us that he does not have two peoples: the church and the nation of Israel. The household of Abraham is the church. It existed among the Jews from the days of Abraham until Pentecost, when its gates were flung wide open to the nations of the earth in the fulfilment of God's promise. By faith, we enter the household of Abraham or, to take Paul's other image, we are grafted into one olive tree (Rom. 11:17-24). There are not two trees. There is one tree and some of the natural branches were lopped off, because of unbelief, and others were engrafted in by faith. If we have believed in Christ, we are the Abrahamic olive tree; we are engrafted into the Jewish olive tree. The church of God is the new Israel. There is but one household, there is but one church, and we enter the church in but one way, by faith.

A second lesson flows from the first. If it is the same church, with the same blessings, then we also have the same covenant privileges for our children that Abraham had for his. After Abraham is declared justified in Genesis 15:6, he asks God for proof. God gives him a covenant to assure him. Later in Genesis 17 God says that circumcision is the sign of this covenant and that the covenant is with Abraham and his children. Therefore, if there is but one church, with one set of promises, and one way of entering, there must be but one covenant. The inclusion of Abraham's children in the covenant is one of the many arguments that prove children of believers are members of the covenant community today, with the same covenant standing as Abraham's children. Each of God's covenant administrations embraced the children. Since children in the old covenant received circumcision, and baptism has replaced circumcision (Col. 2:11-13), I believe the Bible makes clear that children of Christians should be baptized.

But there is also a warning. Circumcision did not save all who experienced it. As in the old covenant, circumcision had to be united with faith, so baptized covenant children must come to Christ by faith and repentance. Their baptism does not save them. Baptism is the sign and seal of God's promise that they are in the covenant and heirs of the promises of the covenant, but they must come to Christ for themselves. As their parents or guardians, we must constantly keep before them the necessity of faith in Christ. If our children eventually prove themselves to be unbelievers, like many of the physical descendants of Abraham, they will not be saved.

Study Questions

1. What Old Testament passage does Paul use in Galatians 3:6, to prove his doctrine that justification is by faith and not faith plus works?
2. Discuss the context of God's declaration of Abraham's righteousness.
3. What does it mean that God reckoned his faith to him as righteousness?
4. Was Abraham justified differently from the New Testament believer?
5. In what two ways are we the sons of Abraham?
6. What does it mean to be a son by imitation?
7. How are we united to Abraham?
8. What second Old Testament passage does Paul quote?
9. What does Paul's language ('Scripture, foreseeing') teach about Paul's doctrine of Scripture?
10. What were the primary blessings promised to Abraham?
11. Are these the blessings of the gospel?
12. What are the two lessons learned from this section?

11

The Curse of the Law

(Galatians 3:10-12)

Paul is proving from Scripture that justification is by faith and not by works of the law. In verses 6-9, he uses the life of Abraham to prove that Abraham was justified by faith and that by faith believers today are his children and heirs. In verses 10-12, Paul uses three other Old Testament passages to demonstrate that if one seeks to be justified by works of the law he will fall under God's curse: **For as many as are of the works of the Law are under a curse; for it is written, 'Cursed is everyone who does not abide by all things written in the book of the law, to perform them.' Now that no one is justified by the Law before God is evident; for, 'The righteous man shall live by faith.' However, the Law is not of faith; on the contrary, 'He who practises them shall live by them.'**

The Law's Curse

Paul expands his argument beyond the ceremonial law. He has already shown that to be under the Mosaic Law in any way brings a person under its full stipulations and sanctions. Here the apostle asserts that the one seeking salvation through law-keeping will not find peace and commendation, but falls under condemnation and the curse of the law, which the Shorter Catechism (19) reminds us is the miseries of this life, the fact of death itself, and eternal damnation. In order to establish this point the apostle quotes from Deuteronomy 27:26: 'Cursed is everyone who does not abide by all things written in the book of the law, to perform them.' This verse concludes a series of curses pronounced at Mt. Ebal. These curses relate to some of the major prescriptions and applications of the Ten Commandments. Verse 26 is a summary statement of the covenant curses.

The purpose of the curses was to remind the people that they were unable to keep the law of God in a way that would make them acceptable to Him. For this reason, an altar for sacrifice was erected on Mt. Ebal, reminding the people of their need of grace, their need of pardon through an atoning sacrifice. Therefore, they lived by grace. Paul derives from what was said at Mt. Ebal the general principle: the person who seeks to come to God by the means of his obedience or the person who does not deal with the fact that he is a sinner, who falls short of the glory of God, is under God's curse.

The indictment of this curse is threefold. First, it reminds us that we are called to a *comprehensive* obedience: 'Cursed is everyone that does not abide by all things written in the book of the law.' The self-serving claim of comparative obedience will not suffice. One cannot claim, 'Well I have kept this part and that part, but I have not really kept this other part, but that is okay.' Remember James 2:10, 11: 'For whoever keeps the whole law and yet stumbles in one point, he has become guilty of all. For He who said, "Do not commit adultery," also said, "Do not commit murder." Now if you do not commit adultery, but do commit murder, you have become a transgressor of the law.'

Second, God's law demands *personal actions* of obedience: 'Cursed be everyone who does not abide by all things written in the book of the law to perform them.' We must personally obey the law. We are under a curse if we do not perform the demands of the law. Some of the Jews revelled in the fact that they had the law and imagined that this by itself made them special. For this reason, Paul reminds them in Romans 2:13: 'For not the hearers of the Law are just before God, but the doers of the Law.' In this verse Paul is not teaching that one can be saved by law-keeping. Rather he is contrasting possession with performance. Therefore, it is not sufficient to be in covenant with God and know the law. One must personally keep all the law if one is to be saved.

Third, God requires *perpetual* obedience: 'Cursed is everyone who does not abide by all things written in the book of the law.' It is not sufficient to have kept all of the law for thirty years and then for the next year or two break the law. The law is a perpetually binding obligation (see Ezek. 18:24).

Therefore, Paul uses Deuteronomy 27:26 to indict anyone who thinks that he can be right with God on the basis of the works of the law. Left to ourselves, we are under the curse of God and there is absolutely no hope that we can be justified by the works of the law.

Faith's Role

Having established from the law the inability of law-keeping to justify a sinner, Paul demonstrates from the Prophets that justification is by faith: 'Now that no one is justified by the law before God is evident, for the righteous man shall live by faith' (v. 11). In this verse Paul quotes Habakkuk 2:4: 'Behold, as for the proud one, his soul is not right within him; but the righteous will live by his faith.' Habakkuk had complained about the sin of the covenant people and God said that He was going to punish them by the Babylonians. Habakkuk was scandalized. He pointed out that the Babylonians were far worse than the covenant people. Why would God use them? God replied that in the future He would make all things right: 'For the vision is yet for the appointed time; it hastens toward the goal, and it will not fail. Though it tarries, wait for it; for it will certainly come, it will not delay' (Hab. 2:3). In verse 4, God anticipates the proud person who says that he does not want to wait for God's timing. He does not want to live by that which he cannot see. He quibbles against the purposes of God. Such people are unwilling to submit; they are unwilling to live by the promise of the word of God; they demand to live by sight, by human effort, by their own rules. This is the type of one whose 'soul is not right within him'.

By contrast the righteous man is the one who lives by faith. Habakkuk is referring to the behaviour of the righteous man and not to how one becomes righteous. The fact is, however, that those who are righteous before God live by a very different principle than the proud. They live by faith. Paul's inference is, if they live by faith, then they have come to that righteousness by faith, which is exactly what he has already proven. So he rightly concludes that if the righteous man continues by faith, he begins by faith; he persists and perseveres by faith. It is faith alone that enables him to live righteously before God. That which is true for the maintenance of righteousness is obviously true for the receiving of righteousness. Therefore, the apostle concludes that no one may be justified by the works of the law.

Paul has already proved in 3:1-5 that sinners do not begin in faith and perfect themselves by works. Instead they begin by faith and continue by faith. They depend completely on the grace of God for all righteousness and acceptance. Regardless how long such have lived the Christian life, the principle remains the same, 'The righteous man lives by faith.' A person does not commend himself to God by his sanctification, by his faithfulness, by all of his church deeds, by his service, by his work as a pastor, by his faithfulness as a husband and father. They can do nothing that will ever commend themselves to God. Once they try to commend themselves to God by the standard of the law, they come under a curse, because the law demands perfection.

Therefore, Paul argues from Habakkuk 2:4 that salvation is by faith alone. Righteousness is received by faith alone and the righteous one lives by faith. This fact does not negate the responsibility of believers to pursue sanctification (Heb. 12:14). God has saved them in order to conform them to the image of His Son, Jesus Christ. If they have been justified, they will long to obey.

The Incompatibility of Law and Faith

Paul anticipates the objection that although one is justified by faith, true faith obeys, therefore works play a role in our justification. He reminds his readers that with respect to justification these two roads (faith and law) will never converge. They are diametrically opposed and there is no middle road that is part faith and part works. He says in verse 12, 'However, the law is not of faith; on the contrary, "he who practises them shall live by them."' With respect to being right with God, the law and the gospel are diametrically opposed. Of course, both are part of God's revelation and therefore are not opposed as divine truth (see Romans 3:21).

The law is good. It instructs believers about how to respond to God in love and gratitude. When they use the law in this God-revealed way, there is no conflict with faith. But as soon as they introduce law-keeping as part of the way one becomes or remains right with God, they must be reminded that law-keeping plays no part. We can no more mix faith and works as instruments in justification than we can mix oil and water.

To prove his point, Paul quotes Leviticus 18:5: 'So you shall keep My statutes and My judgments, by which a man may live if he does them; I am the Lord.' God's law is a way of life in that it shows the believer the path that he is to walk in; it is the way of covenant blessing. Paul, however, absolutizes the statement in Leviticus, because the Judaizers have twisted the law from its God-given purposes by making it the means of justification. When it is abused in this manner, the judgment of the law resounds – 'he who practises them shall live by them.' To practise the law in order to seek righteousness by it brings one under the comprehensive demands of the law.

What Paul declares positively in Romans 11:6, 'But if it is by grace, it is no longer on the basis of works, otherwise grace is no longer grace,' he says negatively in verse 12 here. The moment that we introduce any aspect of law into the equation of being right with God we have actually done away with grace and placed the person under law. Therefore, we may never combine faith and works with respect to justification. Any effort of commending ourselves to God, of earning or currying God's favour, brings us under the curse of the law. We only find peace as we rest in Christ alone.

One practical lesson from these verses is the importance of using the law in our evangelism. We are to use the law to bring people to a conviction of sin. People need to realize that they are under the curse of the law and that their only hope is in Jesus Christ.

A second lesson is the necessity for each of us to be humbled at the realization of our sinful weakness. Oftentimes, the longer we live the Christian life, the more highly we regard ourselves, quickly losing sight that we are sinners saved by grace. We begin to think that God is fortunate to have us on His side! Paul's reminder here is very humbling: 'The righteous man lives by faith.' At the end of the day, regardless of how much we have done and of how many years we have lived the Christian life, we have done nothing to make ourselves acceptable to God. There is nothing of worth in us innately. Whatever usefulness we have is by the grace of God in order that He alone might get the glory. All our achievements, all the things that we have done by God's grace, are simply our giving thanks to Him. When all is said and done, we are unprofitable servants. We have only done what we ought to do. Therefore, we should live humbly and walk as righteous people in dependence upon the grace of the Lord Jesus.

Study Questions

1. What is Paul's purpose in Galatians 3:10-12?
2. What is the purpose of the curses in Deuteronomy 27?
3. How does Paul apply Deuteronomy 27:26 to the matter of justification?
4. What three things does God require for complete obedience?
5. What principle does Paul derive from Habakkuk 2:4?
6. If faith is essential to sanctification, then does law-keeping work along with faith in justification?
7. What verse does Paul use to show that one may not introduce law-keeping as a partial instrument in receiving justification?
8. What does this section teach us about the use of law in evangelism?
9. How does this section humble us?

12

The Curse Bearer

(Galatians 3:13, 14)

Paul teaches in these verses that faith justifies not by what it does, but by what it receives; the ground, the basis, of our justification is the work of Christ. Faith simply brings us into union with Christ. **Christ redeemed us from the curse of the law, having become a curse for us; for it is written, Cursed is everyone that hangs on a tree, in order that in Christ Jesus the blessing of Abraham might come to the Gentiles, so that we might receive the promise of the Spirit through faith**. Christ has purchased for His people the benefits of the covenant.

Christ Redeems from the Curse of the Law (3:13)

The verb 'redeem' and its noun 'redemption' are very important words in the Bible. They mean to ransom, to purchase by a price paid; the price is designated a redemption or ransom; and the reality of being purchased by that price is to be redeemed. Redemption includes deliverance from the curse and purchase of the inheritance.

Paul is dealing with the negative aspect of redemption, what sinners have been redeemed from. An Old Testament background for this aspect of redemption is found in Exodus 21:28-30, a reference to an ox that was in the habit of goring people. 'If an ox gores a man or a women to death, the ox shall be stoned and its flesh shall not be eaten; but the owner of the ox should go unpunished. If, however, an ox was previously in the habit of goring and its owner has been warned, yet he does not confine it, and it kills a man or a woman, the ox should be stoned and the owner shall also be put to death. If a ransom is demanded of him, then he shall give the redemption of his life whatever is demanded of him.' Here is the case of a dangerous ox, whose owner has been warned to keep it under lock and key. If the owner is careless and the ox gets out and kills somebody, the ox is put to death and the owner is also condemned to death, because of his carelessness; it is his fault that his ox has killed somebody. But in this case a ransom, a redemption price, might be paid if the family of the victim determines to accept a financial payment in place of the death of the owner. The guilty man can make that payment and be delivered from the curse of death.

This law illustrates what Paul is teaching about Christ's redeeming His people from the curse of the law. Christ has made a payment, not to Satan (as the ransom theory of the atonement would teach),[1] but to God, because their sin has brought them under His curse. Their violation of the law exposes them to the curse of a just and perfect God. They are liable to punishment, because they are guilty. But Christ has paid a redemption price to deliver His people from the curse of the law.

How did Christ accomplish this redemption? He redeemed them from the curse of the law by becoming a curse for them. These words are perhaps the most astonishing words in the Bible. Here we are reminded of the great transaction of imputation, which Paul delineates in 2 Corinthians 5:21: 'He made Him who knew no sin to be sin on our behalf, that we might become the righteousness of God in Him.' Imputation means to place to one's account. Christ, who was pure, spotless and undefiled, who had obeyed the law of God perfectly in all respects, willingly took on Himself the guilt of the sins of His people. It is not just that He was accursed, but He became 'A Curse.' He took the curse of the sins of His people on Himself, the guilt to which they were liable. The eternal damnation that belonged to them was placed on His soul, put into His

1 The Ransom Theory, which was first taught by Origen, states that Christ's atonement was paid to satisfy Satan's claims and not to propitiate God's wrath.

moral account so that He who knew no sin was made sin, He who was innocent became guilty in the place of sinners. And when did that transaction take place? It occurred when Christ was on the cross of Calvary.

Paul demonstrates the curse-bearing nature of Christ's death by using Deuteronomy 21:23 to relate His death on the cross with being cursed by God. He introduces the quotation with the word 'for,' giving the basis of what he just said: Cursed is everyone who hangs on a tree. In the old covenant the person who was guilty of a capital offence was put to death most often by stoning and then, if the offence was particularly heinous, he was hanged on a post or a tree as a mark of his cursedness. Moreover, enemies of God's people were hanged in this fashion. Joshua hanged the body of the king of Ai on a tree (Josh. 8:29). God revealed this form of punishment because He intended to put His Son to death in this manner in order to signify He was the cursed of the cursed. He was the most cursed of all; cursed like an enemy of God. Christ endured the most humiliating and awful death on the cross to bear our curse. As He hung suspended on the cross between heaven and earth and the sun blackened, this awful transaction occurred. The Father placed on the Son the guilt of the sins of His people and Christ paid the penalty of separation from the Father and was directly exposed to the punishment and wrath of God against sinners. He suffered the pains of hell in order to satisfy the justice of God (Rom. 3:24-26).

This transaction is so wonderful, so mysterious and awful that Luther boldly wrote, 'But Christ took all our sins upon him, and for them died upon the cross: therefore it behooved that he should become a transgressor, and (as Isaiah saith, ch. 53) "to be reckoned among transgressors." And this, no doubt, all the prophets did foresee in spirit, that Christ should become the greatest transgressor, murderer, adulterer, thief, rebel, blasphemer, &c. that ever was or could be in all the world. For he being made a sacrifice for the sins of the whole world, is not now an innocent person and without sins, is not now the Son of God born of the Virgin Mary; but a sinner, which hath and carrieth the sin of Paul, who was a blasphemer, an oppressor and a persecutor; of Peter, which denied Christ;

of David, which was an adulterer, a murderer, and caused the Gentiles to blaspheme the name of the Lord.'[2]

By this work Christ purchased redemption. He offered His own perfect life to redeem us from the curse of the law, and that is the negative aspect of redemption.

Christ Purchased the Benefits of the Covenant (3:14)

In verse 14 Paul speaks positively about the covenant benefits Christ has purchased for His people: 'In order that in Christ Jesus the blessing of Abraham might come to the Gentiles, so that we might receive the promise of the Spirit through faith.' Verse 14 begins with a purpose clause that shows the close connection between the negative work of redemption by which Jesus satisfies the curse and the positive work of redemption by which He has purchased the benefits of the covenant.

When Adam sinned, he not only exposed us to the justice and anger of God, he also forfeited our inheritance. Our redemption would not have been complete if Jesus only delivered us from the curse of God. We would still lack communion with God. Therefore, Paul teaches that it was God's intention to purchase for sinners the benefits of the covenant, 'that in Christ Jesus the blessing of Abraham might come to the Gentiles.'

The blessing of Abraham is the twofold promise of the remission of sin and the gift of the Holy Spirit. God pictured this promise for Abraham and the old covenant community by the inheritance of the land. The fulfilment of this inheritance belongs to all of the seed of Abraham, Jews and Gentiles. Christ by His work of redemption purchased this blessing for all His people, so that by His work the Gentiles become heirs of Abraham. Note that this verse, in fact, contains two purpose clauses: in order that in Christ Jesus the blessing of Abraham might come to the Gentiles; in order that we might receive the promise of the Spirit. Both of the purpose clauses relate to the work of Christ. In the second purpose clause Paul teaches that believers receive the promise of the Spirit by faith; so that in Christ not only do they receive the blessing and the inheritance of Abraham, namely, the remission of

2 Martin Luther (revised by Philip S. Watson, 1953), *A Commentary on St Paul's Epistle to the Galatians*, James Clarke, 269.

sins, but that this reception is guaranteed to them by the gift of the Holy Spirit. He is the pledge God gives to assure them that they have received all that He has promised.

In fact, it is only in the new covenant that believers receive the Holy Spirit in full measure, because He is given by the glorified Christ, who received Him without measure and has been given the privilege of giving Him to the church. Therefore, the Spirit of Christ dwells in each believer today as fully and as completely as He indwelt a few people such as prophets, priests and kings in the old covenant. That is what Joel means when he says that when the Spirit comes all will prophesy and have visions (Joel 2:28, 29). The New Testament believer has the Spirit in exactly the same way that the prophets of the old covenant had the Holy Spirit. In this age every son and daughter of God has the Spirit, which is why the least in the kingdom of heaven is greater than John the Baptist, who was the greatest of the old covenant prophets (Matt. 11:11).

And how do such receive the Spirit? Through faith. With this phrase, Paul comes full circle. He began his argument in 3:1, 2 by asking, 'How was Christ set before you? He was preached and you received Him by faith. And how did you receive the Spirit with His benefits? By faith.' He concludes with the rhetorical questions, 'Do you really think that having begun by faith you are going to complete these things by works?' In verse 14 he continues this argument, showing from the life of Abraham that believers today receive the blessings of Abraham, not through circumcision, not through any ceremonies, but through faith alone.

Study Questions

1. What are some of the faulty understandings of the role of faith in justification?
2. What is the basis or grounds of justification?
3. What does Paul mean by the term 'redeem'?
4. How does Exodus 21:28-30 illustrate redemption?
5. What does Deuteronomy 21:23 teach about the curse of crucifixion?

6. Was Christ truly cursed? What did the curse entail?
7. According to verse 14 what benefits did Christ purchase for us?
8. What is the blessing of Abraham?
9. How does the gift of the Holy Spirit relate to this blessing?
10. Does every New Testament believer have the Holy Spirit in the same way?
11. What does this section teach about the awfulness of sin?
12. What does it teach about the love of God?
13. What should our response be?

13

Law and Grace

(Galatians 3:15-22)

There is much discussion today concerning the relationship between law and gospel, the Mosaic covenant and the new covenant. What are the patterns of discontinuity and continuity between the Old Testament and the New? Dispensationalism asserts the most extreme pattern of discontinuity between the Mosaic covenant and the new covenant, that there is little relationship between them. In its earlier forms, Dispensationalism taught that God offered salvation in the Mosaic covenant to those who obeyed. A modified Dispensationalism says that God offered salvation to those who obeyed in order to teach the people that they could not be saved apart from grace. In the first form, the Mosaic covenant was an administration of salvation, in the latter it served as a probationary period. Neither form believes that the Mosaic covenant is part of the covenant of grace or that the Ten Commandments have any positive role for new covenant believers.[1]

A more recent expression of discontinuity was taught by Dr Meredith Kline. Kline taught that the Mosaic covenant was a covenant of works and not part of the covenant of grace. He conceded that God still saved people by grace through the

1 For a recent study of Dispensationalism, see Kimbro, Reginald C., *The Gospel According to Dispensationalism: A Doctrinal Survey of the System That Permeated Fundamentalism* (Toronto: Wittenburg Publications, 1995). Mathison, Keith A., *Dispensationalism: Rightly Dividing the People of God?* (Phillipsburg, N.J.: P & R Pub, 1995).

time period of the Mosaic covenant, but the covenant itself was a legal covenant. He therefore downplayed the role of the Ten Commandments in the life of new covenant believers.[2]

On the other hand, there are those who see almost no discontinuity between the Old and New Testaments. Some theonomists argue that, apart from the temple cult and sacrificial system, there is little difference between the Mosaic covenant and the new covenant and, therefore, they emphasize the continuity with very little discontinuity. Theonomists of course would have a high view of the role of the Ten Commandments in the life of the believer (interestingly though, some downplay the Fourth Commandment).

In this passage, Paul gives us a great deal of insight into the relationship of law and gospel. He uses the term 'law' to refer to the Mosaic covenant. If law culminates in curse, what then are its role and its relationship to God's grace? Paul answers this question by explaining the relationship between the Abrahamic and the Mosaic covenants. He shows us two things: (a) the Mosaic does not nullify or alter the Abrahamic and (b) the Mosaic is actually subservient to the Abrahamic.

The Mosaic Covenant does not nullify the Abrahamic Covenant (3:15-18)

First, in verses 15-18, Paul proves that the Mosaic covenant does not nullify or alter the Abrahamic. In verse 15, he uses an analogy from human contracts to establish the boundaries of the relationship between the two covenants: **Brethren, I speak in terms of human relations: even though it's only a man's covenant, yet when it has been ratified no one sets it aside or adds conditions to it**. When both sides sign the contract/covenant, it is ratified and is binding on all parties. Someone may not come along later and nullify or change it. Imagine you have bought a house for $200,000 and after you signed the contract the seller came back and said, 'I have changed my mind; I want $250,000.' He legally could not get more money from you nor could he retake possession of the

2 Meredith G. Kline, *Treaty of the Great King: The Covenant Structure of Deuteronomy, Studies and Commentary* (Grand Rapids: Wm. B. Eerdmans, 1963); *By Oath Consigned: A Reinterpretation of the Covenant Signs of Circumcision and Baptism* (Grand Rapids: Wm. B. Eerdmans, 1968).

house. This is analogous to what Paul teaches with respect to the relationship of the Mosaic to the Abrahamic. The covenant that God made with Abraham could not be laid aside by a later covenant made through Moses.

Paul continues in verses 16-17 to demonstrate that the Abrahamic covenant takes precedence over the Mosaic covenant. He begins with the fact that God sovereignly made specific, unilateral (with no conditions attached) promises to Abraham. These promises were not merely for temporal benefits; in addition the temporal promises were types of great spiritual promises (3:9).

Paul notes that God made the promises to Abraham and to his seed. Interpreting the Abrahamic promise in light of Genesis 3:15, Paul teaches that the term 'seed' refers primarily to Jesus Christ: **He does not say, 'and to seeds,' as referring to many, but rather to one, 'and to your seed,' that is, Christ** (v. 16). Paul is not denying that God promised Abraham a seed more numerous than the stars of the heavens (Gen. 15:5). In fact, in Galatians 3:7, he teaches that all believers are the sons of Abraham. Paul by his language in verse 16, however, is teaching that the promises belong not to Abraham's physical seed, but to his spiritual seed, and that it is only in 'the seed' (Christ) that the promises will come to Jew or Gentile. Hence, he builds on the promise of Genesis 3:15 that the seed of women will destroy the serpent, Satan. The seed of the woman is the promised Messiah. Therefore when God swore to Abraham to bless him and make him a blessing to the world (Gen. 12:1-3), God was promising to bring the seed (the Christ) through the descendants of Abraham.

This emphasis on Christ is important for two reasons. First, one could argue that although the promise was made to Abraham, Isaac, and Jacob, since they were now dead, at Sinai God introduced another contract to replace the previous one. Paul argues that there can be no change, because the ultimate recipient of all the promises in the Scriptures is the Lord Jesus Christ, in whom are all the promises of God (2 Cor. 1:20). The promise, therefore, not only is about Christ, it also belongs to Christ. It is the eternal Christ, who has received the promises of the covenant, who is the true covenant maker and covenant keeper. If the Abrahamic covenant is with Him, then the promise continues in Him. Second, Paul reminds us that we have no blessings in the promise apart from Christ. It is as we are in union with the Lord Jesus Christ that we have the things that were promised to Abraham, which are the promises of the gospel. Therefore, the Abrahamic covenant takes precedence over the Mosaic because of the seed to whom the promise was given.

A second argument for the precedence of the Abrahamic covenant is the time sequence. Since the promise was made to Christ and is eternal, what God did at Sinai four hundred and thirty years later cannot invalidate the previously ratified covenant of God, **What I am saying is this: the Law, which came four hundred and thirty years later, does not invalidate a covenant previously ratified by God, so as to nullify the promise** (v. 17).

There is an interpretative problem with Paul's chronology here. In Exodus 12:40, Moses writes: 'Now the time that the sons of Israel lived in Egypt was four hundred and thirty years.' Paul says, however, that the law was given four hundred and thirty years after the promise. How do we reconcile these diverse accounts with respect to dating? Either Moses includes in his chronology the time from Abraham, but telescopes it to the period in Egypt, or, since God renews the promise to Jacob as he is about to leave the land (Gen. 46:1-3), Paul has in mind the repetition of the Abrahamic promise to Jacob as he went down to Egypt. So the period of four hundred and thirty years either began with Abraham while he was in the land or with the renewal of the promise to Jacob as he left the land. Either interpretation is valid.

In verse 18 Paul draws his conclusion: **For if the inheritance is based** (from) **on law, it is no longer based on a promise, but God has granted it to Abraham by means of a promise**. The term 'for' shows the relation of the analogy to the two covenants. The inheritance (the benefits promised to Abraham) would be lost if God changed the terms. God, however, has not changed the terms. He promised the inheritance to Abraham and sealed that promise with an oath (Heb. 6:17, 18). Abraham received it by faith. By promise and oath God guaranteed to Abraham that He would fulfil all He had said. Therefore, the promise and the means (faith) remain in effect. If the inheritance were by law, God would have changed the principle of inheritance.

As far as the Galatians were concerned, it was not God who changed the principle of inheritance, but the Judaizers. Hence, God did not bring in law as a competing way of receiving the promised benefits.

The Mosaic Covenant is Subservient to the Abrahamic Covenant (3:19-22)

If the Mosaic covenant did not nullify or change the terms of the Abrahamic covenant, what then was its role, and is it contrary to the promise of God? **Why the law then?** Remember that 'law' refers to the Mosaic covenant. If the Mosaic covenant is not another way of salvation, what is its purpose? Paul says its purpose was to convince of sin and point to the promised Messiah: **It was added because of transgressions, having been ordained through angels by the agency of a mediator, until the seed should come to whom the promise had been made** (v. 19).

God's people under the Mosaic covenant needed a regular reminder that without grace they were under God's judgment; they needed to be kept under restraint; and they had to be taught to anticipate the coming of the Messiah. Paul answers his question, 'Why Law,' by showing that the law was subservient to promise; God gave it because of sin. He illustrates this from the manner of giving of each covenant. God gave the promise to Abraham directly, but he gave the law indirectly through the mediation of angels and Moses. The reference to angels was a reminder of the overwhelming holiness of God revealed at Sinai. In Deuteronomy 33:2, Moses wrote: 'The Lord came from Sinai, and dawned on them from Seir; He shone forth from Mount Paran, and He came from the midst of ten thousand holy ones; at His right hand there was flashing and lightning for them.' The angelic mediation demonstrated the holiness of God and exposed the sin of the people. The divine, angelic terror at Sinai filled the people with terror. Therefore, they desired that God not speak to them directly, but that He would speak through Moses: 'And all the people perceived the thunder and the lightning flashes and the sound of the trumpet and the mountain smoking; and when the people saw it, they trembled and stood at a distance. Then they said to Moses, "Speak to us yourself and we will listen; but let not God speak to us, lest we die"' (Exod. 20:1, 19).

So God spoke directly to Abraham with promise and oath, but indirectly to the people in the Mosaic covenant. Paul says further that God's speaking through a mediator demonstrated the sin of the people: **Now a mediator is not for one party only; whereas God is only one** (v. 20). The term 'mediator' implies sin. The people, not God, needed the mediator, because of their sin. God does not change; He is one; therefore, He could have come to them as He did to Abraham. He chose to come in a mediator in the Mosaic covenant to show them their sin and their need of the Saviour to come.

This assertion leads to Paul's second question, **Is the law contrary to promise** (v. 21)? Notice Paul's strong denial, **May it never be**. Such a thought is unimaginable. Paul then uses a conditional sentence: **For if a law had been given which was able to impart life, then righteousness would indeed have been based on law.** If it were possible to get life by the works of the law, then there would be a conflict between Abraham and Moses. But law does not impart life; therefore, no man can obtain a righteous standing (justification) before God by works. Law cannot save; it cannot give a new heart. No one can keep it perfectly to be righteous in God's sight.

Therefore, in verse 22, Paul reiterates the purpose of the law: **But the Scripture has shut up all men under sin, that the promise by faith in Jesus Christ might be given to those who believe**. Paul further spells out this concept in Romans 3:19, 20: 'Now we know that whatever the law says, it speaks to those who are under the law, that every mouth may be closed, and all the world may become accountable to God; because by the works of the law no flesh will be justified in His sight; for through the law comes the knowledge of sin.' Therefore, there is no conflict between Abraham and Moses. The law points to the promise that salvation is by faith in Jesus Christ. The promise given in the Abrahamic covenant is not in conflict with the Mosaic covenant, but they work in tandem to promote the promise.

Note Paul's final statement, 'given to those who believe.' He reiterates that justification is not by faith plus works; it is not by some reintroduction of the Mosaic covenant. It is by faith alone.

In summary we learn that the Mosaic covenant was part of the covenant of grace. Its legal element pointed men to the Saviour to come. The demands of the covenant of works, originally made with Adam in Eden, were repeated in the Mosaic covenant: to be right with God one must obey the law perfectly and those who did not would die. The reiteration of these demands in the Mosaic covenant accomplished two things. First, it convinced men and women that they needed a Saviour, because none could obey the law perfectly. Second, it provided the framework under which Christ obeyed the law perfectly throughout His life (His active obedience) and satisfied the judgment of God against sin on the cross (His passive obedience).

Study Questions

1. What are some of the modern conflicts with respect to the Mosaic Covenant and the Covenant of Grace?
2. What does Paul means by the term 'Law' in verse 17?
3. What analogy does Paul use to prove that the Law does not nullify promise?
4. How does he interpret 'seed' in verse 16? Why does he do this?
5. Give a summary of his argument that law does not nullify promise.
6. What two questions does Paul ask with respect to the Law's relationship to the Abrahamic covenant?
7. What is the role of the Mosaic Covenant?
8. Are the two covenant administrations in opposition?
9. What do we learn here about the role of the Mosaic Covenant in the history of redemption?
10. What does this section teach about dispensationalism and other views that claim the Mosaic Covenant is not part of the Covenant of Grace?
11. What do we learn about the role of law and gospel?

14

Why Law?

(Galatians 3:23-25)

We have established that the Mosaic covenant was a legal administration of the covenant of grace, which in no way abrogated or nullified the Abrahamic covenant. These covenants are not different or competing ways of salvation. The Bible reveals only one way that sinners may be saved and that is by faith in the Lord Jesus Christ. What then was the purpose of the Mosaic covenant law? Paul begins to answer this question in verses 19-22: the legal covenant was given because of sin to prepare for and drive people to Christ. He said in verse 19 that it was added because of transgression, and in verse 22 that 'Scripture has shut up all men under sin, that the promise by faith in Jesus Christ might be given to those who believe.' In verses 23-25, the apostle expands on the role of the Mosaic economy in relationship to the unfolding of the covenant of grace, by spelling out the purpose of the Mosaic covenant in the history of redemption.

Mosaic covenant Given to Govern the People of God in Their Immaturity (3:23, 24)

Paul affirms: **But before faith came, we were kept in custody under the law, being shut up to the faith which was later**

to be revealed. Therefore the law has become our tutor to lead us to Christ, that we may be justified by faith. Paul uses two different concepts to describe the working of the Mosaic economy. First, he uses legal terms – 'kept in custody' and 'shut up'. Keep in custody means to guard. Paul uses it in 2 Corinthians 11:32 to describe the way its king guarded Damascus to prevent Paul's escape from the city. Shut up denotes confinement under restraint. These terms depict the bondage of the old covenant. Paul defines the Mosaic covenant as something by which God corralled His people. It was as if they were under house arrest. The law was a restraint that God had placed on them, because of their waywardness of heart, their propensity to fall into idolatry and covetousness. Moreover, it pointed them to Christ and their need of Him.

This imprisonment would last until Christ came. Notice the unusual language, **being shut up to the faith which was later to be revealed** (v. 23) and **Now that the faith has come** (v. 25). Paul says that their bondage was temporary until the faith came. What is this 'faith'? He is not referring to the active principle by which all of God's people are saved, since it was at work in the Old Testament (Heb. 11). This phrase refers to the full revelation of the new covenant; namely, the object of faith. Paul uses a figure of speech. Faith is put for its object, which is the Lord Jesus Christ.

So the bondage was temporary. God kept the people in bondage until the full mystery of the gospel would be revealed in the person of the Lord Jesus Christ. We rightly infer from the contrast that, when Christ would come, the period of custodial relationship, the imprisonment so to speak, would end.

This contrast is made even clearer in the second figure Paul uses in verse 24: **Therefore the law has become our tutor to lead us to Christ**. Paul here uses the word 'pedagogue.' In Greek culture the pedagogue was the slave who was placed in charge of the heirs while they were in their minority. He would take them to school; he would administer discipline. Under this arrangement, although they were heirs, they were treated almost as if they were the slaves. The custodianship of the law functioned like a pedagogue.

So during the period of the Old Testament, God governed His people by the Mosaic administration.[1] By it God restrained them morally and religiously. This covenant was strict and severe. It repeated the stipulations and the sanctions of the covenant of works. The command 'Do this and you shall live' caused people to realize that they could not earn eternal life by their works, because they could not keep these laws. The curses of the Mosaic covenant were prominent in its promulgation, when God threatened them with physical and spiritual punishments. In that respect, it was a dark and foreboding covenant.

Moreover, the concept of being trained as children explains the Mosaic covenant's emphasis on temporal blessings. God used the physical blessings of the Mosaic covenant to reward His people in their minority in order to train them by teaching them to take small steps to please Him. Because they were as children, they needed the ceremonies, the washings, and the sacrifices. These things, however, were an enormous bondage. Can you imagine a woman trying to run a household with all the ceremonial laws of what was unclean? They lived

---

1 In my exposition of Paul's explanation of the Mosaic covenant, I have used the distinction of moral, ceremonial, and civil (or judicial) laws. The distinction is based on the Westminster Confession of Faith, 19:3, 4: 'Beside this law, commonly called moral, God was pleased to give to the people of Israel, as a church under age, ceremonial laws containing several typical ordinances; partly of worship, prefiguring Christ, his graces, actions, sufferings, and benefits; and partly holding forth diverse instructions of moral duties. All which ceremonial laws are now abrogated under the New Testament.''To them also, as a body politick, he gave sundry judicial laws, which expired together with the state of that people, not obliging any other now, further than the general equity thereof may require.'The distinction is based on the concept of moral laws and positive laws. Moral laws are those laws that are a reflection of God, our relationship to Him, and our relationship to one another. These laws perpetually bind the people of God. Positive laws are those laws that God places on His people for certain periods of their history; for example, food laws and the day the church observes the Sabbath. These laws are based on the moral law and apply it, but God may change them. Ceremonial and judicial laws are positive applications of God's moral law. Both have moral principles that we seek to apply today.With this distinction in mind, some ask, 'Is Paul not simply abrogating the ceremonies (circumcision and food laws) when he says that justification is not by works of the law?' In Galatians 3 Paul uses law to refer to the entire Mosaic legislation (vv. 10, 11), which included the moral law of God. In Galatians 2:16, when he writes about 'works of the law,' he alludes to Psalm 143:2, 'For in Your sight no man living is righteous,' to prove that the works of the Law do not justify. In Romans 3:20 he writes that works of the law do not justify, because the purpose of the law is to convict of sin, alluding to its moral scope (see Rom. 7:7, 8). Moreover, he is contrasting the principle of faith (receiving) with works (doing).

under constant pressure in every part of life. But they were treated in this way so that they might be kept morally and religiously pure. Even with these restraints, they kept falling into immorality and idolatry. Implied in this assessment of that temporary arrangement is the concept of the foolishness of a Christian (Jew or Gentile) ever returning to those laws. He would be placing himself under the minority system after he has tasted of the full liberty of the gospel.

Christ has Freed the Church from Bondage (3:25)

Christ has freed the new covenant church from the bondage of the Mosaic covenant. Everything Paul has said points toward the reality of this change. Before faith came the church was under custody and the law was a tutor to lead them to Christ in order that they might be justified by faith. **But now that faith has come, we are no longer under a tutor** (v. 25).

In what way does Christ free His people from the old covenant restrictions? By His meeting all the demands and fulfilling all the types of the law. This fulfilment is part of the concept of the faith that was to come. As we live in the power of the Lord Jesus Christ, we live as mature men and women in Christ and are freed from the bondage of the Mosaic covenant. See how the apostle applies this in verse 25. Because Christ has come, we have been delivered from the law. The tutor has been dismissed. Or as Paul says in Romans, we are under grace and not the law (Rom. 6:14). We are no longer under the tutor. What Paul means is that we are no longer under the law in its temporary capacity as a legal administration of the covenant of grace. The demand of the law to earn life through obedience to it has been fulfilled in Christ. Jesus fulfilled all the moral demands of the Mosaic covenant and so He has fulfilled the covenant of works, obeying it perfectly in order to earn life for His people and submitting to the curse of law by His crucifixion in order to satisfy the justice of God as their propitiatory sacrifice.

Moreover, Christ fulfilled all the *ceremonies*, both those that were figurative, pointing to Him, and those that were necessary to govern Israel in her minority. We have been delivered from all of the minute particulars of the Mosaic ceremonies. He has done away with all of the childish rules that were necessary in the past and has brought us into a maturity in which He governs us by His Spirit. The Mosaic covenant also contained *judicial laws* to govern the people in their minority. God does not obligate the state today to govern by these laws, but the moral principles of these laws ought to guide us in family, church, and state.

What then is the Christian's responsibility to the moral law of God as it is summarized in the Ten Commandments? The moral law, which was written on Adam's heart at creation, was restated in the Mosaic covenant and remains the abiding statement of God's moral rule for His people. The moral law teaches us how to express our love to God and gives us a divine pattern for self-examination. It is a light, a mirror, for us to use.

Because Christians live in the maturity of the gospel, James calls the moral law 'the law of liberty' (James 2:12). We are no longer in the servile bondage of the old covenant people. We serve God as freeborn sons, empowered by the Holy Spirit. He who regenerated us is the one who raised Christ; consequently, the power that raised Christ is the power at work in us. And so for us the moral law is a royal law.

Moreover, what God did in the history of redemption He does in the lives of men and women who come to Christ. As the law brought the people corporately to Christ in the history of redemption, it functions in a similar way with individuals today. God brings sinners to Christ through a law work; nearly every born-again person who has not been regenerated in infancy or in his very early years will come to Christ in this way. The law teaches that God demands perfect obedience from each person and condemns any disobedience. It causes sinners to realise that they cannot save themselves and so they must turn to the Lord Jesus Christ in whom alone is righteousness and perfection.

Let us also note that there remains a role for the threatenings of the law in the life of the Christian. The Westminster Confession says that the law 'is likewise of use to the regenerate, to restrain their corruptions, in that it forbids sin; and the threatenings of it serve to shew what even their sins deserve, and what afflictions in this life they may expect for them, although free from the curse thereof threatened in the law'

(WCF 19:6). It is good for us to remember our sin and the curse from which we have been delivered, to feel periodically the awful reality of a Christless existence; so that we might be filled with gratitude and love for all that God has done for us in Christ. Consequently, we thank God for the law and seek to use it biblically.

Study Questions

1. What two figures does Paul employ to teach the temporary character of the Mosaic Covenant?
2. What two terms does he use in verses 23 to teach the custodial work of the law? What does each mean?
3. What does Paul mean by the phrase, 'the faith which was later to be revealed' and 'that faith has come'?
4. What term does he use in verse 24?
5. What was the work of the tutor in Greek culture?
6. What was the role of the law for the Jewish people in the Old Covenant?
7. How has Christ freed us from the bondage of the law?
8. How has he freed us from the ceremonial law?
9. What was the purpose of the judicial law? How do we apply it today?
10. Are we obligated to keep the moral law?
11. Does law fulfill a similar function in bringing individuals to Christ?
12. What lesson may we derive about rearing children?

15

The Family

(Galatians 3:26-29)

Most people by nature are joiners; we join clubs, societies, and associations; we form close groups of friends in whom we find a certain degree of security and identity. The institution, however, in which people often find the most security and identity is the family. The family, instituted by God at creation, is the most basic societal group. Hence it is not surprising that throughout Scripture God has chosen the concept of family as one of the primary figures by which He reveals our relationship to Him and to one another. The Bible says we are God's household; God is our Father; Christ is our elder brother; we are brothers and sisters of one another.

Those of us reared in good covenant families are equipped to appreciate what we have in the Lord Jesus Christ. Those of us who have not had the blessing of living in a Christian home learn about the beauty of family in another way. Through our relationship with God in the church, we learn what family ought to be. As a young Christian, out of a broken home, my great desire was to have a family so that I might, to some degree, do those things that God had appointed for a family. I learned those things primarily through Scripture, how God relates to us, and secondarily through books. And so we learn from God what family is, and from a good covenant family we may learn a great deal about God.

Paul uses the figure of family in Galatians 3:26-29 to teach us about who we are in Christ Jesus. In these verses he establishes that we become the sons of God by faith. Paul lays out three things: first, by union with Christ we are brought into God's family; second, by union with Christ we are related together in God's family; and third, by union with Christ we receive the full inheritance God has for His family.

By Union with Christ we are Brought into God's Family (3:26, 27)

Paul begins by affirming that by union with Christ God brings sinners into His family: **For you are all sons of God through faith in Christ Jesus. For all of you who were baptized into Christ have clothed yourselves with Christ** (vv. 26-27). Paul refers to the Jews in verse 25, but in verse 26 includes the Gentile Christians ('You are *all*'). Along with the Jews, who have been delivered from their minority status, Gentile Christians enter into the privilege of mature sons, having obtained the inheritance through faith.

The phrase 'in Christ' is Paul's favourite way of describing the reality of Christian experience. It permeates his writings. The structure of the sentence in verse 26 places emphasis on 'in Christ Jesus.' Paul points out that faith is the link that brings us into union with the Lord Jesus Christ. He uses the term 'faith' since the argument is to prove that we are saved by faith alone, not by faith and works. When we are regenerated, we believe in Christ for salvation and this faith brings us into a living union with Christ.

Our union with Christ has been eternally planned before the foundation of the world (Eph. 1:4). Thus we are in union with Christ by election and that union is effected by regeneration. When God changes our heart, our very first reflex action is to believe on the Lord Jesus Christ. Even when God regenerates a child in the womb or an infant, He also creates faith. As that child develops, its faith will manifest itself in faith and repentance. Faith works through our minds, our affections, and our wills, so as soon as an infant's faculties are able to grasp anything of its sin and unworthiness, and of the glory of the grace of the gospel, he or she believes.

Union with Christ is the basis of our acceptance with God in justification. Furthermore, it is the basis of our adoption. Because we are in union with Jesus, the first born and the elder brother, we are accepted not as servants and slaves, but as sons and daughters of God. Paul uses the term 'sons' to include women as well as men. In the Greek and Roman culture the son was the heir, so Paul uses the word 'son' to emphasize the inheritance that belongs to all who are in Christ.

Moreover, our sanctification flows out of our union with Christ. Consider what Paul says in 1 Corinthians 1:30: 'But by His doing you are in Christ Jesus, who became to us the wisdom from God, and (both) righteousness and sanctification, and redemption.' All the benefits of redemption belong to us, because we are in union with Christ. The very union we have with Christ, for which God justifies us, is also the vital means by which God sanctifies us. Indeed, it is a phenomenal thing to contemplate that the Spirit of Christ indwells us so that we are vitally one with Christ our Saviour. The power of Christ is at work in us even as we are covered by the righteousness of Christ.

Paul writes that baptism testifies to this union: **For all of you who were baptized into Christ have clothed yourselves with Christ**. He points out that the most significant meaning of baptism is union; baptism is a sign and seal of our union with Christ. Paul uses baptism with this meaning of union, for example, in 1 Corinthians 10:2: 'And all were baptized into Moses in the cloud and in the sea.' When the children of Israel passed through the Red Sea on dry land, they were baptized into Moses. The children of Israel were declared to be in union with Moses; they were the set apart people of God.

Paul also makes clear he is referring to union when he uses the illustration of clothing. Just as you put on your clothing, your baptism reminds you that you have been clothed with Christ. Now all who are baptized are in a covenant relationship with the Lord Jesus Christ. Baptized children are legally in covenant with Christ. Baptized adults making a profession of faith are in covenant with Christ. Paul is not claiming that every baptized person is regenerated. An important function of baptism is to serve as a sign or a picture of union with

Christ. To those who possess the reality by faith baptism also functions at the level of a confirming sign.

Baptism then declares to those who are baptized that they belong to Christ, that they are in covenant under Him. And it declares to those who have been regenerated, the full reality of their saving union with Christ. Calvin uses the illustration that man cannot live by bread alone, but by every word that proceeds from the mouth of God. It is not the physical bread that keeps us alive; ultimately it is God. But God uses physical bread. It is not baptism that regenerates us, but that God uses our baptism in such a way that it confirms to us the reality of our union. It functions as a secondary means.

Let us note the importance of our Baptism. It testifies to us of our union with Christ, our remission of sin, our adoption, and our glorification (L.C. 165). It obligates us to die to sin and pursue holiness (L.C. 167). When we have doubts, we look to our baptism for God to confirm to us that He has clothed us with the righteousness of the Lord Jesus Christ. We look to our Baptism to be reminded that we have died with Christ and have been buried with Him, therefore we are dead to sin (Rom. 6:1-4).

Because of this reality we are to reflect often on our baptism as instructed in the Larger Catechism. Hence the Larger Catechism teaches the important duty of improving our Baptism, not that we can add to it, but we are to use it in a manner to profit from it. Since the efficacy of Baptism is not tied to its moment of ministration, but is life -long, we are to make life-long use of it.

'How is our baptism to be improved by us?' 'The needful but much neglected duty of improving our baptism, is to be performed by us all our life long, especially in the time of temptation, and when we are present at the administration of it to others; by serious and thankful consideration of the nature of it, and of the ends for which Christ instituted it, the privileges and benefits conferred and sealed thereby, and our solemn vow made therein; by being humbled for our sinful defilement, our falling short of, and walking contrary to, the grace of baptism, and our engagements; by growing up to assurance of pardon of sin, and of all other blessings sealed to us in that sacrament; by drawing strength from the death and resurrection of Christ, into whom we are baptized, for the mortifying of sin, and quickening of grace; and by endeavouring to live by faith, to have our conversation in holiness and righteousness, as those that have therein given up their names to Christ; and to walk in brotherly love, as being baptized by the same Spirit into one body' (L.C. 167). Thus the Larger Catechism teaches the important duty of improving our Baptism, not that we can add to it, but we are to use it in a manner to profit from it. Since the efficacy of Baptism is not tied to its moment of ministration, but is life-long, we are to make life-long use of it.

By Union with Christ we are Related to One Another (3:28)

The second matter that Paul teaches here is that in Christ we are joined together in the family of God *in spiritual equality*: **There is neither Jew nor Greek, there is neither slave nor free man, there is neither male nor female; for you are all one in Christ Jesus**. As he is dealing with those who really belong to the people of God, he establishes that baptism, not circumcision, is the sign of membership of His family. Baptism is the great badge of unity. Circumcision has become that which divides between Jew and Gentile (Eph. 2:11, 12). Paul implies, what he asserts clearly in Ephesians 2:11, 12, that baptism has replaced circumcision. We are diverse members; we have different gifts, abilities, and functions, but we are all part of the one body. Just as the toe is different from the ear, the finger from the eye, but all part of one body, the body of Christ is a diverse unity (1 Cor. 12:12-25).

Because of union with Christ, we are one body, one family, and there are no second class citizens in the family of God. That is what the apostle is driving at with these three pairs of distinctions. He says there is neither Jew nor Greek, slave nor free man, male nor female. He begins with the *racial* distinction that has created the problem in Galatia, Jew and Gentile. Because Christ has abolished this division (Eph. 2:11-22), with respect to standing in the church there are no racial or ethical divisions.

The same is true *economically*. Paul says that there is neither slave nor free. Now the New Testament does not abolish the economic institution of slavery. The Bible governs that institution, but it does not abolish it. In the church, however, we are not to relate to people on the basis of their social or economic standing: 'My brethren, do not hold your faith in our glorious Lord Jesus Christ with an attitude of personal favouritism. For if a man comes into your assembly with a gold ring and dressed in fine clothes, and there also comes in a poor man in dirty clothes, and you pay special attention to the one who is wearing the fine clothes, and say, "You sit here in a good place," and you say to the poor man, "You stand over there, or sit down by my footstool," have you not made distinctions among yourselves, and have become judges with evil motives' (James 2:1-4)?

The same holds true for *gender relations*, there is neither male nor female. Circumcision created a distinction between male and female, but this sacramental distinction no longer remains. Women as well as men are baptized to testify to their equal standing within the church of Christ. No one in the body of Christ is spiritually superior to another. We note, however, that this abolition of distinction of standing is not an abolition of distinction of function or authority. God has appointed authority structures between master and servant, employer and employee. In the family God has commanded children to obey their parents and wives to be in submission to their husbands. In the church, God teaches that office bearers are to be men and that women are not to teach or exercise authority over men (1 Tim. 2:11-15). Therefore, within the equality that belongs to all in the body of Christ, there remains a diversity of authority and rule.

Moreover in the church, we may rightly glory in our heritage and culture. There is nothing wrong with cultural distinctives, as long as we do not make them marks of superiority in the Church. The fact that Jew and Gentile became one does not mean that a Jew stops enjoying his heritage and that a Roman Christian cannot still glory in certain things in Roman culture and civilization. The church is not the great melting pot in which we must lose all cultural distinctions, but rather a place where they come together under the headship of Christ and actually are part of the beauty of the church. Heaven will be like a great bazaar, an international market, in which all the cultures of the earth will be represented. Of course, all that is unbiblical will have been removed and all that is biblical will be brought to perfection. So we may rejoice in our culture, not arrogantly, but with humility, recognizing that there are good things in various cultures and that some cultures are superior to others. In the church, however, we do not draw lines on the basis of superiority or inferiority of culture.

Because of Union with Christ we Receive a Full Inheritance (3:29)

The third matter Paul states here is, because of this union, we have entered into the fullness of our inheritance: **And if you belong to Christ, then you are Abraham's offspring, heirs according to the promise**. Because of union with Christ, we are the seed of Abraham. The term translated 'offspring' is 'seed.' Because of faith in Christ, we are reckoned as descendants of Abraham. In other words, the Gentile Christian is as much a descendant of Abraham as the Jewish Christian.

The inheritance then belongs to us on the basis of promise believed and not by works performed. Our inheritance is not something that is postponed until heaven; it begins now. There are at least three things involved in this inheritance. First, there are the spiritual benefits that are ours in Christ. We have already enumerated these: regeneration, faith, justification, adoption, sanctification, union, redemption, assurance, boldness in prayer, all these things are ours right now as part of our inheritance.

Second, there is eternal life itself. We have begun to participate in eternal life, but at our death we will enter into the personal glorification that will be perfected at the second coming of Christ.

Third, the inheritance includes the earth itself. The earth does not belong to the wicked, instead they use it by usurpation. The earth belongs to the family of God. God in His providence has not necessarily given great possessions to His people now, but what He has given to them is theirs to enjoy. The Bible knows no bifurcation of spiritual and material. Part of our inheritance, if we are in Christ, is that we may enjoy the beauty of this world that Christ has made. We can enjoy food, music, gardens and trees, history, geography, and geology; all of these things are ours in Christ. God will not withhold any good thing from us. He delights in blessing us. Our problem is that we turn blessings into gods. The fault lies not in the created world; it lies in our hearts. We need to understand that as the sons and daughters of God we have been given this world to enjoy as part of our inheritance.

And so we are in the family of God; it is a glorious reality. We should think often on it and aim to live in the full reality of union with the Lord Jesus Christ.

Study Questions

1. What is the basis of our being in God's family?
2. What phrase does Paul use to express out union with Christ?
3. What does union with Christ mean?
4. How do we attain union with Christ?
5. What is the relation of union with Christ to justification, adoption, and sanctification?
6. How does baptism confirm our union with Christ?
7. Discuss the sign and seal of baptism as it relates to covenant children, the unconverted, and the converted.
8. How does union with Christ affect our relationships within the church?
9. Is Paul abolishing authority and functional structures?
10. How does union relate to our inheritance?
11. What is our inheritance?

16

Heirs of God

(Galatians 4:1-7)

A person may place someone in his will for a number of reasons; he may be an heir naturally by birthright, an heir by adoption, or an heir by some special relationship with the benefactor. His inheritance might have a particular degree of certainty, but there is no guarantee, even if he were a natural born heir, that he would not be disinherited. In the first century, one could obtain the inheritance by being a natural born heir or by becoming an adopted heir. There was, though, one major difference: while a natural born heir in the Roman culture could be disinherited and often was, an adopted heir could not be disinherited. This legal concept of an irrevocable inheritance for an adopted heir underlies Paul's doctrine of adoption. When Paul teaches about adoption, he not only is dealing with the reality that we have been brought into God's family, he also is dealing with the fact that, as God's children, we have received an inheritance that cannot be annulled. Reference to Roman practice also explains why Paul speaks of adopted sons – in Roman culture it was the son who was the heir. His reference to sons does not exclude women from the inheritance; as we saw in the previous section, in Christ there is no male or female; all have equal standing with respect to the inheritance. The very fact that Paul applies the concept of the adopted son to women demonstrates that men and women share equally in the inheritance.

Paul concludes chapter 3 by declaring that we are sons and heirs by faith. The reality of our position is sealed to us by our baptism. Paul continues this theme of sons and inheritance in chapter 4 as he relates the inheritance to our adoption. In verses 1-7, Paul deals with three things: the preparation for adoption, the purchase for adoption, and the pledge of adoption.

The preparation for adoption (4:1-3)

In verses 1-3, Paul discusses the preparation of adoption: **Now I say, as long as the heir is a child, he does not differ at all from a slave although he is owner of everything, but he is under guardians and managers until the date set by the father. So also we, while we were children, were held in bondage under elemental things of the world**. Paul reaches into the Roman culture of his day for an analogy. He reminds us that a child of a wealthy family, while in his minority, before coming into his inheritance, did not enjoy privileges beyond many of the slaves. He had not obtained his inheritance. He did not have the right to make his own decisions or to spend his inheritance the way he may have wanted. In fact just as slaves were under stewards, administrators, or foremen, the minor child was under guardians and tutors. Paul deals with the role of the slave tutor in 3:24, 25.

So just as slaves laboured under a hierarchical management system, in effect the heir in his minority lived, worked, and studied under this hierarchy. In reality, one could detect little difference externally in the household with respect to the son and the slaves, and this condition continued until the date set by the father when the son would enter into his maturity and receive his inheritance.

In verse 3 he applies the analogy to what he has been saying about the old covenant people. In his use of the pronoun 'we' he refers to the Jews. While they were children, 'they were held in bondage under the elemental things of the world.' The phrase 'elemental things' refers to the ceremonies of the Mosaic administration. As we learned in chapter 3, these things were temporary; they were designed to keep the heirs in a state of servility until they reached maturity. Elemental things are the ABCs, they are the alphabet, so to speak. Their description, being 'of the world,' implies they were externals. They were not designed to change the heart (2 Cor. 3:6, 7). The old covenant law was an external code written on tablets, containing a list of dos and don'ts; it was an external restraint and thus it was called the 'elemental things of the world.'

The purchase of adoption (4:4, 5)

In verse 4, Paul changes the analogy from minors coming into an inheritance to adoption: **But when the fullness of time came, God sent forth His Son, born of a woman, born under the Law, in order that He might redeem those who were under the Law, that we might receive the adoption as sons.** Adam was a son of God and, if he had kept the covenant of works, he would have been confirmed in that estate of sonship. But Christ is the only true born Son of God; even Adam would have been confirmed the son of God by adoption. The old covenant people were the sons of God and although they were adopted in the old covenant, the inheritance and full freedom of adoption was not yet theirs. Their approach to God was to a great degree governed by the rituals of the priesthood and sacrificial system. The priests would go into the holy place daily on their behalf. The high priest once a year would go into the presence of God, into the holy of holies, on their behalf. They were the sons of God, but they had not yet obtained their inheritance; they had not reached the age of maturity.

The date set by the father is tied to the purchase of adoption. What is the set time? It is the time that God had appointed when Christ would come and do all that was necessary to bring the church into her majority, here called the fullness of time. The primary meaning behind the expression 'the fullness of time' is the time that God eternally decreed for his Son to become incarnate and accomplish all that had been decreed for the salvation of the people of God. The fullness of time then is the time God set to bring His people into the fullness of their inheritance by the work of the Redeemer.

That time was indicated by the prophetic clock. The prophetic clock began ticking with the first announcement, in Genesis 3:15, of the miraculously provided Deliverer. As the clock ticked, the picture grew bigger. To change the figure, it is like the way your computer loads a program or brings up a web site. It begins with partial pictures that go from the top down. When it is fully loaded you have the complete picture. The images load according to the speed of your computer. Well that is what I mean by the prophetic clock. The Old Testament displays one image after another until the picture is complete, from the outlines of the patriarchal revelation to the clearer pictures of Isaiah and Daniel, to the final details of the post exilic prophets. The picture becomes increasingly clearer. By the time of Christ's birth, the picture was so clear that many of the faithful covenant people knew that they were going to see Christ in their generation. They waited by faith, because the alarm clock was about to go off.

That is the idea behind this phrase, the fullness of time. It is a God-decreed time, the wisely chosen time that God has appointed, the time in which He would complete the unfolding of the revelation of redemption. The old covenant church was the custodian of that revelation. She was the clock keeper and would be so until the alarm would go off when the fullness of time arrived.

So the fullness of time should be thought of, not in terms of a prepared time, but of a prophetic time, of the God-set time. This concept, however, does not rule out that it was a prepared time. If God had wisely determined the time for the advent of the Redeemer, he was also preparing the world for that advent. Thus in a secondary sense it is not wrong to think of the fullness of time as the culturally prepared time. God not only prepared the Jewish people, he prepared the scene in terms of establishing the worldwide use of the Greek language, improved means of transportation, and other consequences of Roman rule, for the advent of the Christ.

Paul next describes what occurred at the fullness of time: 'God sent forth His Son, born of a woman, born under the law.' With these simple words Paul proclaims the glorious mystery of the incarnation of the Son of God. God's sending His Son states the pre-existence of the Son, and implies the divinity and eternality of the Son. The Son was with the Father and the Father sent Him into the world. The Son is not someone whose existence began at birth.

The Son came to earth by being born of a woman. Those two simple phrases 'sent forth' and 'born of a woman' sum up the mystery of the incarnation. The eternal Son of God was sent into the world through a process of taking a human nature in the womb of the virgin Mary. This fact is the greatest mystery of divine revelation: in the womb of the virgin Mary, God the Son took to Himself a human nature with a true body and a reasonable soul. As a result he was one person existing with two distinct natures. Luther captured the mystery in his advent hymn, 'All Praise to Thee, Eternal Lord':

> Once did the skies before thee bow;
> A virgin's arms contain thee now:
> Angels who did in thee rejoice
> Now listen for thine infant voice.

The Shorter Catechism summarizes the event thus: '*How did Christ, being the Son of God, become man?* Christ, the Son of God, became man, by taking to Himself a true body, and a reasonable soul, being conceived by the power of the Holy Ghost, in the womb of the virgin Mary, and born of her, yet without sin' (S.C. 22). Shorter Catechism 21 delineates the result: 'The only Redeemer of God's elect is the Lord Jesus Christ, who, being the eternal Son of God, became man, and so was, and continueth to be, God and man in two distinct natures, and one person, for ever.'

The Son was born under the law. Although Jesus is the heir of all things, He was born under the Mosaic covenant with all its obligations. He humbled Himself and entered into that estate. He submitted to the regulations of the Mosaic administration. He fulfilled all the prophecies and types. He is the perfect prophet, priest, and king. He offered His life as the perfect sacrifice. The Shorter Catechism describes these things as His humiliation: '*Wherein did Christ's humiliation consist?* Christ's humiliation consisted in His being born, and that in a low condition, made under the law, undergoing the miseries of this life, the wrath of God, and the cursed death of the cross, in being buried and continuing under the power of death for a time' (S.C. 27).

By submitting to the law as the covenant of works, Christ was under contract to obey the law of God perfectly and to bear the curse of any law breaking. In particular, He obeyed the moral commandments perfectly (His active obedience) and He satisfied the curse of God's judgment (His passive obedience).

In His capacity as one born under law, Jesus purchased our adoption. Verse 5 contains two purpose clauses: (a) 'in order that He might redeem those who were under the Law,' and (b) 'that we might receive the adoption as sons.' The same Greek word is used for 'in order that' and 'that.'

The first purpose statement describes Christ's work: He came to redeem. There are two major aspects involved in our redemption: the removal of the curse and the restoration of the inheritance. We explained the concept of redemption with respect to the removal of the curse in our comments on Galatians 3:13. Note here it relates to the restoration of the inheritance. This second aspect of redemption is spelled out in Leviticus 25:25: 'If a fellow countryman of yours becomes so poor he has to sell part of his property, then his nearest kinsman (kinsman redeemer) is to come and buy back what his relative has sold.' God beautifully illustrates this transaction in the story of Ruth and Boaz. Naomi had lost her inheritance through the negligence of her husband. The kinsman redeemer, Boaz, pays the debt (redemption) and restores the inheritance.

As Naomi lost her inheritance through the failure of her husband, all men lost their inheritance in Adam. Although he was a son of God, by his rebellion he became a son of Satan, a member of the dark kingdom. Consequently, none of us by birth are heirs of God, but all are sons of Satan. For the inheritance to be restored full payment had to be made. This payment was Christ's active and passive obedience. Christ obeyed the law perfectly and delivered us from the curse; He paid off the debt. On the basis of His work of redemption we obtain the inheritance.

The second purpose clause (that we might receive adoption as sons) relates our adoption to Christ's work of redemption. By adoption Paul is describing the unique relation God bears to all those who are in Christ. Paul discusses the inheritance in terms of adoption, because none whom God savingly adopts can be disinherited. Paul describes adoption in terms of the Jews, but in verse 6 he relates it to the Galatians (And because *you* are sons). When the old covenant people entered into the reality of their adoption, God incorporated the Gentiles into the Church. In the old covenant they were incorporated by becoming part of the Jewish people, like Ruth (cf. Ezek. 47:21-23). Now, Jews and Gentiles are incorporated by being in Christ Jesus. The Gentiles who were far off are now joined to the children of the family of the old covenant. Christ has redeemed all His elect people that they might receive the adoption as sons.

The Shorter Catechism, defines adoption: 'Adoption is an act of God's free grace, whereby we are received into the number, and have a right to all the privileges, of the sons of God' (S.C. 34). Not only are we received into the number of, we also possess all the privileges of the sons of God. These privileges are our inheritance. As we noted in 3:29, we have already begun to participate in the inheritance. No longer are we heirs in waiting; because the work of redemption has been completed, we have begun to participate in eternal life. Because of union with Christ, we are seated with Him in the heavenly places (Eph. 2:6). Moreover, as part of our inheritance we have received regeneration, faith, justification, adoption, and sanctification, along with the hope of glory.

What is more, we also have the subjective reality of the inheritance. We are God's sons and daughters with all family privileges. We have the privilege of communion with God, the privilege of prayer, of coming freely and boldly into the Father's presence. We have a personal enjoyment as well as the solace, comfort, and joy that come from justification and adoption. These personal benefits are described in Shorter Catechism 36: '*What are the benefits which in this life do accompany or flow from justification, adoption, and sanctification?* The benefits which in this life do accompany or flow from justification, adoption, and sanctification, are assurance of God's love, peace of conscience, joy in the Holy Ghost, increase of grace, and perseverance therein to the end.'

We are no longer under tutors and pedagogues, managers and stewards. We are the sons of God and the joint heirs of the Lord Jesus Christ. Since, however, we do not fully enjoy the inheritance in this life God gives us a pledge of our adoption.

The pledge of adoption (4:6-7)

When we purchase a house, most often we are not able to pay the entire amount at one time; therefore, we make a down payment. The purpose of the down payment is to secure from us a pledge or commitment. The lender relies on the probability that, if you have invested something in this purchase, you are not likely to walk away from it. So the down payment serves as the surety that you are going to keep the contract. In Galatians 4:6, 7, God tells us that He has given the down payment of our inheritance; namely, the Holy Spirit, as the pledge of our adoption: **And because you are sons, God has sent forth the Spirit of His Son into our hearts, crying, 'Abba! Father!' Therefore you are no longer a slave, but a son; and if a son, then an heir through God.**

God gives the Holy Spirit as the pledge of adoption. Notice the relationship of adoption and the reception of the Holy Spirit, in verse 6: 'Because you are sons, God has sent forth the Spirit of His Son into our hearts.' We receive the Holy Spirit because we are sons of God. The phrase 'sent forth' is the same word Paul uses in verse 4 to describe the Father sending the Son. The Bible also speaks of the Son giving the Spirit, but because the Father is the one who adopts sinners into the family, He is portrayed here as giving them the Spirit of His Son.

As the language of God's sending His Son implies the divine pre-existence of the Son, the language here implies the same with respect to the Holy Spirit. Moreover, the Spirit is called 'the Spirit of His Son'. This language reminds us of the unity of the God-head. The Shorter Catechism in Question 6 summarizes this truth: 'There are three persons in the Godhead: the Father, the Son, and the Holy Ghost; and these three are one God, the same in substance, equal in power and glory.'

Furthermore, Paul describes the Spirit as the Spirit of God's Son to show that He comes on behalf of Christ; He comes because of the completed work of Christ *for* us and He comes to complete the work of Christ *in* us. Jesus prepared His disciples for this reality in His discourse in the Upper Room (John 14–16). He said that it was expedient for them that He go away so that He might send another comforter. That other comforter is the Holy Spirit. Christ has the authority to give us the Spirit because He completed His mediatorial work.

The privilege of giving the Spirit is part of His reward. Jesus Christ is now in heaven as the glorified God-Man. Yet as our Redeemer, He is confined to one place at one time. Thus, it is by the indwelling of the Holy Spirit that Christ is with us and in us.

In whatever way the old covenant church participated in the work of the Holy Spirit, they could not participate in the indwelling of the Spirit in the way that we do because the indwelling that we have is contingent upon the completed work of Christ. The Spirit was not yet given in this manner to complete the work of Christ by bringing us into union with the Lord Jesus. The glorious truth is that the Spirit of God indwells you and me, individually, and as a church corporately. As truly as the Shekinah cloud came down from heaven and filled the temple, the Spirit of the triune God brings us into perfect union with Christ.

Then Paul speaks of the work of the Spirit. He boldly proclaims, **God has sent forth the Spirit of His Son into our hearts, crying, 'Abba, Father.'** In Romans 8:14-16, Paul says: 'For all who are being led by the Spirit of God, these are the sons of God. For you have not received a spirit of slavery leading to fear again, but you have received a spirit of adoption as sons by which we cry out, "Abba, Father." The Spirit Himself bears witness to our spirit that we are children of God.' In Romans Paul reminds us that, because of the work of the Spirit, we cry 'Abba, Father.' In Galatians 4:6, however, it is the Spirit who cries for us 'Abba, Father.' He comes to us as a pledge, a seal; He is the guarantor of our adoption. There is no more graphic way for the apostle to explain this sealing work than to say that the Spirit comes into us crying 'Abba, Father.' The Spirit, with these words, 'Abba, Father,' bears testimony to our hearts and minds that our sins are pardoned, that we are accepted in Christ, that we are the children of God, and that we are full heirs with Him.

Paul uses both the Aramaic term, 'Abba' and the Greek term, 'Father.' Here we have a beautiful expression of the universality of the gospel, in contrast to the Judaizers' concept of God. The Judaizers would have had a problem saying 'Abba,' although God was the Father of the old covenant people. Paul, however, joins the Jewish expression of intimacy with the Gentile expression of fatherhood. As all are one in Christ (3:28) and indwelt by the Spirit, whatever our language, we know that God is our Father and we may address Him intimately.

The Spirit is the pledge of our adoption. He is in us as the Spirit of Christ, not only to effect the union, but also to bear testimony to us that we are the children of God. Therefore, no one can take the Spirit from us. If we have the Spirit, says Paul in Romans 8:9, we have Christ: 'But if anyone does not have the Spirit of Christ, he does not belong to Him.' Because we have the Spirit, we are Christ's. He is the pledge to us of our current inheritance and of our future perfect and glorious inheritance.

This work of the Spirit relates directly to our assurance of salvation. The Westminster Confession of Faith, chapter 18, paragraph 2, comments on assurance: 'This certainty is not a bare conjectural and probable persuasion grounded upon a fallible hope; but an infallible assurance of faith founded upon the divine truth of the promises of salvation, the inward evidences of those graces unto which these promises are made, the testimony of the Spirit of adoption witnessing with our spirits that we are the children of God, which Spirit is the earnest of our inheritance, whereby we are sealed to the day of redemption.' The Spirit is the earnest, the seal, and the guarantee of our inheritance that we are God's now and that God will keep us until the day of our glorification. Thus it is the indwelling Spirit of Christ who reminds us that we are in union with Christ and that our sins are forgiven.

Paul concludes by personalizing the argument: **Therefore you are no longer a slave, but a son; and if a son, then an heir through God**. He speaks here particularly to the Gentiles, declaring that no man or woman in Christ Jesus is a slave. They are not enslaved to the elemental things of Judaism. This is the conclusion of the matter. The purpose of the Spirit indwelling us is that we might respond to God with assurance and confidence, that we might live confidently in the world, whatever the circumstances in which we find ourselves by God's providence.

Some versions follow the reading, 'heir through God', but The New King James translates the reading, 'heir of God through

Christ.' I prefer the second reading, although ultimately they say the same thing. The reading 'through God' reminds us that God is the sovereign source of the grace of our adoption. The reading 'heir of God through Christ' teaches that our adoption and inheritance are based on the perfect work of the Lord Jesus Christ. Each of the two readings teaches that God alone has procured our adoption.

In verse 7, the apostle relates how the testimony of the Spirit relates to two other matters. In the Shorter Catechism, we read that God uses three things to give assurance: the promises of God, growth in sanctification, and the testimony of the Holy Spirit. Verse 7 is a promise, **Therefore you are no longer a slave, but a son; and if a son, then an heir through God**. This is a great promise to all who have believed. How do we know that we have truly believed? The promises are attached to the inward workings of grace. We know that if we discover God's work in us (this does not mean that we must wait for the mature marks of grace – the desire to be delivered from sin is sufficient), the promise belongs to us.

The Holy Spirit ties together the promise and the character of the one to whom the promise belongs. Notice that verse 7 begins with the word, therefore. Because He is the Spirit who bears witness to us, we know that we are sons and heirs. His witness begins with a sense of filial disposition. He testifies to us that we are children of God and we respond to that witness with a desire to know and love God as our Father. Then the Spirit applies the promises by causing us to love them and by showing to us His sanctifying work in our lives. The result is that we have confidence in our relationship with God. We know that our sins are forgiven and that we are the sons of God.

We therefore ought to live as freeborn heirs and not as slaves, with an exuberant boldness, confident of our current inheritance and our eternal hope.

Study Questions

1. What analogy does Paul use in 4:1, 2?
2. To whom does he apply the analogy in verse 3?
3. What are the 'elemental things of the world'?
4. What does Paul mean by 'fullness of time'?
5. What is implied in the phrase 'God sent forth his Son'?
6. What does Paul mean by 'born under the Law'?
7. What are the two purpose clauses in verse 5?
8. What does the first purpose clause teach was the reason Christ was born under the law?
9. What does Paul teach in the second purpose clause?
10. What is adoption?
11. Of what things does our inheritance consist?
12. Relate the Spirit's coming to the completed work of Christ.
13. What does Paul mean by saying the Spirit cries 'Abba Father'?
14. Relate the work of the Spirit to assurance of salvation.

17

A Stern Warning

(Galatians 4:8-11)

I love lighthouses; their architecture, their unique designs, and the isolation of their locations all combine in my mind to create a certain romance and mystique. But of course we know that the distinctive architecture, designs, and desolate locations of lighthouses were not intended to create mystique, but rather to serve very practical purposes. Lighthouses, with their distinct markings, were placed in desolate places along the coastal regions of the world so that sailors might know where they were and avoid dangers. These vivid beacons were a great warning system designed to keep boats from running aground or breaking up on rocks and reefs.

In Galatians 4:8-11 Paul is giving warnings like a lighthouse. He is beaming a bright light in order to alert the church about the shallows and rocks of legalism. For the Galatian church, if we think of her as a ship, was about to run aground and perhaps be destroyed. The apostle wrote the letter in order to warn the Galatians against the legalism of the Judaizers, Jewish professing Christians that were coming among the Gentile converts and teaching them that they had to be circumcised and observe the Jewish ceremonies and customs in order to belong to Christ.

Of course, that is what legalism does. Legalism is any system by which a sinner seeks to earn or keep God's favour. We all by nature are legalists. People would rather be in bondage to something than live under the full freedom of the Lord Jesus Christ. Hence legalism is an ongoing problem in the church. Some wrestle with legalism because they do not understand their full acceptance in Christ before God on the basis of what Christ has done. Others wrestle with legalism because their conscience has been wrongly instructed. We still have need of the lighthouse that warns us about the dangers of legalism.

A reminder (4:8)

Paul reminds his readers of the bondage from which they have been delivered: **However at that time, when you did not know God, you were slaves to those which by nature are no gods** (4:8). The term 'however' contrasts what he is now saying with what he has just said. He has concluded a discussion of the law of God, its relationship to faith, and particularly the role of the Mosaic Ceremonial Law in terms of the old covenant church. He demonstrated that the Old Testament believers were in their spiritual minority; they had not entered into the full inheritance, which would come only with the first advent of Christ.

The Gentile Christians in Galatia, along with the Jewish Christians, have received the inheritance by adoption and have been delivered from bondage, but before they were converted they were in a form of slavery much worse than that of the Old Covenant people. Note how Paul refers to conversion, **When you did not know God**. What a glorious concept! Paul describes the essence of conversion as knowing God. He reminds them that they did not always know God. They had been delivered from spiritual slavery: **You were slaves to those which by nature are no gods.** Although Israel was in bondage, at least they were in a bondage to God. The bondage of paganism was far worse. All pagan religions are products of sinful imaginations and bind their followers in superstitious bondage. Before their conversion, the Galatians were in bondage to those who were not gods; in reality they were in bondage to demons. Paul declares the foolishness of all false religions, the foolish nature of every unconverted heart. Man-made religions with their false gods bring a whole series of superstitious regulations, with a constant striving to appease gods, and a constant fear of running afoul of them. Moreover, these gods are capricious, jealous, and wrathful, and to serve them is to be bound by Satan himself.

The warning (4:9-11)

Paul warns of the danger of returning to bondage through Christian legalism. In verse 9 he poses a question: **But now that you have come to know God, or rather to be known by God, how is it that you turn back again to the weak and worthless elemental things, to which you desire to be enslaved all over again?** By this question, Paul goes to the heart of the problem of their defection. He reminds them that they have come to know God, because He first knew them. The term 'know' refers to God's covenant love and favour. Because God placed his favour on them, they had come to know (love) God. Paul makes the same point with the term 'foreknew' in Romans 8:29: 'For whom He foreknew, He also predestined.' Foreknowledge is the eternal love of God that He placed upon a specific people. Each one on whom He placed his love, He chose to salvation. If you are a Christian, it is the grace of God that seized you, that opened your eyes to see your own sin and the beauty of the Lord Jesus Christ. So Paul is incredulous. How is it, having been known by God, that the Galatians can turn back to the weak and worthless elemental things and become enslaved to them all over again?

We noted in our comments on 4:3 that these elemental things are the rudimentary elements or principles, the ABCs, of the old covenant church in her Mosaic childhood: the things God gave to prepare the church for Christ. In verse 10 Paul details what he has in mind: **You observe days and months and seasons and years.** Paul is not talking about the Christian Sabbath; he is talking about the seventh day Sabbath, the new moon festivals, the annual feast, seventh year remission, and the year of jubilee. In other words, to embrace circumcision was to place oneself under the old order with all its ceremonial observances. These Gentile Christians in Galatia were trying to be Jewish with all these ceremonies; in effect they were trying to earn God's favour. Although they had been delivered from the bondage of false gods they now were returning to the bondage of weak and worthless elements. Here is an analogy. When you were a child you graduated from a tricycle to a two wheeler with training wheels. Those training wheels were very important to help you learn to keep your balance. But you can remember the day when you took off the training wheels; the training wheels became weak and worthless. You would not put them back on your bike. The ceremonial law served its purpose, but now it is weak and worthless.

Paul concludes with the warning in verse 11: **I fear for you, that perhaps I have laboured over you in vain.** Paul is not an impersonal lighthouse, a revolving light in the bleak darkness. He is on the shore, jumping up and down and waving his arms. He is shouting at the top of his voice, because the Galatians are heading toward destruction. He reminds them that God had used him to call them and bring them into the glory of grace. Was it possible that he had laboured over them in vain, that they are really unconverted? If they continue on their present course, they will prove themselves to be so. He is not saying that they are going to lose their salvation, but that by choosing a system of legalism they will manifest that they were not saved in the first place.

Christian legalism is dangerous for four important reasons. First, it denies the sufficiency of Christ. In Him is everything that we need. He is our righteousness, our wrathbearer, the justice satisfier. He, the eternal Son of God incarnate, is the suitable and sufficient Saviour of sinners. To add anything to His work for our acceptance with God is to denigrate Him and His work. Second, legalism denies the moral authority of God. He alone possesses the right to tell us the ways in which we should walk and how we should live. Third, it denies God's absolute authority over the conscience. God alone is Lord of the conscience; legalism allows others to usurp that role. Fourth, it denies the sufficiency of the Scriptures, by adding man-made beliefs and requirements to them.

All of the errors of Christian legalism are not soul damning, but all are dangerous and soul damaging. There are a number of ways we can be guilty of Christian legalism and bring ourselves under bondage.

Study Questions

1. What is Paul's reminder in verse 8?
2. To what does he make a contrast with the word 'however'?
3. What language does Paul use to describe conversion?
4. What is the slavery of false religion?
5. Why does Paul tell them they have been known by God? What is the meaning of this language?
6. Why does Paul refer to the ceremonial laws as weak and worthless?
7. What things does Paul have in mind? What makes them weak and worthless?
8. What analogy helps us to understand the significance of this language?
9. What awful danger does Paul warn about in verse 11?
10. For what four reasons is legalism wrong?
11. What are some types of legalism in the evangelical church today?

18

The Pastor's Heart

(Galatians 4:12-20)

Having issued an urgent warning, the Apostle Paul changes his tone and tack in verse 12. He has been vehement in his denunciation of the Judaizers. In his extremely logical and intense argumentation, he moved from a defence of his own apostleship and special revelation, to a personal demonstration of the validity of justification by faith alone, to the exegetical arguments, by which he shows the relationship of law to gospel, justification, and adoption.

In the previous section, Paul warns about the danger of a new legalism. Now he changes his tone: **I beg of you, brethren, become as I am**. As he often does, the apostle opens his heart. He wants to assure them of his love; he writes as a pastor, exposing his affections so that they will understand his motivation. Moreover, he appeals to the tie that bound them to him as a further reason why they should follow his teachings and not those of the false teachers.

Notice the warmth and the affection in the first part of verse 12, '**I beg you, brethren**.' When Paul addresses them as **brethren**, he is declaring that he thought more highly of them than they might infer from his previous statements. He embraces them as fellow members of the body of Christ, covered by the perfect work of the Lord Jesus Christ. He is saying, 'I have warned you, but understand I am speaking to you as Christians, even if I had to use extremely strong language with you.' His example reminds pastors that in their pastoral work there always must be a distinction between probing, searching application and scolding. A minister is not to scold God's people. True, he must search their hearts, but then he will bring them to Christ. He will seek to convict with gentleness and affection. Even when he must speak urgently and vehemently, he must never forget that he is speaking to God's people.

Paul urges his readers: **Become as I am, for I also have become as you are**. They must follow him in renouncing Jewish ceremonies and in embracing the righteousness that is found in Christ alone. He reminds them that when he came to them initially, he was all things to all men. He did not come and live among them as a Jew. Culturally, he became like them in every way he could (with moral and biblical integrity) in order to minister to them. But more importantly, he came among them renouncing Judaistic righteousness. Certainly if anybody could boast about self-righteousness, it would have been Paul. He, however, renounced it all as useless. Therefore he says, 'Don't begin to mimic Jews, but rather follow my example.'

The Galatians' esteem and love for Paul (4:12-16)

Paul looks back to how they responded to him when he brought the gospel to them (vv. 12-16). He wants to clear away any notion that he has a grudge against them and asserts that he is not speaking out of vindictiveness. **You have done me no wrong** (v. 12). He could say this because he was confident of their esteem and love.

He first expands on their esteem: **but you know that it was because of a bodily illness** (literally, weakness of the flesh) **that I preached the gospel to you the first time; and that which was a trial (a temptation) to you in my bodily condition you did not despise or loathe, but you received me as angel of God, as Christ Jesus *Himself*** (vv. 13-14). Paul is ambiguous as to the nature of his infirmity. Many interpret his remarks as references to an eye disease, suggesting that his eyes ran and were ugly and unattractive. The reference to 'weakness of the flesh' could be to some physical affliction. It seems, however, when we look at the historical context, we ought to interpret the phrase more broadly. Paul's missionary journey among the Galatians was marked by intense persecution by the Jews. They drove him out of Antioch (Acts 13:50). He went to Iconium, where they threatened his life: 'And when an attempt was made by both the Gentiles and the Jews with their rulers to mistreat and to stone them, they became aware of it and fled to the cities of Lycaonia, Lystra, and Derbe, and the surrounding region; and there they continued to preach the gospel' (Acts 14:5-7). In Lystra they stoned him and left him for dead: 'The Jews came from Antioch and Iconium; and having won over the multitudes they stoned Paul and dragged him out of the city supposing him to be dead. But while the disciples stood around him, he arose and entered the city and the next day he went away with Barnabas to Derbe' (Acts 14:19). The entire ministry in southern Galatia was marked by intense persecution, bodily weakness, and affliction of the flesh. Those who accepted the gospel responded to him as if he were an angel; in fact, they responded to him as if he were the Lord Christ. Paul reminds them that they responded not to the man, but to the message; he was the messenger of God. They esteemed him in spite of all appearances.

Moreover, they loved him. He continues: **Where then is that sense of blessing that you had? For I bear you witness, that if possible, you would have plucked out your eyes and given them to me** (v. 15). He reminds them that when he preached in weakness they were greatly blessed and they loved him. The reference to plucking out their eyes gave rise to the interpretation that Paul suffered from an eye disease. The eye, however, is the most tender and affectionate part of the body. Paul could be saying that they loved him so much that they gladly would have sacrificed the tenderest part of their body on his behalf. He asks them if his rebukes and warning now made him their enemy: **Have I, therefore, become your enemy by telling you the truth** (v. 16)? He reminds them that he was their beloved, esteemed friend. Were they going to treat him as an enemy, because he has told them the truth about the gospel?

Paul's love for them (4:17-20)

Paul also reminds them that he loves them even if he has rebuked them. In verse 17, he contrasts himself with the false teachers: **They eagerly seek you, not commendably, but they**

wish to shut you out, in order that you may seek them. It was true that the false teachers were courting them. But why? They sought to build themselves up at Paul's expense. They sought to erect a wall between Paul and the church in Galatia, because they wanted the people's loyalty. They slammed shut the door of gospel liberty because they wanted popularity.

We learn here something of the pathology of false teachers. They present themselves in such a way so as to build a following among God's people. A true pastor does not seek his own, but God's glory and the well-being of those to whom he ministers. As Paul says, **But it is good always to be eagerly sought in a commendable manner, and not only when I am present with you** (v. 18). False teachers bask in the sunlight of attention when they are present, but when they move on they could not care less about the people they have left. For this reason Paul points out that even when he is apart from them he longs for their well-being. Here he expresses pure pastoral love, a love that always seeks the best for the beloved.

Paul expresses his goal for them in verse 19: **My children, with whom I am in labour until Christ is formed in you**. What a statement! Paul bares the heart of a true pastor; he struggles for his people as a woman in labour. He struggled with them in this letter, that Christ might be formed in them. In fact, he dealt harshly with them because he loved them.

His language reminds us that the ministry is daily giving birth. There is much work to be done and pastors cannot be men pleasers and timeservers. Pastors are like mothers giving birth and they must labour and travail over the lost and over the sheep that Christ has given to them.

Paul concludes this section with a further manifestation of his heart: **but I could wish to be present with you now and to change my tone, for I am perplexed about you** (v. 20). Because he loves them, he longs to be there in order to protect them from the false teachers. He regrets having to deal roughly with them, but he is perplexed that they are willing to listen to the legalists. Hence, Paul uses arguments of affection to win back the Galatians.

Study Questions

1. What does he imply by addressing them as brethren?
2. What is Paul exhorting the Galatians to do in the first part of verse 12?
3. In what ways were they to mimic Paul?
4. How may one understand Paul's 'bodily condition'?
5. Why is it important that we esteem our pastors?
6. How does Paul express their affection for him?
7. Is rebuking contrary to loving?
8. What does Paul teach about the pathology of false teachers in verse 17?
9. How did Paul commend his love to them? Why does he say 'not only when I am present'?
10. What figure does he use in verse 19? What does this teach about the work of the pastor?
11. How does Paul express his love in verse 20?

19

The Allegory

(Galatians 4:21-31)

You have heard said that a picture is worth a thousand words. I do not subscribe to that exact proposition, but I recognize that pictures, concrete illustrations, often are the things that cement the conclusion of an argument or drive home to our consciences its force. In Galatians 4:21-31, Paul paints an allegorical picture to confirm his argument. In this section, the Apostle is concluding the series of arguments to deter the Galatians from running headlong back into Judaism. He has worked out carefully the doctrine of justification received by faith alone based solely on the work of Christ. He has gone on to describe the relationship of law as covenant to the new covenant in Christ. He has established that our adoption and justification are by free grace and not according to works. He has written of the liberty that is ours in Christ; a liberty that surpasses both the bondage of the minority of Israel and the bondage of paganism. He establishes that if a Gentile Christian turns to the ceremonies of Judaism, he is placing himself under bondage as terrible as that slavery in which he had existed in his paganism. Then Paul opens his heart to them, by affectionately appealing to them that they heed his teaching and walk with him. Now he concludes the argument with a historical sketch and its spiritual lessons.

The historical sketch (4:21-24)

Paul begins this section with a challenge: **Tell me, you who want to be under the law, do you not listen to the law?** (v. 21). Paul challenges them to think about what they were saying and doing. By his reference here to law, Paul means the first five books of the Bible (the Pentateuch). In particular, Paul refers to Genesis, which is the prologue to the entire Mosaic covenant. He reminds them that the Old Testament also speaks of grace and gospel.

In verses 22 and 23 Paul refers to Genesis 16:22: **For it is written that Abraham had two sons, one by the bondwoman and one by the free woman. But the son by the bondwoman was born according to the flesh, and the son by the free woman through the promise**. Abraham had two sons, Ishmael and Isaac. In Genesis 16, impatient Abraham takes matters into his own hands and seeks the promised seed through Hagar, Sarah's handmaid. Hagar bears a son to Abraham, Ishmael. God, however, declares to Abraham that Ishmael is not the son of promise. Instead God would miraculously provide the son of promise. Thus in Genesis 17:18-19, when Abraham pleads with God to accept Ishmael as the seed, God says, 'No, the seed is going to be the one provided according to the promise.'

The other part of the story that Paul alludes to is recorded in Genesis 21, which tells of the occasion when Ishmael mocked Isaac, perhaps disdaining him as the covenant bearer. In response God commands Abraham to excommunicate Ishmael from the visible covenant community and to send him away. In answering Abraham's doubts, God tells him that the promise is going to be accomplished in Isaac. He is the son of the promise.

By reviewing the historical background, we can determine the principle Paul is establishing. Abraham was justified by faith (Gen. 15:6); he believed the promise of God, that he was going to give him a seed and through that seed the entire world would be blessed. He believed the promise of God and it was imputed to him as righteousness. Therefore, Paul, in Galatians 3:6, constructs the doctrine of justification showing that Abraham is the father of those that believe. But what does Abraham the believer do in Genesis 16? He tries to accomplish God's purpose by the flesh. Now he is no longer living by faith; rather, he is living by the flesh. He is using ungodly means in a vain attempt to accomplish God's purposes.

But God does not subscribe to the dictum that the ends justify the means; therefore, the son of that relationship, Ishmael, is called the son of the flesh. By this language Paul does not mean that he was conceived out of lust, but out of an attempt to fulfil God's purposes by a fleshly endeavour. Since Ishmael was the son of a slave, he was a slave; he was in bondage. Hence those who seek to accomplish God's purposes according to the flesh will only produce bondage. On the other hand, Isaac, whom God provided supernaturally, was the child of promise. In him God fulfilled His promise. He was the son of Sarah, the freeborn wife. He was the heir, who would enjoy the full liberty of the household.

The spiritual lesson (4:24-28)

In verse 24 Paul begins to draws out the spiritual lessons of the story: **This is allegorically speaking: for these women are two covenants, one *proceeding* from Mount Sinai bearing children who are to be slaves; she is Hagar. Now this Hagar is Mount Sinai in Arabia, and corresponds to the present Jerusalem, for she is in slavery with her children. But the Jerusalem above is free, she is our mother. For it is written, 'Rejoice, barren woman who does not bear; break forth and shout you who are not in labour; for more are the children of the desolate than of the one who has a husband.' And you brethren, like Isaac, are children of the promise** (24-28).

Readers are often thrown by the language of allegory. The problem arises because some ascribe a technical meaning to the term 'allegory'. In the history of interpretation, terms often, over time, take on more technical and precise meanings. Take for example the word 'bishop'. In the New Testament, the term 'bishop' refers to the overseer of the flock; it is the word for pastor. Later in the history of the church, the term takes on a technical definition of a hierarchical church office. The later use, however, gives no warrant to impose that meaning on the term as it is used in the Bible.

This analogy helps us to understand Paul's use of the term 'allegory'. In the history of interpretation allegory described the method of interpretation that sought to avoid the literal meaning of Scripture in order to steer clear of an apparent harshness in the literal reading or to get a more spiritual meaning. It became part of what is called the fourfold sense of Scripture: a method that included the historical, the allegorical, the analogical (moral application), and finally the tropological (the Christological meaning of the text). Medieval interpreters used this method predominantly.

This definition of allegory is not what Paul means. Rather, he says that there is a clear relationship between an historical event and New Testament spiritual principles. He is drawing an analogy. Note, he does not ignore or explain away the history. Rather, he says the historical incident illustrates and contrasts the consequences of attempting to fulfil God's purposes by human endeavour or by faith.

The analogy between Abraham's actions and what the Galatian Christians were tempted to do is clear. Abraham was justified by faith, but sought to accomplish the promise of God in the flesh. His attempt produced bondage and he was left still without an heir. The Galatian Christians had received justification by faith. Earlier in his argument the Apostle asked: 'You began by faith; are you going to finish in the flesh?' Now, they were considering fulfilling God's promised salvation by human effort, by the works of the flesh. Paul warns that they are doing exactly what Abraham tried to do. The moment they submit to circumcision, the moment they concur that Jewish ceremonies are necessary for acceptance with God and sanctification, they, like Abraham, are resorting to the arm of the flesh to accomplish the purposes of God. The end will be bondage.

Hagar represented the Mosaic covenant. The biblical account extends this analogy. When Ishmael and Hagar were put out by Abraham they lived in the wilderness of Paran, which was in the Sinai Peninsula, in the desert outside the Promised Land. Thus, Paul says, she was in bondage and lived outside the church. She lived near Sinai and so pictured the old covenant later given to Israel on that mountain. Thus the historical location of the bondwoman with her slave son in the wilderness outside of the land in the territory of Sinai graphically illustrates the spiritual state of people trying to accomplish salvation by human effort.

Paul takes his argument a step further when he says that this **Hagar is Mt. Sinai and corresponds to present Jerusalem.** Unbelievable! The Judaizers were telling the Galatians that they must become Jews. They had to get connected to Jerusalem; after all, look at all the glorious things the Old Testament Scriptures say about Jerusalem. Of course they failed to grasp the great truths that were taught in Ezekiel and Jeremiah that Jerusalem was predestined to become derelict and desolate. This first happened in the Babylonian captivity and it would happen again soon after Paul wrote, because of her rejection of the Messiah (cf. Matt. 24:2). Therefore, the Jerusalem of Paul's day was a picture of Mt. Sinai and bondage. If the Galatians turn to Judaism, they will be returning to bondage, even as Paul asserted earlier. As Jerusalem is to be cast off, they will be cast off as well if they apostatize.

Next, Paul demonstrates that physical Jerusalem has been replaced by the church: **But the Jerusalem above is free, she is our mother**. The church has become God's Jerusalem. Mt. Zion serves as a type of the church of the Lord Jesus Christ. As we are Abraham's seed, the new Israel, we are God's holy city, Jerusalem. This is the other part of the spiritual lesson: the church is the heavenly Jerusalem, represented by Sarah and Isaac, the free born son of promise. Paul declares that the church is the mother of the elect. God begets His people to Himself through the church. Paul proves this part of the analogy by quoting from Isaiah 54:1: **Rejoice, barren woman who does not bear, break forth and shout you who are not in labour, for more are the children of the desolate than of the one who has a husband**. As Sarah received a son supernaturally, the church shall grow supernaturally.

Notice the appropriateness of this proof text. What kind of woman was Sarah? She was a barren woman. The child of promise did not come through her ability to conceive. She had never been able to conceive. Moreover, she was past the age of conception. Only at that time did God give her the promised son, who was the heir of the promise. And thus is it not fitting that Sarah is a spiritual picture of the church, with her free born sons and daughters, who have been saved by faith in the promise? So Paul concludes the first part of the analogy in verse 28: **And you brethren, like Isaac, are children of**

promise. The Galatians, like Isaac, were products of grace. They were born of God and not of the flesh.

Paul's argument is not some ill-founded, illegitimate allegory, but a historically based analogy. The writer to the Hebrews also links the old covenant church with Sinai and the new covenant church with Jerusalem above, Mt. Zion, the city of God (Heb. 12:18-24). His argument reminds us that although men may deride her, she is God's glorious church. Moreover, he is referring to the church in her visible expression, which is the only way we can see her in this life. She is the mother of God's elect. Her children are born through her and are incorporated into her. In our day she is often weak and contemptible. In her more spiritual form, she lacks the pomp and circumstance, the power and the authority, the wealth and resources of the world. Nevertheless, we rejoice because she shall become the mother of a multitude. All the nations, according to Isaiah 54, shall be brought to Christ through her ministry.

The contemporary application (4:29-31)

In verse 29 Paul refers again to the story of Sarah and Hagar: **But as at that time he who was born according to the flesh persecuted him who was born according to the Spirit, so it is now also**. As Ishmael persecuted Isaac, the Judaizers were persecuting those who held to justification by grace alone.

What was the result? Ishmael was put out of the church: **But what do the Scriptures say? 'Cast out the bondwoman and her son, for the son of the bondwoman shall not be an heir with the son of the free woman**' (v. 30). When Ishmael mocked Isaac, God confirmed the request of Sarah that Ishmael be put out of the house, which was the church at that time. Consequently, the son of the bondwoman had no place in the church and those who resort to works for part of their acceptance with God will have no place in the church either. Paul concludes: **So then, brethren, we are not children of a bondwoman, but of the free woman** (v. 31). All those who cling to Christ alone are children of the free woman and part of God's church. If they resort to human effort they will become children of bondage and be put out.

As a note of doctrinal application, we learn how we should think about the present city, Jerusalem. Jerusalem, in terms of

God's saving purposes, is not the city located at the eastern end of the Mediterranean Sea. Jerusalem is the church of the Lord Jesus Christ. The Jews are in Israel so that we might evangelize them (Rom. 11:14). They live in Jerusalem and Israel so that we may have a target group to whom to take the gospel. But to say that they are a unique part of God's unfolding redemptive purposes violates the principle that the apostle lays out here.

Study Questions

1. Why does Paul refer to Genesis as part of the law?
2. What two events in Abraham's life does he use?
3. What principle does Paul establish?
4. What does Paul mean by allegory?
5. Does this usage of allegory give us warrant to interpret the scripture allegorically? Why or why not?
6. What is the relation Paul makes between Hagar, Mt. Sinai, and Jerusalem of his day?
7. Whom do Sarah and Isaac represent?
8. How does he apply this allegory to the Galatians? To whom does he compare the Judaizers?
9. If Ishmael was put out of the church, what does that say about the Judaizers?
10. Who then are the true members of the church?

20

Stand Fast in Liberty

(Galatians 5:1-12)

There are certain incompatibilities in the physical world – oil and water, heat and ice; things that do not mix. The same holds true in the moral realm. As physical darkness and light are incompatible, moral darkness and light are incompatible; truth and falsehood cannot coexist. In Galatians 5, the apostle Paul details another spiritual, moral incompatibility, namely, salvation by free grace and salvation by grace plus works or human achievement. In 5:1-12, he concludes the argument of the book with this exhortation to stand firm in liberty. In verses 1-4, he outlines the principle of incompatibility; in verses 5 and 6, he proves this incompatibility; and in 7-12 he condemns human effort in salvation.

The incompatibility of faith and works (5:1-4)

Paul begins in verse 1 with an exhortation: **It was for freedom that Christ has set us free; therefore keep standing firm and do not be subject again to a yoke of slavery**. Having demonstrated that those who seek salvation through Old Covenant law-keeping entangle themselves in bondage, Paul exhorts us to stand uncompromisingly in the freedom that belongs to us in Christ. He reminds the Christians that Christ has delivered them from the bondage of slavery. In Him they entered into the freedom of the sons of God. If they turn to the weak and elemental laws of Judaism, they will enslave themselves. Consequently they must stand firm in the freedom of the gospel.

He follows with a warning that one cannot mix grace and works. In fact to do so is soul-damning: **Behold I, Paul, say to you that if you receive circumcision, Christ will be of no benefit to you. And I testify again to every man who receives circumcision, that he is under obligation to keep the whole law. You have been severed from Christ, you who are seeking to be justified by law; you have fallen from grace** (vv. 2-4). He highlights the warning with the phrase, **Behold I, Paul**. On the basis of his apostolic authority, he solemnly warns them that if they receive circumcision in order to contribute to their standing before God, Christ will be of no profit to them. In verse 3 he stresses the warning and gives a reason: **And I testify again to every man who receives circumcision, that he is under obligation to keep the whole law**. His apostolic testimony is that Christ will not profit them because they are placing themselves under the Old Covenant, as minor heirs, under bondage. They will be under all the demands of the Old Covenant.

The net effect will be to sever themselves from Christ: **You have been severed from Christ, you who are seeking to be justified by law; you have fallen from grace**. He says that if they receive circumcision as necessary for acceptance with God, they are seeking to be justified by law-keeping. Therefore they will be severed from Christ, which is the same as saying Christ will be of no benefit to them. In other words they will have fallen from grace. Paul uses the term 'Grace' as the principle of salvation. He does not mean a truly converted person would lose his salvation. Paul is asserting the spiritual truth that one cannot mingle grace and works. To step one toe, one millimetre, over the line of grace into the realm of human endeavour destroys the principle of grace. One who persists in adding works for his acceptance with God demonstrates that he has not been converted.

Positive proof of the incompatibility of faith and works (5:5-6)

In verses 5 and 6, Paul offers two grounds to prove that to seek acceptance with God through circumcision is to fall from grace. **For we through the Spirit, by faith, are waiting for the hope of righteousness. For in Christ Jesus neither circumcision nor uncircumcision means anything but faith working through love**. First, in verse 5 he asserts that the focus of faith is righteousness. He contrasts himself and all true Christians with the Judaizers and the Galatians who are succumbing to the temptation to follow the Judaizers. He lays out the great hope of life; namely, the hope of righteousness. What is this hope of righteousness? It is the hope of our standing before God. It is the hope that on the day of our death and the final Day of Judgment we will be accepted into God's presence.

By the term 'hope' Paul expresses confidence; the confidence that comes from or is based on the imputed righteousness of Christ. The confidence of the Judaizer, his hope of righteousness, was based upon performance. It was faith plus works; it was faith plus circumcision and the Jewish ceremonies. And Paul declares that such an attempt obligates them to live by a works system and their confidence in part rests on their performance.

Paul, however, contrasts himself and all true believers ('**we**') with that system. He says that the hope of all true believers arises from faith and faith alone. This confidence is Spirit-bred, **for we through the Spirit**. His confidence is based on the faith that has been worked by the Holy Spirit in his heart in the work of regeneration. It is a spiritual exercise of the heart, and it is a reflex action of the one who is born again. It is not a confidence in the flesh or in carnal things; it is not a confidence in Jewishness or in circumcision. Paul says the same thing in Philippians 3:4-7: 'If anyone else has a mind to put confidence in the flesh, I far more: circumcised the eighth day, of the nation of Israel, of the tribe of Benjamin, a Hebrew of Hebrews; as to the Law, a Pharisee; as to zeal, a persecutor of the church; as to the righteousness which is in the Law, found blameless. But whatever things were gain to me, those things I have counted as loss for the sake of Christ.' He rejects every other basis of acceptance for Christ alone.

Notice as well that the nature of faith is receptive. Paul says that through the Spirit we have faith that waits for the hope of righteousness, not a faith that works for the hope of righteousness. Faith takes hold of the promises of God and rests in them alone for acceptance with Him.

Paul offers the second part of his proof in verse 6: **For in Christ Jesus neither circumcision nor uncircumcision means anything, but faith working through love**. Paul reiterates that faith alone brings us into union with Christ Jesus. Circumcision does not effect this union. It matters not whether one is Jewish or Gentile, circumcised or uncircumcised. Circumcision possesses no spiritual value. Faith effects the union and the sacrament of baptism is the sign and the seal of regeneration and union with Christ to the one who possesses the reality. Although works contribute nothing to our acceptance with God, they play an important role. They are the evidence of a living faith; faith works through love. So just as faith is a spiritual exercise in contrast to the carnality of works and self righteousness, the evidence of that union in Christ is not a physical badge of Jewishness or circumcision, but a lively faith that manifests itself by working through love.

The Roman Catholic Church misconstrues this statement by teaching that it is a faith formed by love. Now there is a great difference here between 'faith working through love' and 'faith formed by love'. The latter statement claims that faith is a mental assent that must be perfected by true love of God and neighbour. When faith is so perfected it receives the promised salvation. Note however, the distinction between 'faith working through love' and 'faith formed by love'. Paul is not describing the perfecting of faith, but the way true faith manifests itself. He parallels James, 'Even so faith, if it has not works, is dead, being by itself' (James 2:17). True faith manifests itself in loving obedience. The Westminster Confession of Faith says 'Faith, thus receiving and resting on Christ and his righteousness, is the alone instrument of justification; yet is it not alone in the person justified, but is ever accompanied with all other saving graces, and is not dead faith, but worketh by love' (WCF 11:2). True faith manifests itself in a life of love to God and to our neighbour, which obeys the law of God. Christ says, 'If you love me you will keep my commandments' (John 14:15). In the chapter on 'Faith,' the Westminster Confession teaches that the faith which obeys the commandments is the same faith that receives Christ for righteousness:

'By this faith, a Christian believeth to be true whatsoever is revealed in the word, for the authority of God Himself speaking therein; and acteth differently upon that which each particular passage thereof containeth; yielding obedience to the commands, trembling at the threatenings, and embracing the promises of God for this life and that which is to come. But the principal acts of saving faith are, accepting, receiving, and resting upon Christ alone for justification, sanctification, and eternal life, by virtue of the covenant of grace' (15:2).

That is what Paul means when he says that faith works through love. Our obedience does not commend us to God, but is the evidence that our faith is genuine. And hence the apostle has proven that grace and works are incompatible for acceptance with God. But in doing so he teaches the correct role of works in the Christian life.

Before we go to the next point, we need to examine ourselves here. Paul gives the marks of the one who has been converted. First, the basis of your hope is a resting in Christ, and Christ alone, for justification. You bring nothing to the table, no works, no effort, and no knowledge. Are you resting in Christ alone for your acceptance with God? Second, he gives you a way to examine your faith. Is your faith a lively faith? In other words, do you have a care and zeal to live and walk by the law of God? We all struggle; there is a remnant of sin within us and we do not always obey. But do you have a desire to obey God's law? Is there a delight in you for the law of God? Is there a pleasure in His testimonies and judgments and commandments? If you lack this desire, then the faith that you profess is not true faith. It is a deceived faith.

Condemnation of combining faith and works (5:7-12)

In verses 7-12 Paul offers four arguments condemning the attempt to mix works with faith. First, he condemns the way of human effort because it is not of divine authority: **You were running well; who hindered you from obeying the truth? This persuasion did not come from Him who calls you** (vv. 7, 8). He points out that they had started out in the right direction and were running well. He reminds us that the Christian life is a race, in which we are pressing on to the prize of our high calling in Christ (cf. Phil. 3:12). Why had they turned aside? He asks, 'What happened? Who has hindered you from the truth?'

He answers this question negatively: **This persuasion did not come from Him who calls you**. If they have been persuaded to trust in works along with their faith, it was not God who thus persuaded them. The term 'call' refers to the effectual call of God in the gospel. The persuasion of that call is to rest in Christ alone. Therefore, the teaching to add works to faith was not of God.

Second, he reminds them, in verse 9, of what he said earlier in verse 4: you cannot mix grace and works: **A little leaven leavens the whole lump of dough**. Grace is not like Ivory Soap. The makers of Ivory Soap boast that it is 99.44% pure – that is great soap. But Paul says in Romans 11:6 that to add anything to grace is wrong: 'But if it is by grace, it is no longer on the basis of works, otherwise grace is no longer grace.' It just takes a little leaven to leaven a lump of dough. Just as a little bit of yeast will leaven a loaf of bread, a little leaven of works is enough to destroy the soul. If you rest in anything but Christ for your acceptance before God, you are damning yourself.

The third proof Paul offers is the divine judgment on the false teachers: **I have confidence in you in the Lord, that you will adopt no other view; but the one who is disturbing you shall bear his judgment, whoever he is** (v. 10). Paul distinguishes here between the deceived and the deceivers. Paul has been very hard on the Galatians. Now he expresses his confidence. Although he has severely warned them, he alleviates some of the pressure that he has brought to bear upon them. In reality he thinks better of them, because he understands the effectual power of sovereign grace. His confidence is in the Lord, as he also expressed elsewhere: 'For I am confident of this very thing, that He who began a good work in you will perfect it until the day of Christ Jesus' (Phil. 1:6). The seriousness of the warning remains, but God will keep them and they will not adopt another view.

Notice as well that Paul distinguishes between the leader and the led. If they continue in this wrong direction, they will be damned. But the judgment of the leader is all the more severe. The false teachers will incur heavy judgment from the hand of God. Because they are disturbing the people of God their judgment will be severe. He expresses their judgment in verse 12: **Would that those who are troubling you would even mutilate themselves**. The term '**mutilate**' means to 'castrate'. Let those who insist on circumcision castrate themselves. According to Judaism this would make them unacceptable to God, for a eunuch had no place among God's people (Deut. 23:1). Castration was a pagan rite, not a covenant rite. They want to cut your foreskin; let them castrate themselves. They have no place among God's people.

The fourth thing Paul argues is that those who add works to grace will always persecute the church: **But I, brethren, if I still preach circumcision, why am I still persecuted**? (v. 11) Judaizers argued that Paul had a double message – they said that he preached circumcision to the Jews and no circumcision to Gentiles. Paul says, 'That is absurd! Why are these people persecuting me? Why do the Jews throughout the world persecute me? Why have I been stoned and imprisoned if I am preaching a message of faith plus circumcision?' Paul implies that he was persecuted because he preached free grace. If he preached otherwise, the stumbling block of the cross would have been abolished.

The background of this argument is 4:29: **But as at that time he who was born according to the flesh persecuted him who was born according to the Spirit, so it is now also**. The persecution of Paul proves that he is preaching grace. The cross is a stumbling block, an offence to those who want to contribute to their own salvation (1 Cor. 1:17-25). Paul says that the true preaching of grace leaves the cross as a stumbling block in the minds and hearts of men and women. It abases them, depriving them of all self-righteousness. The moment we back off that message, persecution will cease.

If God came to sinners today and said, 'Cut off your hand and I will bring you to heaven,' they would line up to do it, because they would have contributed something to their salvation. Ultimately, it is their hatred of God and grace that cause them to refuse free grace.

And so by these four arguments Paul condemns the combination of faith plus works. Such a message has no divine authority, rather it is destructive.

Thus Paul completes his argument against the Judaizers with this warning against mixing faith and works. May each of us stand fast in the liberty that is ours in Christ Jesus!

Study Questions

1. What is the theme of this section?
2. Why does the combination of faith and works bring one back into bondage?
3. What does it mean to be severed from Christ? To fall from grace?
4. What two arguments does Paul give to prove the incompatibility of faith and works?
5. What is the confidence of the one who truly believes?
6. Why does he insert the phrase 'through the Spirit'?
7. What does Paul say is the true evidence of faith?
8. What does he mean by the phrase 'faith working through love'?
9. What four arguments does he give to condemn the combination of faith and works?
10. Why does Paul have confidence that they will stand fast in the principle of faith alone?
11. How does he express God's judgment of the false teachers?
12. Why does he appeal to the fact that he is persecuted by the Jews?

21

The Shape of Liberty

(Galatians 5:13-15)

Freedom must have form. We can illustrate this principle from a train. A train is quite restricted in its movement. It is bound to its tracks. It may only go where those tracks go. As long as the train operates within the perimeters of its tracks, it is free to do that for which it has been built. Off the track, even though in a sense it is unfettered and no longer restrained by those perimeters, it has no freedom. It has lost the ability to do that for which it was made. In fact, it actually can do great damage. As the apostle Paul continues to instruct us in the freedom that is ours in Christ, he now discusses the nature of Christian liberty. It is a liberty with pattern. It is a freedom with form.

Having concluded his argument against the Judaizers in Galatians 5:1-12, he begins to teach how believers are to use the freedom that is theirs in Christ Jesus. Perhaps he anticipates the objection of the Judaizers: 'If justification is by grace alone, people will live lawless lives.' In verses 13-15, he sets forth three things: the practical experience of freedom, the regulation of freedom, and the abuse of freedom.

The practical experience of freedom (5:13)

Verse 13 lays out the practical experience of freedom in Christ. **For you were called to freedom, brethren: only do not turn your freedom into an opportunity for the flesh, but through**

love serve one another. Paul begins by reminding us that liberty is the very essence of what it means to be in Christ. He says that it is the consequence of our calling; namely, God who has called us effectually in Christ has called us to liberty in Christ. The title 'brethren' signifies that the apostle is speaking to the church, to those who are in covenant with God through Christ, and have received justification and adoption. The liberty of the gospel is the freedom that comes from justification and adoption. As Paul says in Romans 5:1: 'Therefore if any man is justified by faith he has peace with God.' We are freed from the curse, bondage and condemnation of sin. Furthermore, because of our adoption, we have bold access into the presence of God (Gal. 4:6, 7). He also implies that we are free from all man-made laws.

This freedom, however, is not licence to sin: **Do not turn your freedom into opportunity for the flesh**. Paul will develop the deeds of the flesh in the next section. He uses this term *flesh* to refer to the remnant of sin that remains in each believer. In a person's flesh resides all of the passions and the lusts that constantly war against the Spirit. Paul says that we are not at liberty to do the deeds of the flesh. Christian liberty is not a freedom to sin or to have a nonchalant attitude towards sin.

The grace of God is glorious and when we confess sin God pardons us. We, however, are not free to think that we can commit this or that sin because we are forgiven. This is one of the problems, as I see it, with Sonship Theology.[1] Those who hold to this theology say that all the Christian needs to do is tell himself that he is justified and God is always pleased with him regardless of what he does. God is not pleased with us regardless of what we do. God always accepts us if we are in Christ regardless of what we do, but He is displeased with His people when we continue in sin and do not seek to please him.

1 Sonship Theology teaches that all we need for sanctification is to affirm our justification. Many teach that we are not to strive for holiness since that would be legalistic. They often have a low view of the law of God. See my chapter, 'Critique of Sonship,' in *Growing in Grace: Sanctification*, ed by Joseph A. Pipa Jr and J. Andrew Wortman (Greenville, SC: Southern Presbyterian Press, 2001), 151-178; Chad Van Dixhoorn, 'The Sonship Program for Revival: A summary and Critique,' *Westminster Theological Journal* 61, no. 2 (Fall 1999): 227-446.

Neither is this a freedom to abuse 'Christian liberty'. Just because one has the freedom to use alcohol in moderation, one does not have an excuse to abuse alcohol. We are never free to sin.

Moreover, we must not abuse this liberty with selfishness. Paul puts it positively, he says, 'Through love serve one another.' In other words, our Christian liberty is a freedom from sin to love and serve God and our neighbour. Paul is going to develop the positive service to one's neighbour in the next verse. Before we leave verse 13, I want to emphasize that our liberty is not to be exercised at the expense of our neighbour. My liberty does not allow me to live in a manner that ignores those around me both in and outside the church. I may not ignore their feelings, their privileges, or their rights. Even if they ignore my rights, I never have an excuse to ignore their rights or feelings. Liberty does not behave selfishly.

As young Christians come out of legalism into the realization of the true liberty that belongs to them in Christ, they discover that they are free to go to a movie or drink a glass of wine, but they often overdo it. They flaunt their freedom, regardless of the sensitivity of other Christians. Christian liberty is always to be exercised in a way that considers others and never compels someone to act contrary to conscience.

Liberty is then to be exercised in love. Practically, you need to understand the difference between prudence and hypocrisy. You are not being a hypocrite if you exercise your liberty privately out of respect to the Christian community where you live.

Consequently, we see that we must not exercise liberty sinfully or selfishly. We have been delivered from sin; we are free to serve God in holiness; we are free to love our neighbour.

The regulation of freedom (5:14)

In this verse, Paul teaches how God regulates our freedom: **For the whole law is fulfilled in one word, in the statement, 'You should love your neighbour as yourself.'** How do we avoid the abuse of our liberty? We regulate our lives by the law of God. Liberty expresses itself through love, and love expresses itself in obedience to the law.

Paul picks up on Christ's summary of the Law in Matthew 22:40: 'On these two commandments depend the whole Law and the Prophets.' Christ summarized the second great commandment by quoting Leviticus 19:18: 'You shall love your neighbour as yourself.' Paul quotes this verse as the summary of our responsibility to our neighbour.

A neighbour is anyone with whom we come into contact. The neighbour may be an enemy; the neighbour may be a Christian friend; the neighbour may be someone we do not know, but with whom we come in contact. We are to love our neighbour as we love ourselves.

Is Paul telling us that we need a healthy respect, a healthy measure of self-esteem and self-love? No! He is simply and realistically saying that normally we all already have a measure of self-love and self-esteem. Therefore, do not let your love for yourself outpace your love for your neighbour. In other words, 'Therefore, however you want people to treat you, so treat them, for this is the Law and the Prophets' (Matt. 5:12). We are to love others with a disinterested love.

But you will notice that Paul does not leave our responsibility in the realm of love unformed. No! He tells us that love is formed by the law. The commandment to love our neighbour is the summary of the last six commandments. Therefore, the whole law is fulfilled in this one commandment. The measure of our love is the moral law. Both Romans 13:8 and James 2:2-11 teach that law is fulfilled in love and love is fulfilled in law. Love expresses itself objectively when directed and guided by the law of God.

Not only does obedience shape love, but love also shapes obedience. Love for God and neighbour is the motive of obedience. Law keeping is to be from the heart and not some mechanical act performed perfunctorily. I am not saying that if one does not feel like obeying he does not have to. To obey formalistically is sin, but to disobey is a greater sin. Therefore, we must not commit the second sin, by disobedience. Rather, we confess the lack of love and ask God to give us proper motives.

The law of God regulates our love, which regulates our liberty. But does Paul only require us to love our neighbour? John answers the question in I John 4:20, 21, 'If someone says, "I love God," and hates his neighbour, he is a liar; for the one who does not love his brother whom he has seen cannot love God whom he has not seen. And this commandment we have from Him, that the one who loves God should love his brother also.' The commandment to love our neighbour does not rule out the commandment to love God and keep all the commandments. The matter of love to neighbour, however, is the measurable standard of love. Moreover, in the context Paul is dealing with the way we treat one another. You cannot love God if you do not love your neighbour according to the law of God. But, if in fact you are treating your neighbour according to God's law, you will respond to God according to all his moral law.

Therefore, it is not only the second half of the law that regulates our liberty, but the entirety of God's moral law as summarized in the Ten Commandments. The first four commandments teach us how to love God.

The abuse of liberty (5:15)

In verse 15, Paul applies what he taught in verse 14: **But if you bite and devour one another, take care lest you be consumed by one another**. Apparently, Judaizing legalism had created in the Galatian Church a great deal of dissension, back biting, and petty arguing. Legalism, in fact, always produces this mentality within the church. Legalism engenders a self-concern and produces schism and a party spirit. Apparently in the Galatian congregation, they were chewing up each other. They were acting like animals biting and devouring. You may have seen a pack of dogs turn on each other and get into a terrible dogfight. That is what they were doing in the congregation of the Lord Jesus Christ.

This bestial behaviour was destroying the people of God. Paul says that, if we abuse our liberty in this way through selfishness, we will be consumed and will consume. Is this self-centredness not the cause of so many church splits? Of course there are times when churches divide over doctrine. But even when the cause is righteous, one must be careful to act out of love. If we live together, striving to serve one another in love, we will live together in harmony.

Our Christian liberty is a glorious thing. We should be willing to die for it. It lies at the very heart of the gospel. But let not that for which we are willing to die be marred by our abuse of it; rather let us live in the liberty that is regulated by love and serve one another.

Study Questions

1. What is the liberty, which Paul describes in verse 13?
2. What two ways do we abuse liberty?
3. How does one abuse liberty in license? In Christian liberty? In selfishness?
4. What has God given to regulate our love?
5. What is the relation of law and love?
6. What statement of Christ does Paul have in mind?
7. What Old Testament passage does he quote?
8. How does love of self serve as a standard of love for neighbour?
9. Why does Paul refer to the last six commandments and not the first four?
10. What situation does he seem to be addressing in verse 15?
11. How does this in-fighting relate to the abuse of our liberty?
12. What causes the great majority of church splits?

22

The Battle

(Galatians 5:16-18)

In Tolkien's classic *Lord of the Rings*, when Frodo finally gets to the mountain of doom and is to throw the ring into the fire, he balks. His lust for the ring grips him and a great battle ensues. Only because he wrestles with Gollum for the ring, is it cast into the fire. Frodo's lust hindered him from accomplishing his quest. Our quest is the pursuit of righteousness and God's glory and to accomplish it we must wage war against our lusts.

Our hearts and souls resonate with the struggle of the apostle Paul: 'For the good that I wish, I do not do; but I practise the very evil that I do not wish' (Rom. 7:19). Hardly a day passes that we do not mourn our lack of love, do not mourn the fact that we fall into the same temptations that we fell into the day before. Sometimes we despair of any success in the quest.

In this section the Apostle Paul realistically faces the problem and teaches the resources that are ours in the Lord Jesus Christ. If the exercise of our liberty is not a licence to sin or to harm others, but rather is to be used for God's good and holy purposes, how do we deal with the remnant of sin? Paul answers this question in Galatians 5:16-18.

He lays down the rule in verse 16: **But I say, walk by the Spirit, and you will not carry out the desire of the flesh**. Paul contrasts walking by the Spirit and carrying out the desires of the flesh. The Bible uses the term 'walk' to refer to our conduct, how we live. We are to walk or live by or in the Spirit. In other words, we are to live our Christian lives in dependence upon the Holy Spirit, led by Him. (We will return to this concept in verse 18.)

Let us examine the contrast more fully. The Apostle is reminding us that each one of us has a remnant of sin. In the Bible the word 'flesh' may mean our physical nature, our body, but it also has a theological meaning. It may describe our depravity. For example, Romans 7:18: 'For I know that nothing good dwells in me, that is, in my flesh.' Or as Jesus says to Nicodemus: 'That which is born of the flesh is flesh' (John 4:6). Every person born of a mother and father is by nature fleshly or sinful. The Bible says there are two types of people: the natural man, who is flesh, and the regenerate man who has been born again. In our new nature, however, we have a remnant of sin, which Paul calls 'the desire of the flesh'. This remnant of sin is active in our appetites and in our lusts and is a great source of temptation. Satan acts on it and it responds to the sinful enticements of the world.

Every Christian has this remnant of sin warring within him. Paul's antidote or rule is that one resists the lust of the flesh by walking by the Spirit. As a Christian you have a new nature; you are new man (Eph. 4:24). Everyone who is born again is indwelt by the Spirit of Christ, who works in him, activating, strengthening and leading. As we seek God's grace through the use of the means of grace, the Spirit of Christ will strengthen us in our warfare.

We are involved in a war and the rule that Paul gives to guides us is that we must walk by, in dependence on, the Holy Spirit. **If you walk by the Spirit, you will not carry out the desires of the flesh**. The verb 'carry out' is a verbal form that expresses completed action. In other words, although you will fall into sin, sin will never have dominion over you. You will not complete the desire of the flesh. Why? The Spirit is in you lusting after holiness, hungering and thirsting for righteousness. You will grow in grace and in victory.

In verse 17, Paul spells out that which I have already anticipated: **For the flesh sets its desire against the Spirit, and the Spirit against the flesh; for these are in opposition to one**

another, so that you may not do the things that you please. Here he details the battle that rages within; a great battle, between the Spirit and the flesh. The flesh is lusting, warring against our new nature. We are attacked in two ways. First, the flesh labours to hinder our obedience, to trip us up, to cause our affections to grow cold, to throw stumbling blocks before us. Second, the flesh entices us to sin. As James tells us in James 1:14, 15: 'But each one is tempted when he is carried away and enticed by his own lust. Then when lust has conceived, it gives birth to sin; and when sin is accomplished, it brings forth death.'

William Perkins traces five steps of lust that lead to sin and the manner of the opposition. The first act of lust is suggestion. Suggestions often pop into our minds. They do not have to originate with Satan; we have enough resident lust to tempt us every day. The second acting of lust is for us to take delight in the suggestion. The suggestion comes and we delight in the prospect it lays before us. The third step is consent. The first two often occur without any resistance. But, if you are a Christian, you will not consent without some resistance. I am not referring to times of spiritual declension, but the experience of the Christian that is seeking to serve the Lord. If we do consent, it will never be wholeheartedly. It is at this point we experience the war. If you did not begin to battle at step two, delight, you will here. A battle will begin to rage between the desires of the flesh and what God has revealed He desires for you. The fourth step is the act. Even if you give in, you will not wholly consent to the act. You will suffer conviction and sorrow. And the fifth step in James's description of declension is what Perkins describes as perseverance. He says that you will never persevere in it; if you have been renewed by the Holy Spirit, you will not persevere in that sin. It will not become the habit of your life as it is with the unregenerate.[1]

Paul reminds us at the end of verse 17 that we may not do the things that we please. The term 'please' means 'wish'. He refers to the born again person and explains there is conflict. Although we wish to satisfy our lusts, we may not give into them. Because of the warfare, we never obey God perfectly,

1 William Perkins, 'A Commentary upon the Epistle to the Galatians,' Works, II (London: printed by John Legatt, 1631), 326b.

never with pure motives or affection. In fact our repentance was never perfect. This reality constantly brings us back to Christ.

Even as Paul lays down the reason, he comforts us, by reminding us that this battle is not simply between our new natures and the remnant of sin, but between the Holy Spirit and the remnant of sin. The two references to Spirit are not to our spirits, but to the Holy Spirit. He is the general who leads our new nature in this battle; He is the one who gives us strength to resist.

In verse 18, Paul deals with the result: **But if you are led by the Spirit, you are not under the law**. This phrase is one of Paul's more controversial. What does he mean when he says that you are not under the law? Some suggest that he means because we have the Holy Spirit we do not need the objective law of God. Paul, however, begins this section by reminding us of the remnant of sin that resides in us. Our hearts are unreliable guides, because of the lust of the flesh.

So what does he mean? He is asserting that we are no longer under the condemning power of the law. As he says in Romans 8:1, immediately after describing the conflict due to the flesh, 'There is therefore now no condemnation for those who are in Christ Jesus.' We are freed from the condemnation of the law.

Moreover, the law no longer excites our lust. One of the roles of law is to excite the lusts of the unregenerate: 'But sin, taking opportunity through the commandment, produced in me coveting of every kind; for apart from the law sin is dead' (Rom. 7:8). Because we have been freed from the law, law is no longer a catalytic agent, stirring up sin within us.

Third, our acceptance with God is not dependent upon our perfection with respect to the law. In fact our imperfect obedience is accepted as perfect. All of your struggles, your cold prayers and sinful motives are accepted in Christ Jesus if you are resting in Christ alone for righteousness and walking by the Spirit.

Furthermore, the great result of the Spirit working in us is we increasingly die to sin and the lusts that remain within us. We shall grow from grace to grace, from strength to strength, victory to victory. If in fact you long to be free of sin, you desire to love and serve God, then know that, at the end of the day, you shall succeed. God is going to get the victory; Spirit is at work within you.

Notice, however, if we are going to deal with these lusts, we must be careful that we are **led by the Spirit**, or as Paul says in verse 16, 'walk by the Spirit.' We are led by the Spirit as we submit to what He commands in Scripture and depend on Him for all that we are to do. In the first place, we must be sober and watchful: 'Keep watching and praying, that you may not enter into temptation; the spirit is willing, but the flesh is weak' (Matt. 26:41). We must know as well our besetting sins; what particular indwelling sin troubles us. What places and people and occasions must we avoid to avoid temptation?

Moreover, we pray for the Spirit to do His work within us. Christ has promised us: 'If you then, being evil, know how to give good gifts to your children, how much more shall your heavenly Father give the Holy Spirit to those who ask Him' (Luke 11:13)? It is the Spirit, who will excite our affections; it is the Spirit, who will put to death the lusts that are within us. If we cry out to God to give us this work and to increase His work by the Spirit within us, He will not hold back. The Saviour has promised us that if we pray according to the will of the Father, He will grant what we ask. Is it the will of God that you be holy? Is it the will of God that you be led by the Spirit? Of course! He will give you the Spirit in a full measure for grace and strength. We pray as well that God will keep us from temptation and when we are tempted he will deliver us from evil (Matt. 6:13).

We must also use the means of grace because the Spirit does not usually work apart from them. Daily private Bible study, prayer, and meditation; family worship; and most importantly corporate worship are the means that God has appointed to work grace in our lives. We must as well practise mortification of the flesh. Make peace with no sin. We must bring every sin, every lust to the cross to be crucified with Christ. We ask him to drive the nails into the heart of our favourite sin that we might die to it and it to us. We choke off its lifeline; we deprive it of all support. If you are not at war with your lusts and the remnant of sin in you then most likely you remain unconverted. Mind you, I am not talking about always winning the war, but if there is no warfare within you, that is an indication that you are not born again.

On the other hand do not let the reality of the battle discourage you. The fact you have these interior wars is to you a sign that you are alive.

Study Questions

1. What is the rule or principle Paul lays down in verse 16?
2. What does Paul mean by flesh?
3. What does he mean by walking by the Spirit?
4. What is the reason for the conflict?
5. What are the five steps in this conflict?
6. What does he mean that we do not do what we wish?
7. What is the role of the Holy Spirit in this struggle?
8. What does Paul mean when he says we are not under the law?
9. How does the Spirit lead us?
10. What are things we should be doing to be led by the Spirit?

23

The Deeds of the Flesh

(Galatians 5:19-21)

Satan, the world, and the flesh are the troika of evil opposing Christians. To be well equipped, we need to know the enemy that roams about seeking to destroy us. We must understand as well the temptations that arise from the world system. And particularly, we must know the enemy that lies within. In fact, there is no more dangerous enemy than the one within. One of the great difficulties in fighting the insurgents in Iraq was the enemy's ability to appear to be an ally; the danger lies in his appearing to be one of the good guys. A great moral enemy dwells within us. In the previous section, Paul warns about this enemy and the necessity of warfare. He calls the enemy the flesh; the remnant of sin that resides in each one of us. We are to wage war against this enemy by the Holy Spirit who indwells us. Paul continues to prepare us for this war by identifying the deeds of the flesh: **Now the deeds of the flesh are evident, which are: immorality, impurity, sensuality, idolatry, sorcery, enmities, strife, jealousy, outbursts of anger, disputes, dissensions, factions, envying, drunkenness, carousing, and things like these of which I forewarn you just as I have forewarned you that those who practise such things shall not inherit the kingdom of God.**

Evident sins (5:19)

Paul says the deeds of the flesh are evident or obvious. By deeds of the flesh, he refers to those actions, words, and deeds that are the outworking of our sinful nature. These things mark the lifestyle of the non-Christian and are the enemy within against which the Christian must war.

Notice Paul is not talking about obscurities; he is not talking about things which Christians may differ. He catalogues thirteen deeds that clearly violate the law of God. It is obvious that they are sins, and furthermore our own consciences will bear testimony to us; it will be evident when we have a problem with these things. And so the deeds of the flesh are clearly things against which we must be vigilant.

The best way to establish the true character of the sinful nature is to consider its outworking. The Bible does not simply accuse us of being sinners. God says by nature we are sinners and that nature manifests itself in thoughts, words, and deeds. Since they are evident, each of us may discover the nature of his heart by examining its deeds by Scripture. Psalm 119 tells us that the law of God is a light unto our path; it is light to search our hearts (v. 105). James tells us that the law of God is a mirror that gives a clear testimony with respect to the nature of our heart (James 1:23-25). How then do you examine your heart? You take this list, and others like it, and prayerfully examine your thoughts, words, and deeds. We need regularly and carefully to examine ourselves by the light of God's Word. An unexamined life is a life in danger. There may be an unscriptural examination that leads to a morbid introspection, but true biblical examination leads us to discover the sin in our heart so that we may go to Christ for pardon and grace to obey.

Furthermore, we may not explain these things away as quirks of personality or an excusable response to a unique circumstance. No! These things are evident; they are deeds of the flesh, contrary to the holy will of God.

The catalogue of sins of the flesh (5:19-21)

As Paul catalogues the deeds of the flesh, he details four categories: sins of a sexual nature, sins of religious conduct, sins of a social nature, and sins of appetite.

Sins of a Sexual Nature (v. 19)

Paul lists three sins of a sexual nature; immorality, impurity and sensuality. All three violate the seventh commandment.

Immorality – by this term Paul includes all abuses of lawful sexual relations: fornication, adultery, and those things that tempt one to these acts. He also condemns all perversions of sexual relations: homosexuality (1 Cor. 6:9, 'effeminate, nor homosexuals'), bestiality, and pornography. *Impurity* (uncleanness) – Paul asserts that not only actions violate the law of God, but in addition all lusts and fantasies, worked out in thought, word, and deed, are sinful. The term *impurity* encompasses immoral conversations, as well as books, movies and music that promote sexual impurity. The term also condemns lustful thoughts and fantasies (Matt. 5:28). *Sensuality* (licentiousness) – by this term Paul exposes the shamefulness of immodest dress (1 Tim. 2:9; 1 Pet. 3:2, 3), suggestive behaviour (Prov. 7:10, 11; Isa. 3:16), and shamelessness (Ezek. 16:15-34; Rom. 1:24).

Sins of Religious Conduct (v. 20)

Paul list two sins that have to do with our religious conduct: idolatry and sorcery. He is applying the second Commandment. *Idolatry* – the term *idolatry* includes false worship in all its forms. By this term Paul includes the worship of false gods and the false worship of the true God. He condemns seven things. First, he condemns the failure to worship the true God: atheism (Ps. 14:1; Eph. 2:12); polytheism and the worship of all false Gods (Exod. 20:3; Jer. 2:27, 28); all non-Trinitarian cults (Mormons, Jehovah's Witnesses), Jews, and Muslims. Second, idolatry is the worship of the true God through images (Isa. 40:18-20; Exod. 32:1-5). God is a spirit and we are not to make images of Him or worship Him through such images (Exod. 20:4-6; Deut. 4:15-20; L.C. 109). Third, idolatry is the refusal to come to the true God through the Lord Jesus Christ, God's appointed mediator (John 14:6). Fourth, it is the failure to worship the true God according to Scripture (Deut. 12:21-32; John 4:21-24). Fifth, it is the failure to worship the true God from the heart by the Spirit (Isa. 29:13; Matt. 15:7-9). Sixth, it is the failure to put God first in trust, affection, and priorities – trusting in things for our security or happiness (Deut. 8:17; Eph. 5:5), loving other people more than God (Matt. 10:37), putting things before God (Matt. 6:24-33). Seventh, it is the failure to believe what God has revealed in his word and base our lives on it (Heb. 4:2; Isa. 8:19, 20).

Sorcery – Paul uses the term from which we derive the word 'pharmacy'. The root word for 'sorcery' refers to the use of formulas and potions to work magic and to cast spells and curses. This particular term is translated 'witchcraft' or 'sorcery'. Paul forbids all occult activity – use of mediums, fortune telling, astrology, and psychic games like 'ouija boards' (Lev. 20:6; Deut. 18:10, 11; Isa. 8:19; 47:12-15). He forbids all superstitions and superstitious acts, like 'knocking on wood' or crossing one's fingers, as well as attributing the outcome of events to luck or fortune (James 1:17).

Sins of a Social Nature (vv. 20, 21)

In this list Paul details eight sins. I call these the deadly eight. Deadly because like cancer they often destroy secretly. These sins are often considered to be more respectable. These are the kinds we most easily excuse as quirks of personality, failing to realize that they, although on the surface more minor in their symptoms, are deadly,

Enmities – Enmity is a state of bitterness and vindictiveness towards another person. It was Esau's attitude towards Jacob. He was filled with enmity. After Jacob deprived him of his inheritance, he began to nurture resentment. He had a settled opposition of bitterness towards his brother and planned his death (Gen. 27:41, 42). Sometimes the spirit of bitterness or enmity can be short-lived; most of us wrestle with it in our relationships. Somebody does something to offend us and in turn we nurse a bitter spirit against them. Enmity lies at the root of many relationship problems in marriage, at work, and in the church. But when a person nurtures enmity, it marks his character. The bitter spirited person constantly feels animosity towards those who have wronged him and wishes ill against them. Few things do more damage to relationships than enmity.

Strife – This characteristic marks the person who, by his speech, causes tension and difficulties within relationships. Like a person infected with the flu, he moves among a group of people and spreads contagion. He creates strife by harsh words, slander, and gossip. Laban's use of harsh words against Jacob is a telling example (Gen. 31:25-29). Solomon says, 'A fool's lips bring strife, and his mouth calls for blows'

(Prov. 18:6). Few things do more to damage relationships than slander or gossip. By such speech walls are built between people and strife is the result.

Jealousy – The jealous person is discontent with his own lot and resents what others possess or receive. He is upset, because his gifts or importance are not recognized by others. Jealousy produces resentment, a feeling that comes out of a 'me first' attitude. Now one may experience a proper jealousy, when his rights are violated or wickedness is perpetrated. Men and women may be jealous in their covenantal relationship of marriage if one violates that marriage contract. Parents may be jealous of the allegiance of their children. Pastors and elders may be jealous for the truth of God and his righteousness. God is jealous when his people disobey his law (Exod. 20:5, 6) Paul, however, is talking here about the jealousy that marked Diatrophes, 'I wrote something to the church: but Diatrophes, who loves to be first among them, does not accept what we say' (3 John). The desire for pre-eminence is the root of much jealousy. Moreover, it is a violation of the tenth commandment, for it springs ultimately from discontent with God's providence.

Anger – The fourth deadly sin is anger. Anger is the expression of enmity, impatience, or discontent. It often manifests itself in passionate outburst of wrath and malice. Jesus says that anger is a violation of the sixth commandment (Matt. 5:22). One of the more egregious examples is Simeon and Levi's massacre of the inhabitants of Shechem (Gen. 34:25-31). Others, like Nabal, possess no self-control (1 Sam. 25:25, 37). There are, however, the silent angry, those who are perpetually angry, although they, like Esau, might hide it (Gen. 27:41). Just below the surface they are a boiling cauldron of anger and resentment. Having more self-control they are careful when they show their anger. They are like a Coral Snake, beautiful in appearance, but deadly in its bite.

Disputes – The disputatious nature often manifests itself in the false teacher who seeks to discredit true religion by throwing up intellectual doubts and stumbling blocks. For example, Elymas the magician who contradicted Paul in Acts 13:8. When the proconsul, Sergius Paulus, desired to hear what Paul had to say, Elymas sought to turn the proconsul away from the faith. The disputatious person wants to turn people away from the faith or lead them into some narrow, sectarian view of the faith. To accomplish his purpose he throws up obstacles. Paul describes these people in 1 Timothy 6:3-4: 'If anyone advocates a different doctrine and does not agree with sound words, those of our Lord, Jesus Christ, and with the doctrine conforming to godliness, he is conceited and understands nothing; but he has a morbid interest in controversial questions and disputes about words, out of which arise envy, strife, abusive language, evil suspicions, he is conceited and understands nothing.' But one can also be disputatious while contending for truth. For this reason Paul warns that the elder must not be quarrelsome or pugnacious (1 Tim. 3:3; Titus 1:6). In 2 Timothy 2:24, 25, Paul adds, God's servants 'must not be quarrelsome but be kind to all, able to teach, patient when wronged, with gentleness correcting those who are in opposition, if perhaps God may grant them repentance leading to the knowledge of the truth.' This attitude expresses itself as well in our other social contacts, the person who is always disagreeable and arguing, regardless of the issue.

Dissensions – Dissension describes the result of strife breaking out in a group, along with lack of respect for the leadership. It begins with disputing, but suddenly and subtly one is undermining authority and creating questions that lead to doubt. Satan used this strategy with Eve (Gen. 3:1-4) and Paul warns in Romans 16:17: 'Now I urge you brethren, keep your eye on those who cause dissensions and hindrances contrary to the teaching which you learned, and turn away from them.' As we have seen in this Epistle, false teachers plagued Paul, following him from church to church, creating dissension. They began by disputing, seeking to raise doubts about Paul's authority. They were able to stir up sedition and treachery in the churches, causing dissatisfaction. It takes only one such person, who appears to be very upright and pious, to ruin a Christian community.

Factions – Paul describes factions in 1 Corinthians 1:10, 11: 'Now I exhort you, brethren, by the name of the Lord, Jesus Christ, that you all agree that there is no division among you, but that you be made complete in the same mind and in the same judgment. For I have been informed concerning you, my brethren, by Chloe's people, that there are quarrels among you. Now I mean this, that each one of you is saying, "I am of

Paul," and "I of Apollos," and "I of Cephas," and "I of Christ."' Each clique considers itself spiritually superior to the others and subtly a party spirit develops. Such behaviour destroys and is most often connected with error or narrow sectarianism (as we see in Titus 3:9-10: 'But avoid foolish controversies and genealogies and strife and disputes about the Law, for they are unprofitable and worthless. Reject a factious man after a first and second warning, knowing that such a man is perverted and is sinning, being self-condemned.')

Envy – Envy is jealousy gone to extreme. It is wicked malice; the motivated ill-natured desire to destroy others because you cannot abide them and their success. James says that people murder and fight because of envy (James 4:1, 2). I think some of the most tragic words in the Bible are in Matthew 27:18, when Pilate realized that the Jews were condemning Jesus Christ because of envy. Envy caused them to murder the Lord Jesus Christ. Envy creates murder in the heart and will commit physical murder when it can get away with it. From envy Cain murdered Abel (Gen. 4:3-8).

Thus, Paul catalogues the deadly eight. Notice he places them in a list that includes more outrageous sins (idolatry, immorality, etc.). But in God's sight these social sins are as evil as the others. Hence we ought to hate them as God does.

Note as well the relationship of thought to words and actions. Enmity leads to strife, jealousy leads to outbursts of anger and disputing. Disputing leads to dissension, which leads to factions. Our Saviour warns us of these causal relationships in Mark 7:20-23: 'That which proceeds out of the man, that is what defiles the man. For from within, out of the heart of men, proceed the evil thoughts, fornications, thefts, murders, adulteries, deeds of coveting and wickedness, as well as deceit, sensuality, envy, slander, pride and foolishness. All these evil things proceed from within and defile the man.' In Romans 1:24-32, Paul demonstrates the relationship of social sins to idolatry and sexual immorality. Sin will never stay still. Sin is either being put to death or it is increasing in influence.

Sins of Physical Appetite (5:21)

The two sins mentioned here are actually forbidden by the Seventh Commandment and could be placed under immorality. Paul, however, places them at the end of his list in order to emphasize them.

Drunkenness – Paul condemns the abuse of or addiction to alcohol or any other substance that alters your behaviour to a degree that you lose self-control. The Bible, from beginning to end, forbids drunkenness. Note well, it is not a sin peculiar to our age or culture. Paul says it is a sin against the body. Under drunkenness he would include gluttony or any other form of addictions (tobacco or pain pills), as well as the abuse of other physical things.

Carousing – Carousing refers to following the ways of the world in the pursuit of sinful pleasures and appetites; deliberately pursuing those things that are immoral by going to places and associating with people who are debauched. In Ephesians 4:17-19 Paul writes, 'So this I say, and affirm together with the Lord, that you walk no longer just as the Gentiles also walk, in the futility of their mind, being darkened in their understanding, excluded from the life of God because of the ignorance that is in them, because of the hardness of their heart; and they having become callous, have given themselves over to sensuality for the practice of every kind of impurity with greediness.'

Before leaving the catalogue, note that the list is representative, **and things like these**. Paul often catalogues sins (Rom. 1:23-32; 1 Cor. 6:9-11; Eph. 5:5; Col. 3:5, 6). Although there are many parallels, threads that run through all the lists, in each Paul emphasizes things particular to those to whom he wrote. In other words, Paul does not intend for us to take any one or even all of them together as exhaustive. Hence the phrase, 'and things like these.' He puts it this way to remind us that just because we do not find our particular sin in the list, we may not conclude that it is not serious. Moreover, we may not exempt ourselves from his warning if we are guilty of only one or two of the sins listed. James teaches: 'For whoever keeps the whole law and yet stumbles in one point, he has become guilty of all' (James 2:10).

The Warning (5:21)

At the close of verse 21, Paul condemns those who practise the deeds of the flesh: **Of which I forewarn you, just as I have forewarned you, that those who practise such things shall**

not inherit the kingdom of God. This is a sober warning, found in many of Paul's letters. Paul had warned them in the past and continued to do so. There is always the possibility within the congregation of God's people, that even the most outwardly spiritual and moral person could fall into the practice of some of these sins.

The clause 'inherit the kingdom of God' refers to eternal life. Paul warns that those who practise theses things are not saved; they are lost and going to hell. Therefore it is important that we understand what he means by 'practice'. Practice does not mean wrestling with a sin and at times falling into it. We all wrestle with the lust of the flesh and we daily battle with the sins Paul lists. Paul has said that the flesh lusts against the Spirit and the Spirit against the flesh. In the heart of all believers are the seeds of sin. Like weeds, they press through to the surface of our lives; although I should mention that, in our wrestling, it is not normal Christian experience to fall into the outward acts of idolatry, immorality, sorcery, drunkenness, and carousing.

Neither am I denying that a genuine Christian can fall into the practice of serious sin for a period of time. David lived for well over a year impenitent for his act of adultery; Peter fell into the sin of denying Christ and there are many other examples in Scripture. Therefore it is possible that a genuine Christian can fall into the practice of one of these sins for a period of time. Admittedly, such a Christian while in such a state has no right to assurance of salvation. Moreover, when he is warned, like David, he repents. If a professing Christian continues to harden himself in the practice of sin, it is evidence that he is unregenerate.

What then does Paul mean by the practice of these things? First, if anyone of these sins or any other expression of a wicked heart marks your life, it is the quality, the pervasive characteristic of your life, you are practising it. We can illustrate the difference between a person who has a garden and raises some vegetables and a farmer. The farmer's life is marked by the pursuit of agriculture in order to make a living; the back yard gardener is a hobby farmer. His life will be marked by his vocation. Consequently our lives are not the characteristic of the practice of any of the deeds of the flesh.

Second, note that it is not just outward acts that bring a person under condemnation. Thoughts and speech may mark the person as one who practises sin. There are those who outwardly are very moral, but their inner life is marked by lust, fantasy, anger, jealousy. They simply lack the nerve to act out of their lusts. Moreover, the persons whose speech is marked by immorality, gossip, slander, and dissension are equally condemned.

Third, the person who forsakes the practice of sin, but does not truly repent of it, remains under this condemnation. He is like the person whom the demon leaves, but finding the house empty, returns with seven more evil than himself (Matt. 12:43-45). People will reform morally for any number of reasons. The outward forsaking of certain patterns of behaviour, because they are unacceptable in the church or society, or because they are destructive to one's life, is not evidence that one has been converted. Moralists will simply substitute different practices in the place of those laid aside.

Lists like this one should bring us to the cross of the Lord Jesus Christ. God is willing to save all who call out to Him in repentance and faith. Moreover, as Christians we come daily and often to Christ for cleansing as well as to receive the power to resist the deeds of the flesh.

Study Questions

1. Why does Paul say that the deeds of the flesh are evident?
2. What do we learn about the importance of self-examination?
3. Some of the deeds listed seem to be personality faults. May we explain them away by saying, 'That is just how I am'?
4. List the three sins of against morality and define each.
5. List the seven sins under idolatry and define each.
6. List the eight deadly sins and define each with an example.

7. What are the two sins of appetite?
8. Why does Paul add the phrase 'and things like these'?
9. What is the warning?
10. What does it mean to practice sin?

24

The Fruit of the Spirit

(Galatians 5:22-23)

Spring reminds us why we garden. We seek for fruit: for the flower, for the vegetable, for the herb, for those plants that bring us joy, beauty, and nourishment. Similarly, we ought to seek fruit in the spiritual world, in our minds, hearts, and souls. God has invested in us in order that we might bear fruit for His glory and honour; we are to be a people who live well for Him and bring forth the blessed fruit of righteousness. In Galatians 5:22, Paul turns his attention to the necessity of fruitfulness. He has described the barren, winter landscape of the natural man, the deeds of the flesh. He has taken us through this war zone and shown us the devastation of the human heart. Having shown us the landscape, he leads us into God's garden. In verse 22-23, he contrasts the 'fruit of the Spirit' with the 'deeds of the flesh': **But the fruit of the Spirit is love, joy, peace, patience, kindness, goodness, faithfulness, gentleness and self-control. Against such things there is no law. Those who belong to Christ Jesus have crucified the sinful nature with its passions and desires.**

The general nature of the fruit

After introducing the fruit of the Spirit, in verse 22, Paul lists nine features: love, joy, peace, patience, kindness, goodness, gentleness, faithfulness, and self-control. By these terms he depicts the Christian graces or virtues, which are produced by the Holy Spirit. He is not describing personality traits. Unregenerate people may be loving, kind, and patient. In fact, it might be difficult to distinguish the kindness of a renewed man from that of the unregenerate person. The difference lies, in the first place, in the motive, the spring of it, which is love. Love is the chief grace and out of love flows all the other graces.

Second, Paul is not listing nine diverse fruits, of which a Christian may possess a few. The term, fruit, is in the singular. The nine together are the fruit that mark the Christian, like a cluster of nine grapes. By the cluster concept, we begin to discover the difference between the kind and patient non-Christian and the truly renewed man or woman. The Christian possesses all the fruit. The renewed person should have some balance, some symmetry of character, although by no means will he be perfect. Each has his or her areas of weakness, but there will be some element of each of these graces in the life of every Christian.

Third, like the catalogue of the deeds of the flesh, this catalogue is representative. In many of his epistles, Paul lists similar catalogues of God's good fruit (Col. 3 and Eph. 5; cf. 2 Pet. 1:5-8). As we examine our hearts, we must not stop with these nine, although they are a good place to start.

Fourth, Paul focuses on the character of the heart. Indeed, the character of the heart will manifest itself in outward acts, but the heart of the matter is the heart. Note that we are not talking about a legalistic conformity to external standards (outward acts), but about the heart that is being transformed. Closely related, Paul is not talking about a formalistic role playing; we all can put on our 'Sunday go to meeting face.' We know how to play the role; we can give the appearance of being patient, kind, and gentle. Instead, Paul describes the internal reality of who we are.

Fifth, the author of these graces is the Holy Spirit. Here Paul names them the fruit *of the Spirit*, teaching that the production of the fruit is a supernatural work. The Spirit plants the seed of this fruit when He regenerates us and immediately He begins to cultivate these graces in us. Therefore, the fruit is a necessary evidence of the new birth. The person who is not developing this fruit over a period of time is unregenerate.

Since it is the work of the Holy Spirit, it is also a sovereign work; Christ teaches the sovereignty of this work in Matthew 13:23: 'And the one on whom seed was sown on the good soil, this is the man who hears the word and understands it; who indeed bears fruit and brings forth, some a hundredfold, some sixty, and some thirty.' Just as God causes our children to grow at different rates and to mature at different paces, He causes us to grow at different speeds spiritually. None of us, of course, should be content with our degree of fruitfulness. We mourn our lack of growth and we hunger and thirst for righteousness. But we must never forget that God is sovereign in our sanctification.

The specific nature of the fruit

I will group the nine fruit into three categories of three fruit each: the foundational graces (love, joy, and peace); the social graces (longsuffering, kindness, and goodness); and the controlling graces (faithfulness, gentleness, and self-control).

The Foundational Graces

Love – The first three fruit are formative of all the others and love is the source of them all. We learned in Galatians 5:6 that faith works through love, and in verses 13 and 14 that our obedience must spring from love. Love, therefore, is the motivating principle of the other eight because love is the form that faith takes and it is love that gives rise to all the others. Along with love, the features of joy and peace particularly mark our relationship to God but they spill over into our relationship with others.

What is love? We can define love as the affectionate disposition and commitment that seeks the well-being of its object. It is an act of the will, but it grows out of a disposition of affection and kindness. At times the disposition will be lacking. At such times you must act out the commitment. We must always obey and to do so is to love God and our neighbour. We ought, however, to cultivate the affectionate disposition. We are to have this disposition even towards our enemies, since this is the manner in which God dealt with us. We love because God first loved us (1 John 4:10). Our love for God is kindled by the realization of His love. As we receive Christ by faith, we are overwhelmed by God's glorious love and love Him in return. We cannot separate faith and love. Faith is the action, by which we receive justification, but it is attracted to God because of His loveliness and it is accompanied with a love for God, a love for the Saviour, a love for the Holy Spirit. This love is not the instrument of justification, but it acts along with justifying faith.

Above all, we are to love God: '"You shall love the Lord your God with all your heart, and with all your soul, and with all your mind." This is the greatest commandment' (Matt. 22:37, 38). This love is the fountainhead of all obedience and is particularly expressed in the first four of the ten commandments, although love of God is working in all aspects of obedience.

Out of this love flows love for our neighbour: 'the second is like it, "you shall love your neighbour as yourself"' (Matt. 22:39). Because we love God, we love our neighbour. This love is governed by the last six of the ten commandments.

Joy – Love produces, and is accompanied by, joy. Since we find delight in the object of our affections, it is fitting that joy is the next aspect in the list. Joy is an attitude of delight, security, and comfort that we have as we trust in God. Because we trust God, we may maintain this delight and security in all circumstances. Joy comes out of the realization that God is our portion and our inheritance; therefore, we are complete in Him (Ps. 73:25-28). He loves us and will only do for us that which is best (Rom. 8:28); therefore, we may rejoice even in our trials (Phil. 4:4; James 1:2). We are enabled to say with Eli, upon hearing that awful prophecy about the destruction of his household, 'It is the Lord; let Him do what seems good to Him' (1 Sam. 3:18). Joy is not the gritting of the teeth and enduring. Rather it is resting with a quiet submission in God, who has promised he will never leave us or forsake us (Heb. 13:5).

Peace – The Bible often joins joy and peace. They are twins. Peace is that sense of well-being that comes out of being reconciled to God. It delivers us from anxiety (Ps. 94:19). It promotes and brings contentment and prompts us to be at peace with our neighbour. It is important to understand that this sense of well-being arises from being reconciled to God. Peace, in the first place, is an objective reality. Peace comes when God, who has been opposed to us as His enemies, lays down His weapons against us. He does this because Christ Jesus has satisfied His justice and made us His friends and His children (Rom. 5:9-11; 2 Cor. 5:18, 19). This peace is an objective reality: 'Therefore, having been justified by faith, we have peace with God through our Lord Jesus Christ, through whom also we have obtained our introduction by faith into this grace in which we stand' (Rom. 5:1, 2).

Peace with God leads to a peace of conscience. Our consciences have been cleansed from the defilement of sin, our guilt has been removed and we are right with God. As we realize we are reconciled to God, we experience subjective peace. We see further the relation between peace and joy. It is impossible to have joy without this peace of conscience. Real joy can only be produced by the conscience that knows that it is at peace with God. As we read in the Shorter Catechism 36: 'The benefits which in this lie do accompany or flow from justifications, adoption, and sanctification are, assurance of God's love, peace of conscience, joy in the Holy Ghost, increase of grace, and perseverance therein to the end.' Peace frees us from anxiety about our sins and gives us boldness before God; and hence we are delivered from worry and anxiety.

As we truly experience the peace of God, we will become peace-makers. As Paul exhorts us: 'If possible, so far as it depends on you, be at peace with all men' (Rom. 12:18; cf. Heb. 12:14; Matt. 5:9). Thus when we are defrauded, we will bend over backwards to seek peace; we will not insist upon our rights; we will seek to bring reconciliation between people as well as between them and our God.

These three features are foundational, for it is out of them, love flowing into joy and peace, that the other elements of the fruit of the Spirit develop.

The Social Graces

Peace is the link with the next triad: patience, kindness, and goodness. These three graces describe, in particular, our attitudes and behaviour toward those around us.

Patience – Paul begins with patience. The term is better translated 'longsuffering'. The Bible teaches that before we were in Christ, God bore long with us. He was patient and longsuffering. Think how longsuffering He is with us currently as His backward children. He bears long with our foolishness and waywardness. People provoke us all the time; they are rude, inconsiderate, sometimes deliberately, but often unintentionally. Our enemies also attack us; they will misconstrue what we do and say and slander us. The temptation is to resent and seek vindication. We are too easily provoked when our rights have not been considered or we have been ill-treated. We need to quit thinking about rights and start thinking about grace. As we orient our thinking to grace, we will not be so easily provoked. Love covers a multitude of sins. We can learn to think, 'He did not mean to do or say that, I am going to forget about it.'

When love cannot cover the actions of another, what do we do? Either we are unable to forget about it or it is of such a serious nature that we must not forget about it. Love covers that sin another way, by dealing with it according to Matthew 18, by going to the brother or sister, in private to discuss the problem. Ninety-nine percent of the time, the problem will be settled and there will be peace and true reconciliation. When there cannot be true reconciliation, we may either pursue it with witnesses or leave the matter in the hands of the Lord. But regardless, let us learn to exercise patience.

Kindness – The second social grace is kindness. Kindness is the gracious attitude that seeks the well-being of our neighbour. It is the positive step beyond long-suffering; the exercise of compassion and tenderness. Although some versions translate a later fruit as 'gentleness', this fruit is really the exercise of gentleness. The Psalmist reminds us of God, 'And thy gentleness makes me great' (Ps. 18:35). We promote greatness in our children and one another by gentleness and kindness, by having a heart that reaches out to and longs to see good things come to those around us. We combine a kind countenance with kind words and acts as we interact with those whom God brings into our lives. As we do so we manifest the grace of the Lord Jesus Christ.

Goodness – The third social grace, closely connected to kindness, is goodness. Goodness is the moral characteristic or disposition that motivates us to do righteous acts to others, to behave towards each other on the basis of the law of God, and to do good and to seek the well-being of our neighbour. Goodness motivates us to seek our neighbour's good, to see righteousness prevail in our relationships, to promote that which is lovely and of good repute (Phil. 4:8). True holiness is not ugly; it does not have rough edges; it is not unbalanced. But we are often unbalanced. We can be censorious and self-righteous, but the holiness that is shaped by the Fruit of the Spirit indeed is lovely, clearly resembling the character of the Saviour.

The Discipline Graces

The last triad of the fruit of the Spirit is faithfulness, meekness, and self-control. I call these three the graces of discipline. These three, perhaps more than the others, fly in the face of our contemporary culture. To modern man, the practice of these is like someone dragging finger nails down a chalkboard. Faithfulness does not characterize our age. Our age is marked by selfishness and treachery, self-assertion and not meekness. Neither does self-control come to mind in our narcissistic and hedonistic society. Consequently, this last triad profoundly confronts our culture. Love, joy, and peace are not antagonistic to the culture. In fact, many might even marvel at your love and joy. Moreover, the social graces do not directly confront our culture. The exhibition of the graces might irritate our neighbour and they might seek to take advantage over us, thinking we are weak, but they will not be necessarily provoked. These last three, however, will provoke unbelievers to animosity.

Faithfulness – The first is the discipline of action. Faithfulness describes one who is honest and dependable. Faithfulness, which springs out of God's veracity, is a divine attribute. Hence, in the Hebrew the same term is translated 'faithful' and 'truthful'. God's faithfulness is His truthfulness. He tells us in His word who He is, what He has done, and what He will do. He cannot and does not lie and hence you may depend upon everything He says. Because He is true, He is dependable. He keeps every promise and fulfils every threat. The Bible, God's word, is an extension of His faithfulness. Since it is His word, it must be true and dependable as well.

What does it mean, therefore, for us to be faithful? First, it refers to how we live before God; we receive, believe, and love all that He has said in His word. We take it to be our faithful standard of doctrine and practice. Second, faithfulness demonstrates itself most frequently in how we live among those around us. The faithful Christian is the honest person; and committed to honesty. His 'yes' is to be 'yes' and his 'no' is to be 'no'. The Psalmist says, 'He swears to his own hurt, and does not change' (Ps. 15:4). The Christian should desire to be known as one who keeps his word. Not only must we avoid the more flagrant types of lying, but also we must avoid self-exalting exaggerations, as well, the little white lies we use to avoid giving offence. We must try to answer people tactfully, but truthfully. Paul says speak the truth in love (Eph. 4:15). We are not compelled to say everything we think or to tell all the truth, if it is going to harm someone. But we must never tell a non-truth. If we cannot think of another way of answering a question except with a white lie, we must tell the truth.

Faithfulness means we honour our obligations; paying our bills on time is an important part of faithfulness. Faithfulness includes dependability; if you say you are going to do something tomorrow, then unless you are providentially hindered, you will do it tomorrow. We must be careful not to over commit. We must learn to say, 'I am sorry, I cannot do that, not by tomorrow,' or 'I will try, but I can't promise you that I will have that done by tomorrow or by the end of the week.' You must learn to say 'no'. You must learn not to over commit, so when you do commit you are able to accomplish that which you have promised.

Another aspect of faithfulness is loyalty. We remain loyal to our husbands and wives, loyal to friends, regardless of the difficulties. We remain loyal to a commitment, even when something more advantageous comes along.

Meekness – The second discipline is one of attitude, 'meekness.' Meekness is not dissimilar to longsuffering and kindness (some versions translate this term 'gentleness'), but it is distinct and it has to do with a disciplined attitude about ourselves before God and one another. Meekness is the attitude that humbles oneself under God's Word and before one's neighbour. Meekness before God is the attitude expressed by Isaiah: 'But to this one I will look, to him who is humble and contrite of spirit, and who trembles at My word' (Isa. 66:2). James also describes our attitude to the word of God when he writes, 'But let everyone be quick to hear, slow to speak and slow to anger' (1:19). We are to submit to the will of God expressed in His word and the will of God worked out in His providence. It is the attitude expressed by the Psalmist: 'O Lord, my heart is not proud, nor my eyes haughty; nor do I involve myself in great matters, or in things too difficult for me. Surely I have composed and quieted my soul; like a weaned child rests against his mother, my soul is like a weaned child within me' (131:1, 2).

We also are to exercise meekness in our relationships. We are not to think more highly of ourselves than we should, but ought to esteem our brethren more highly than ourselves. Because we are sinners our hearts are deceitful; we tend to appraise our gifts and abilities more highly that we ought. We must labour for a sober assessment to know our weaknesses. Meekness, however, is not a denial of our strengths and gifts. There is nothing wrong with saying, 'Thank you,' when somebody compliments you. Neither is there anything wrong with volunteering to do something that you believe you can do well. Meekness is a sober self-assessment.

Moreover, meekness manifests the humility that submits to the opinion of others and does not always insist on its own way. It would be the opposite of being disputatious. Neither does one get his feelings hurt when he is not recognized or others are exalted over him. Hence it is the opposite of jealousy and envy.

Self-control – The discipline of affection and appetite is self-control. A person who is truly self-controlled governs himself. Self-government begins with submission to the will of God and His word. We learn to control our emotions regardless of the circumstances. Emotions are reactive; we cannot immediately control the emotive response, but we can learn to discipline its expression. We should seek to bring our responses and reactions into a quiet, peaceful submission to God and not be blown about by every adverse circumstance. We can learn to control our emotions by learning to control the venting of our emotions. Paul says, 'Be angry, and yet do not sin' (Eph. 4:26). He modelled that admonition when he had a flash of righteous anger and spoke somewhat harshly to the high priest. When he was rebuked and told not to speak to the high priest in that manner, he immediately brought his anger under control and responded, 'I was not aware, brethren, that he was the high priest; for it is written, "You shall not speak evil of a ruler of your people"' (Acts 23:5).

We also must learn to control our appetites. God has given us all things to enjoy, but He has also called us to a temperate life style. We are not to overindulge in the use of the things of the world. We must not be obsessed with satisfying appetites and pleasures. We are to be moderate in our use of the gifts of God. We must not be slaves to our appetites (not gluttons or drunks) or enslaved to substances like caffeine or tobacco.

We must also exercise discipline over our bodies. Paul does not deny the usefulness of bodily discipline when he says it is of little profit (1 Tim. 4:8). Consequently, we ought to do some form of exercise to maintain regular health and stamina. Therefore, if we are bearing fruit, we will be disciplined in our actions, attitudes, affections and appetites.

Fruit-bearing and liberty (5:23)

Paul concludes the catalogue of the fruit of the Spirit by saying that **against such things there is no law** (5:23). He demonstrates that the fruit of the Spirit is the mark of true liberty. He began this section by saying, 'For you were called to freedom, brethren; only do not turn your freedom into an opportunity for the flesh, but through love serve one another' (5:13). Freedom comes as we walk in the Spirit (v. 16). Paul reminds us of what he said in verse 18: 'But if you are led by the Spirit, you are not under the law.' In others words, the fruit of the Spirit is the mark that you are led by the Spirit. Therefore, if you manifest the fruit of the Spirit, you demonstrate that the Spirit is in you. You are not under the law as its slave. You are freed from its condemning and irritating power. You are free to bear the fruit of the Spirit.

Moreover, these graces are not under the law, which means they do not compete with the law. As we are accepted for Christ's sake as justified men and women, our imperfect fruit-bearing is acceptable before God for Christ's sake. In other words, perfection in the fruit of the Spirit is not what commends you to God. You are to strive for perfection, but your fruit will not make you more acceptable to God. Because you are in Christ, God takes delight and pleasure in you and your fruit. He will cultivate it; He will prune you and develop you, but He takes delight in your fruit and its growth. So do not be discouraged with your small beginnings. God will continue His work in you.

Study Questions

1. What contrast does Paul make in verse 22?
2. What are the five general marks of the fruit of the Spirit?
3. What two things do we learn because the fruit is the supernatural work of the Holy Sprit?
4. What is the first triad? How are these foundational to the rest? Define and discuss each.
5. What is the second triad? Why do I call them the social graces? Define and discuss each.
6. What is the third triad? Why will these create greater animosity in our culture? Define and discuss each.
7. What does Paul mean when he says, 'against such things there is no law'?

25

Mortification of the Flesh

(Galatians 5:24-26)

As we are well aware, life is full of struggles. We struggle with family difficulties, with financial difficulties, with time allotments and priorities in life; but the greatest struggle for the Christian is the struggle between the Spirit and the flesh, which Paul describes in Galatians 5. Moreover, if one wishes to cultivate the fruit of the Spirit, one must put to death the deeds of the flesh. This struggle is the backdrop for verses 24-26: **Now those who belong to Christ Jesus have crucified the flesh with its passions and desires. If we live by the Spirit, let us also walk by the Spirit. Let us not become boastful, challenging one another, envying one another**. At its heart, this struggle has to do with sanctification. The work of sanctification is twofold: vivification and mortification; we are to grow in conformity to the image of Christ (vivification) and we are to put to death the remnant of sin that remains within us (mortification). In this section we will discuss the necessity of the work of mortification.

The necessity of mortification

Paul states that if we belong to Christ, we have crucified the flesh with its passions and desires. As noted in previous comments the term 'flesh' refers to the remnant of sin that is in us. Even if our lives are not marked by the practice of the deeds of the flesh, there remains a remnant of sin within us against which we must struggle. Paul reminds us that the flesh manifests itself in our appetites and our lusts, what he calls our *passions and desires*. The term 'passion' means appetites – desires for food, rest, fulfilment, etc. The remnant of sin manifests itself in our appetites. Our lawful appetites usurp their rightful place and become inordinate, giving rise to immoderation and intemperance. 'Desires' refer to the desire by which perverted appetites express themselves in a triad of lusts: the lust of the eye, the lust of the flesh, and the boastful pride of life. Through this troika the remnant of sin wages war within us every day. Such lusts give birth to sin.

Paul boldly states: 'If you belong to Christ, you have crucified the flesh with its appetites and lusts.' The figure of crucifixion brings to mind one of the most torturous forms of capital punishment ever invented. In other words you may not spare sin, you must put it to death.

Paul uses the language of crucifixion for both a practical and a theological purpose. Practically, crucifixion describes a slow, but certain death. As long as the crucified person remained on a cross, he could not escape death. Although his death would be very slow and painful, it was not the loss of blood or pain that would kill the one being crucified; he died by asphyxiation. Hanging, with all one's weight, from outstretched arms causes the lungs to contract and the ability to breathe is hindered. Struggling for breath, the victim, using the footrest, may push himself up. But he could only do that for a brief period before the body would sag again. Between the pain and the slow suffocation his body grew weak; unable to push up he would suffocate gradually and inexorably. That is why the soldiers broke the legs of the victims on the cross. With broken legs, the victim could no longer push up and would suffocate more quickly. Hence if one remained on the cross, one would die. Therefore, Paul uses the figure of crucifixion to describe the painful, but certain work of dying to sin.

Paul also uses this term for a theological reason. He reminds us that because of our mystical union with Christ, we have been crucified with Christ (Rom. 6:1-11). Because Christ is our covenant head, we died in Him; we were buried with Him; we were raised with Him. Therefore when we are converted, the efficacy of Christ's death, burial, and resurrection becomes ours.

Notice he says that 'we have crucified ourselves.' Paul uses a Greek tense that teaches a past act that is habitual, which implies that death to sin is slow, but certain. Because we were crucified with Christ and because crucifixion is in a sense an ongoing act, we must continue to crucify the flesh. We may not climb down off the cross.

If we are Christians, we will continue this work; it is a necessary part of the Christian life. Notice the construction of verse 24: 'Now those who belong to Christ Jesus crucified the flesh.' The phrase translated 'belong to' is literally 'are of Christ Jesus'. It means that we belong to Him by redemption, faith, and repentance. If you have been saved by grace, you have crucified the flesh and you will continue to crucify the flesh. This act is not an option, it is not even an 'ought'. It is the reality of Christian experience.

Can it be said of you that you are involved in the crucifixion of the remnant of your sin? We are not consistent in this work, but it must be a work that concerns us. If it cannot be said of you that you are crucifying the flesh, if you have no motivation to die to sin, you do not yet belong to Christ.

The work of mortification

What then is this work of mortification? It is the spiritual work of daily putting to death the remnant of sin that manifests itself in our persons. The spiritual, daily, waging of war against the remnant of sin that is within us that we might indeed die to sin. Paul discusses this work in a number of parallel passages. In Romans 8:12 he writes: 'So then, brethren, we are under obligation, not to the flesh, to live according to the flesh, for if you are living according to the flesh, you must die; but if by the Spirit you are putting to death the deeds of the body, you will live.' Again you see the necessity. If you are in Christ, if you are walking by the Spirit, you are going to be putting to death these deeds. And in Colossians 3:5 he writes, 'Therefore consider (literally, "put to death") the members of your earthly body as dead to immorality, impurity, passion, evil desire, and greed, which amounts to idolatry.' We slay the deeds of the flesh.

The work consists of doing a number of things. First, it grows out of the regular practice of self-examination. We must regularly submit to the searchlight of the law of God, asking God to search our desires, motives, and behaviour.

Second, our self-examination must lead us to hate our sin and to mourn over it. God hates our sin; we must hate our sin. The Psalmist says in Psalm 119:104: 'I hate every wicked way.' We must hate every wicked way. The abhorrence leads to mourning, a sorrowing over sin that leads to repentance. We must never be satisfied with our level of spiritual attainment, but continually be hungering and thirsting for righteousness.

Third, act in faith in Christ. This step is often left out. All we do in mortification, we are to depend on Christ to apply His death to our sins. Our pursuit of sanctification is to be done in dependence on the Lord Jesus Christ. Thus Paul exhorts in Romans 6:12: 'Reckon yourself dead to sin.' Faith begins here, telling oneself I am crucified to this sin and I am not under its dominion. Moreover, bring to the cross that particular lust that is tempting you, ask Christ to put the nails into the lust. You also act in faith as you claim other promises like, 'greater is He who is in you than he who is in the world' (1 John 4:4, cf. Rom. 8:31).

Fourth, use the means of grace, prayer, the word, and the sacraments. God has appointed these means to strengthen us against temptation and sin.

Fifth, cut off all occasions and circumstances of sin. When we pray in the Lord's Prayer, 'Lead us not into temptation,' we are asking God to cut off all the occasions of sin, to keep us out of harm's way. Yet how often do we foolishly put ourselves in harm's way. If you are going to be serious about mortifying the flesh, you must avoid every circumstance, every occasion that is a temptation, anything that stirs up and incites your lust.

Sixth, isolate and attack. As we examine and know ourselves, we will learn what our weaknesses are, our besetting sins. As a wise warrior, we isolate each one and seek to kill it. We will never kill it permanently in this life, but we can weaken it.

The effects of mortification

A Spiritual Reality

Paul began this section with a warning against biting and devouring one another (5:15). This behaviour marked the Judaizers and was spreading by their false teaching into the congregations. Such action is a product of the flesh (5:13). The way we guard against this behaviour is to 'walk by the Spirit' (5:16). By mortification we will put to death the deeds of the flesh and will live by the Spirit. In other words, we will cultivate the fruit of the Spirit. He reverses the order in verse 25: if we are crucifying the flesh, we will be living by the Spirit, **If we live by the Spirit, let us also walk by the Spirit**. The reality is that because we crucified the flesh, we can live by the Spirit. Paul arranges verse 25 in what is called a chiasm. A chiasm is a grammatical structure that follows an order of thought like 'a-b-b-a.' Writers use this structure for emphasis. The literal translation of verse 25 is 'If we live by the Spirit, by the Spirit we also walk.' Paul is emphasizing the responsibility to walk by the Spirit, but that responsibility is premised on the spiritual reality that we live by the Spirit. That reality is a powerful motivation: if you want to be led by the Spirit, by the power of the Spirit crucify the flesh.

If you are a Christian, you have the Holy Spirit. Paul makes this clear in Romans 8:9, 'However you are not in the flesh but in the Spirit, if indeed the Spirit of God dwells in you. But if anyone does not have the Spirit of Christ, he does not belong to Him.' Therefore, if you belong to Christ, you are crucifying the flesh and living by the Spirit. Your union with Christ is secured in you by the presence of the Spirit of Christ within you. It is the Spirit of Christ who regenerates us and begins to transform our nature. The very reality of what it means to be a Christian is that we are indwelt by the Holy Spirit.

Notice he uses the plural 'we.' All who are in Christ possess the Holy Spirit. What is true of us individually is also true of the Church. The Church is the temple of the Holy Spirit. Because we live by the Spirit, the Christian life is a supernatural experience. The powerful third person of the Godhead indwells us. As we saw in verse 17, He wars against the flesh within us.

The Responsibility

The reality leads to the exhortation, 'let us also walk by the Spirit.' The word literally is to walk in a straight line. Follow after the Spirit. How does the Spirit lead you? He leads you through Scripture. He leads you as He prompts you and works within you to respond to the truth that is within Scripture. If you are going to walk by the Spirit, you will favour the things of the Spirit. As Paul says in Romans 8:5-7, set your mind not on the flesh, but on the things of the Spirit. We follow Him as we obey God's law set down in the Scriptures. The Scriptures are the light for our path. They are the way in which God would have us to walk and it is the Spirit who prompts us then to walk in them. He leads us through the Scriptures and walking in the Spirit is simply then seeking to live according to the Word of God.

To walk by the Spirit is also to live in dependence on the Spirit. We are actively to depend upon the Spirit of Christ within us in order to love and obey. Paul says in 2 Thess. 2:13 that sanctification is 'by the Spirit and faith in the truth.' We seek to do all in a conscious dependence upon the Spirit.

Practical Consequence

In verse 26, Paul lays out the consequence of walking in the Spirit: 'Let us not become boastful, challenging one another, envying one another.' If you are mortifying the flesh, living in the Spirit, you will not behave arrogantly. The word translated 'boastful' sometimes means vain ambition. It means you have vain thoughts about yourself; you are puffed up, arrogant, and conceited. It is the attitude that breeds jealousy, disputes, dissentions, factions. It is the opposite of meekness. Paul says boastfulness has two consequences: challenging and envying one another.

To challenge one another is to be pugnacious, given to outburst of anger. If we are full of vain ambition and self-seeking, when someone crosses us or if he does not recognize us in the way that we think we should be recognized, we become angry and challenge him. We challenge those who are in authority over us with resentment and anger; we challenge those who are under us by manipulation and intimidation.

The other consequence is envy. Envying is the bitterness and resentment arising when others receive honour or promotion that we believe we deserve. Vain ambition leads to envy every time we resent someone getting the opportunity or position that we thought we deserved, or when someone we consider inferior is promoted over us. Often, out of envy, we put them down or use innuendo to cast doubt on their person or ability.

Obviously we must guard our hearts against these things. The apostle would not have wasted his time to warn about something that is irrelevant. In Galatia the false teachers were driven by vain ambition and envy. They were attacking Paul and producing a similar spirit amongst the Galatian Christians. Only as we walk in the Spirit, can we be delivered from vain ambition, which is provocative and envious.

Study Questions

1. What does Paul mean by passions and desires?
2. What are the two reasons he uses the figure of crucifixion?
3. What inference do we make from the statement in verse 24?
4. What is the work of mortification?
5. What six things does it include?
6. How does verse 25 relate to verse 24?
7. What is the reality that Paul describes in verse 25?
8. What does it mean to walk by the Spirit?
9. What is the practical consequence of being led by the Spirit?
10. How do challenging one another and envying one another relate to vain ambition?

26

Maintaining Healthy Body Life

(Galatians 6:1-5)

Examples are very important, aren't they? Those of you who are fathers of young children probably have spent many a Christmas Eve or the night before a birthday, reading obscurely written instructions on how to put together a toy. Often what has saved the day is the picture on the front of the box or perhaps a diagram that is included with the instructions. We learn by example; we copy things that we see. This is also true for developing spiritually. It is a biblical principle which modern educators have chanced upon. We call this principle modelling.

The apostle Paul (master pastor that he was) often gave examples to illustrate the principles that he had inculcated. Here he exhorts us to live in holiness and in harmony, as we serve one another in love. He concludes the exhortation by relating walking in the Spirit to how we treat one another. In the first five verses of chapter 6, he gives an example of serving one another in love, particularly as we deal with sin within the body of Christ: **Brethren, even if a man is caught in any trespass, you who are spiritual, restore such a one in a spirit of gentleness; each one looking to yourself, lest you too be tempted. Bear one another's burdens, and thus fulfil the law of Christ. For if anyone thinks he is something when he is nothing, he deceives himself. But let each one examine his own work, and then he will have reason for boasting in**

regard to himself alone, and not in regard to another. For each one shall bear his own load (6:1-5).

An example (6:1-2)

Paul begins with an exhortation on how sin should be handled in the body of Christ: **Brethren, even if a man is caught in any trespass, you who are spiritual restore such a one in a spirit of gentleness; each looking to yourself, lest you too be tempted. Bear one another's burdens and thus fulfil the law of Christ (6:1, 2).** Paul's exhortation is an example for implementing his concluding exhortation in chapter 5, **let us not become boastful, challenging one another, envying one another.**

The term **Brethren** encompasses men and women and assumes membership within the church. The verb **is caught** suggests one suddenly falling into sin, but would apply to anyone within the body of Christ who falls into a grievous sin or into the practice of sin.

Obviously, Paul is not talking about the daily sins that are, relatively speaking, minor and covered by love. His language suggests a more sudden fall into a serious sin or the practice of a specific sin. It might be something that happens publicly and needs to be addressed immediately, as in the case of Peter (Gal. 2:11-14). At other times it might be addressed privately either because it was a private offence or in order to avoid embarrassing someone by rebuking him in public.

Paul says it is the responsibility of spiritual persons to restore such a one. Whom does he mean by the term **you who are spiritual**? This term takes us back to 5:25: 'If we live by the Spirit, let us walk by the Spirit.' The **spiritual** refers to those who are seeking to walk by the Spirit, putting to death the deeds of the flesh, and cultivating the fruit of the Spirit. He is not talking about some super-spiritual person, but rather everyone who seeks to live his life for the glory of God.

Thus the spiritual man or woman is to restore the one who has fallen. Now the word **restore** means to mend. This word is used for mending a broken bone. It means to set back to right, to put in order. Sometimes such a putting right is painful ('Faithful are the wounds of a friend,' Prov. 27:6).

Christ details the process for restoration in Matthew 18:15-17: 'And if your brother sins, go and reprove him in private; if he listens to you, you have won your brother. But if he does not listen to you, take one or two more with you, so that by the mouth of two or three witnesses every fact may be confirmed. And if he refuses to listen to them, tell it to the church; and if he refuses to listen even to the church, let him be to you as a Gentile and a tax-gatherer.' We should use this procedure only in the most extraordinary circumstances.

You begin the process by meeting with the individual, discussing your perception, seeking to learn his side of the story. If after listening, you still think he has sinned, you tell him that it appears to you that he is violating the word of God and needs to repent and turn away from what he is doing. You might add that you would be glad to assist him and to encourage him in the process. But if he refuses to repent and his behaviour continues, or if he says he repents, but the behaviour continues, you return with one or two witnesses. The use of witnesses fulfils the biblical injunction that all accusations be confirmed by two or three witnesses (Deut. 19:15). In other words, you repeat step one in the presence of witnesses. If step two fails, you bring it to the church (the elders of the church). If the person refuses to listen to the elders, he is to be excommunicated.

Notice, as well, that Paul tells us the attitude the spiritual ones are to exhibit in this process: **Restore such a one in a spirit of gentleness; each one looking to yourself lest you too be tempted**. Such people do not approach a brother or sister in an arrogant, challenging manner. They come humbly, in gentleness. They approach them as a fellow traveller, a sinner saved by grace, who genuinely cares for them. The word translated **gentleness** is the word Paul uses in the last triad of the fruit of the Spirit, translated **gentleness** or **meekness**. It is the manifestation of humility before God and men.

Paul enforces the need for humility, by adding, **each one looking to yourself, lest you too be tempted**. It is only by God's grace that we have not fallen into the practice of particular sin. The very temptation that suddenly took this brother or sister by surprise could take us by surprise. So we live humbly aware of our own need. We must not attempt the restoration of another in a self-righteous or censorious attitude.

Paul gives the ground of this duty in verse 2: **Bear one another's burdens, and thus fulfil the law of Christ**. He has in mind Leviticus 19:18 (quoted in Galatians 5:14): '**You shall love your neighbour as yourself**.' Notice that Paul says the Old Testament law is the law of Christ. We reprove our neighbour, because we love him. We, therefore, have this duty to one another. It is much easier to gossip or to fume than to admonish and exhort. But true love enables us to labour for restoration.

The Antidote (6:3-5)

Having shown us the practical example of walking in the Spirit and not challenging one another in jealousy and pride, Paul gives the antidote to selfish ambition in verses 3-5: **For if anyone thinks he is something when he is nothing, he deceives himself. But let each one examine his own work, and then he will have reason for boasting in regard to himself alone, and not in regard to another. For each one shall bear his own load**. The apostle warns of the danger of self-deceit: **If any one thinks he is something when he is nothing, he deceives himself**. Since it is difficult to approach a brother or sister with the proper *attitude,* Paul gives the proper *antidote*. Avoid the self-deception of thinking more highly of yourself than you ought. If you think that you are superior in your gifts, in your moral excellence, in your insights, you will not approach your neighbour gently. There is a real danger here. The heart is deceitful; we often are blind to our sins and deceived with respect to our ability (Matt. 7:1-5).

So how then do we deal with this danger of self-deception? What is its practical antidote? It is self-examination: **But let each one examine his own work, and then he will have reason for boasting in regard to himself alone, and not in regard to another** (v. 4). Paul calls us to the regular practice of self-examination. The unexamined life is a fruitless life, a self-righteous life, and a deceived life.

We, however, must not examine our lives by others. We can always find those we consider our spiritual inferiors. Moreover, we can rationalize our behaviour by comparing it to others or by blaming them for our sinful response. Hence, we do not examine our lives by others. Instead we examine our lives by the standard of God's word and our response will be before God alone: **Let each one examine his own work and then he will have reason for boasting in regard to himself alone and not in regard to another**. There is no profit in our thinking that we are superior to another person either in terms of gifts or sanctification. We answer to God alone. Any wrong boasting is vain.

To enforce this practice, Paul borrows a principle out of the Book of Proverbs: **For each one shall bear his own load** (v. 5). He alludes to Proverbs 9:12: 'If you are wise, you are wise for yourself, and if you scoff, you alone will bear it.' He seems to contradict himself. He said in verse 2, **Bear one another's burdens**, and now he says, **each one shall bear his own load**. In this apparent contradiction, Paul borrows from the style of Proverbs. The contrast makes the lesson memorable. The law of Christ, to love your neighbour as yourself, calls you to enter into the sufferings and weakness of your brother and sister. The law of self-examination warns you that you answer to God alone for your actions; you bear your own load before him. Paul here demolishes the victim-mentality of modern western culture. We are responsible to God for our actions. Each of us must live his life before God, and we are all going to give an answer for the deeds done by us. And, consequently, we do not boast with regard to another person; we bear our own load before God.

There is a proper boasting and that boasting is the boasting of a clear conscience before God. We each must seek to maintain a pure conscience. How do we come to such a boasting? It is in Christ, not in ourselves. It is in grace, not in our works. It is on the basis of daily confession of sin and assurance of pardon. By these means we keep the conscience clean.

You may also maintain a clear conscience when you are involved in a difficult relationship. Paul says, 'If possible, so far as it depends on you, be at peace with all men' (Rom. 12:18). You examine your conduct by God's word and if, as best you can determine, you are acting biblically, you can maintain confidence that you are doing your best. It is good in such circumstances to seek counsel in order to ensure you are not being deceived. In this manner we will maintain peace in the body of Christ.

Study Questions

1. How does Galatians 6:1-5 relate to chapter 5?
2. What duty does Paul command in chapter 6:1, 2?
3. What type of sin does Paul have in mind? What does it mean 'is caught'?
4. What does the term 'restore' imply?
5. What are the steps we are to follow?
6. What is to be the attitude of the one who seeks to restore a fallen brother or sister?
7. What is the ground of this duty?
8. How may we conduct this duty and avoid pride?
9. What danger is Paul warning against?
10. How do we avoid this danger?
11. Does Paul contradict himself in verse 5? How does verse 5 relate to verse 1?
12. What does Paul mean by 'boasting in regard to himself alone'?

27

Spiritual Farming

(Galatians 6:6-10)

Do you remember the first time you observed a seed sprouting in a glass jar? The growth of a seed is a marvellous phenomenon. It is a fascinating law of creation, governed by God's providence. God has also created seed so that whatever type of seed planted, that is the plant that will grow and bear fruit. You do not pick grapes from a thorn bush; you pick grapes from a grape vine. The Bible is full of figures of speech, similes and metaphors based on the relationship of seed and plant, and Paul uses such a figure in Galatians 6:6-10, in this case the relationship of sowing to harvesting. He uses this particular figure in order to teach us about stewardship within the body of Christ. He is dealing with how we live with one another. Gospel liberty does not allow us to be self-centred. Paul says gospel liberty is not a licence to sin against God and it is not a licence to live self-centredly in the midst of the community. In the previous section (6:1-5), he gave a practical example of how to live together in humility.

In verses 6-10, he offers another practical example, which at first does not seem to fit, but in fact it does, namely, the matter of Christian stewardship, particularly in the provision for the full-time ministry: **And let the one who is taught the word share all good things with him who teaches. Do not be deceived, God is not mocked; for whatever a man sows, this he will also reap. For the one who sows to his own flesh**

shall from the flesh reap corruption, but the one who sows to the Spirit shall from the spirit reap eternal life. And let us not lose heart in doing good, for in due time we shall reap if we do not grow weary. So then while we have opportunity, let us do good to all men, and especially to those who are of the household of the faith. Once again Paul establishes the principle that God uses His appointed means to accomplish His spiritual purposes.

The Exhortation (6:6)

This exhortation apparently comes out of the blue: **And let the one who is taught the word share all good things with him who teaches**. Paul has been discussing serving one another in the body of Christ, being humble, not being proud, not being conceited, and suddenly introduces this element of Christian stewardship. How does this exhortation fit in the flow of Paul's instruction? First, Paul is giving another practical example of how we serve one another in Christian liberty, by discussing how we use our money in the body of Christ. Second, he has said we are to bear our own load, but that does not rule out the need to help financially both pastors and other brothers and sisters. Third, there might have been the problem of ministerial support caused by the claims of the false teachers. Perhaps some were advocating not paying those who supported Paul.

Thus the apostle lays down this very important spiritual principle; namely, that the catechumen should share all good things with him who teaches. He uses the word **catechumen** for the one who has been instructed publicly and privately. It implies the relationship between the one taught and the teacher; those who have benefited from the ministry spiritually owe material support to the minister (cf. 1 Cor. 9:7-14).

Paul establishes two important principles. First, the Bible teaches that there is a 'professional ministry'. By professional, I mean vocational, those who make a living from the ministry. Second, the congregation in its entirety has a spiritual responsibility to pay its minister. In most Presbyterian Orders of Government, the call to the minister includes the phrase, 'That you may be free from worldly cares and avocations, we hereby promise and oblige ourselves to pay you…' The responsibility to pay the minister is a spiritual duty. It is a duty to be taken seriously; a duty that it is sin to neglect.

The Grounds of the Exhortation (6:7-9)

In these verses, Paul enforces the exhortation by anticipating and answering two objections. The first objection he anticipates is that times are hard and I have to pay my own bills and I have other financial responsibilities. He answers this by saying, **Do not be deceived, God is not mocked; for whatever a man sows, this he will also reap**. Paul reminds his readers that God is the sovereign provider of all things and knows what provisions He has given to each individual. God has said that a minimum of 10% belongs to Him and that he knows full well that any man or woman can live on the remaining 90% if they live faithfully before God. So 'do not be deceived.' Quit playing games in which you say that you cannot afford to support the ministry.

Paul also introduces the spiritual principle, that whatever a man sows he will reap. Here he applies it to stewardship and later he will apply it to godliness. The principle is not dissimilar from what Christ often taught: 'With what measure you measure, it shall be measured unto you again' (Luke 6:38; Matt. 7:2; Mark 4:24). Christ emphasizes the grace of God when he adds 'and more shall be given you besides' (Mark 4:24). It is a spiritual law, but spiritual laws still operate out of grace. God expects you to use means and God blesses these uses of means, but God never blesses means in a mechanical manner. He blesses means by grace. The principle, however, remains.

With respect to stewardship, God will provide for the person who is faithfully committed to the work of God and begins his giving on the foundation of a tithe. The person who neglects to tithe because of financial pressures, most often at the end of the year, will look back and see unplanned expenses that will account for much more than a tithe. God will teach you that you can live on the 90% if you seek to live faithfully in dependence on Him.

And of course, the principle that you reap what you sow is further spelled out in the teaching of the Saviour in Matthew 6. He says there that we are not to worry about physical provisions: 'If God so arrays the grass of the field, which is alive today and tomorrow is thrown into the furnace, will He not much more do so for you, O men of little faith? Do not be anxious then saying what shall we eat or what shall we drink or with what shall we clothe ourselves: for all these things the Gentiles eagerly seek but your heavenly Father knows that you need all these things. But seek first His kingdom and His righteousness and all these things shall be added unto you.' God works in your life according to your sowing. You will reap what you sow. When you sow to Him, you put money in heaven, so to speak. When you respond to the Lord in this way, He will provide for you in ways far beyond what you can imagine.

Although describing stewardship, Paul cannot resist applying the principle to godliness in verse 8: **The one who sows to his own flesh shall from the flesh reap corruption but the one who sows from the Spirit shall from the Spirit reap eternal life**. Here we see that the matter of stewardship is not merely a material thing divorced from the heart's relation to God. Paul shows that when we give in support of the ministry, we are either sowing a carnal thing and reaping carnality or we are sowing spiritual things and reaping eternal life. **Flesh** refers to sinful desires (Paul details them in 5:19-21). Giving is a reflection of our heart commitment. It is a reflection of our true love and worship. It shows whether or not we are idolaters. The southern Presbyterians in the U.S.A. used to say with respect to tithing that it was God's antidote to covetousness. You cannot tithe out of faith and live a life of wanton pleasure, grasping for and greedily gripping material things.

Our use of money manifests the condition of our hearts, it reveals what we consider important. Show me your chequebook and I will tell you what is really important in your life. Even if you are not spending money on worldly pursuits, if you are not tithing, you are making a statement about your priorities. Thus he deals with the first objection.

In verse 9 Paul deals with the second possible objection; we grow weary in supporting the church, in doing good, and in denying ourselves, while nothing seems to improve. He writes, **let us not lose heart in doing good, because in due time we shall reap if we do not grow weary**. The term **lose heart** means to faint, to lose hope and give up. What a necessary admonition! When we note all the problems in various congregations, we are tempted to say, 'This church is not worth it.' We also grow weary in giving our time as well as our money. The church is so full of problems and problem people. If we are to reap what we sow, why are we not seeing the harvest? Not growing weary means that we persevere. Paul reminds us that we are to persevere in doing good; persevere in our giving, in our praying, and in other forms of service. There will be a harvest, if not here, certainly in heaven. Perhaps we will see a great harvest here, but regardless there will be a day when we will see the full harvest in eternity. In heaven all the sacrificial service will be considered well worth it. God will keep His word. The farmer must wait a long time for the harvest; he plants seed in the ground; it grows mysteriously and there will be a harvest. We are to persevere.

The Expansion of the Exhortation (6:10)

So then, while we have opportunity, let us do good to all men, and especially to those who are of the household of the faith. Notice Paul relates this verse to what he has written, **So then**. This is the conclusion. He builds on the exhortation that we are to persevere in our sowing, in verse 9, 'Let us not lose heart in doing good, for in due time we shall reap.' Therefore, let us sow while there is opportunity. This exhortation reminds us of the exhortations of the Saviour, 'Walk while it is day' (John 11:9); 'Behold, I say to you, lift up your eyes, and look on the fields, that they are white for harvest' (John 4:35); 'Therefore beseech the Lord of the harvest to send out workers into His harvest' (Matt. 9:38). Today is a time of work and the apostle reminds us to seize the opportunity. Seize the opportunity and do not grow weary; boldly plunge into the labour.

Furthermore he expands from support for the ministry to service in the body of Christ: **Do good to all men, and especially to those who are of the household of the faith**. Yes, you are to care for your ministers, but you are to do much more. You are to direct your charity, your giving of yourself, as well as your service, to those in the church. The phrase **household of the faith** refers to those who are marked out by the faith of the Bible; those in the local congregation who profess that faith. We are to seek to do good to all men, but our first responsibility is to our brothers and sisters in the church. Paul does not mean that we are to focus our attention exclusively on our own congregation; yet we begin in our congregation, next sister congregations in the presbytery and denomination, and then to all evangelical Christians. Neither does he rule out helping those in the world. But our first priority is our brother and sister in the Church.

Study Questions

1. How does verse 6 relate to the context?
2. Why does Paul use the word 'catechumen'?
3. What principle does he establish in verse 6?
4. What objection does he anticipate in verse 7?
5. What principle does he establish in verse 7?
6. How does he apply the principle in verse 8?
7. What objection does he deal with in verse 9?
8. What is God promising in verse 9?
9. In what way does he expand the exhortation in verse 10?
10. What does he mean by 'household of the faith'?

28

Two Types of Religious Persons

(Galatians 6:11-15)

Many things grip our attention, things to which we are willing to commit energy, strength, time and money. They are things on which we focus, and to be passionate about good things is not bad. As Christians, we should have one passion above every other passion; one focus of our lives that is central to every other focus in life; namely the glory of God; a love for God that focuses on the Lord Jesus Christ. Christ is to be the very heart of our existence; He is the very foundation of all of our hopes. In Galatians 6:11-15 the apostle Paul reminds us that we should glory in Christ above everything else. Having completed his exhortations, he concludes his letter to the Galatians. In the conclusion he summarizes the key message of the book in terms of two types of religionists: one who boasts in the flesh and one who boasts in the cross.

Boasting in the Flesh (6:11-13)

Paul begins by exposing the false religionist who boasts in the flesh: '**See with what large letters I am writing to you with my own hand. Those who desire to make a good showing in the flesh try to compel you to be circumcised, simply that they may not be persecuted for the cross of Christ. For those who are circumcised do not even keep the Law themselves, but they desire to have you circumcised, that they may boast in your flesh**' (Gal. 6:11-13).

Paul carefully draws attention to his conclusion. Normally he dictated his letters. He probably signed them in his own hand, but he had a secretary that took his dictation. In this letter, however, Paul writes the summary paragraph and draws attention to the fact that he is writing it. He writes in large letters in order to emphasize the importance of the conclusion of this letter, even drawing attention to the size of the script.

It has been suggested that the apostle Paul, like Charlemagne, had difficulty with a pen. He was a tentmaker, and although he was a brilliant, well read man, he had secretaries and did not have to worry about writing. Others suggest that the large letters were connected with a problem with his eyesight that developed during his preaching tour in Galatia. In either case, he would have written with a larger than normal script, with a great deal of painstaking effort. Whatever may be the cause behind the size of the script, the very fact that he wrote the conclusion himself and draws attention to the size of the letters accentuates the conclusion.

Preachers should do with the voice and body what Paul does with the pen. We need to use our voice and rhetoric to draw attention to serious matters. We need to emphasize the truth with passion in the way Paul does with the pen – an exclamation, underscoring the seriousness of the truth (1 Cor. 2:4).

Moreover, as Paul emphasizes what he has written, he contrasts himself with the Judaizers, '**Those who desire to make a good showing in the flesh try to compel you to be circumcised simply that they may not be persecuted for the cross of Christ. For those who are circumcised do not even keep the Law themselves, but they desire to have you circumcised, that they may boast in your flesh**.' Here he pulls together the theme of the book of Galatians, indicting the Judaizers. Although they confessed to believe in Christ, they taught that Christ's work alone was insufficient for the remission of sins. He delineates their motives; he says there are three things behind their false teaching.

First, they arrogantly promoted themselves. He points this out with two expressions: '**they desire to make a good showing in the flesh**' (12) and '**they desire to have you circumcised that**

they may boast in your flesh' (13). We find an echo here of what he said in chapter 5 about vain ambition. He says they want applause; they want fame; they want to be recognized as great teachers and spiritual leaders. They desire to boast in their followers as trophies.

It is important to understand this motivation of false teachers. There is a difference between a false teacher and a person who falls into error and is correctable. The person that persists in his error after the church has spoken clearly to the issue, like Arius who denied the deity of Christ in the fourth century, is acting out of pride. The false teacher boasts in his new paradigm and in his followers.

Second, Paul says they are hypocrites; they are driven by a double standard, '**For those who are circumcised do not even keep the law themselves**' (v. 13). Like the Scribes and Pharisees rebuked by the Saviour in Matthew 23:1-13, the Judaizers were not living by that which they required of others. The false teachers cultivated a reputation for being zealous for the law of God, but they exercised no care in keeping the law.

Third, Paul accuses them of being ashamed of the cross, of avoiding the scandal of the cross, '**That they may not be persecuted for the cross of Christ**' (v. 12). The cross was foolishness and a stumbling block to the Jews (1 Cor. 1:18, 23). The crucifixion of Christ was a scandal in the ancient world. The Judaizers sought to make Christ more palatable and to make themselves more acceptable to the Jews as Jewish Christians. Basically, he says, they added Jewish elements to the message, attempting to tone it down in order to remove the problem of persecution, to remove the offence of the cross.

And again that is what all works and sacramental religion does. They substitute for the offence of the cross the dignity of human worth and righteousness, or the beauty and glory of church practices. All such attempts debase the Saviour.

These things are what drive false teachers. We do not have to read the hearts of individuals to say, in a categorical sense, that false teachers are proud hypocrites, seeking to teach a system that removes the offence of the cross.

We all must wrestle with this danger. We can play games and deceive ourselves. Is not our silence in witnessing often because we are ashamed of the cross? The church also does this when it substitutes pop psychology and seeker-friendly worship for law and gospel preaching.

Boasting in Christ (6:14-15)

The best antidote to boasting in the flesh is to boast in Christ. The true religionist boasts in Christ, **May it never be that I should boast in anything, except the cross of our Lord Jesus Christ, through which the world has been crucified to me and I to the world. For neither is circumcision anything nor uncircumcision, but a new creation** (vv. 14, 15). By the term 'cross,' Paul is not referring to the wooden vehicle of crucifixion. He is using a figure of speech, using the instrument of the Saviour's atoning work to depict the gospel. In another place, he says, 'Woe is me if I do not preach the gospel' (1 Cor. 9:16). He is talking about the substitutionary atonement of Christ, by which the justice of God was satisfied and sinners can be justified.

Paul gives us two reasons why he glories in the cross. First, the cross separates him from the world. He says that the cross, the work of Christ on the cross, separates him from the world, '**through which the world has been crucified to me, and I to the world**' (v. 14). He means that through the cross, the world (the world system with its values and temptations) has lost its appeal, its charm. He once clung to the world; namely, his self-righteousness, his Judaism. But he says in Philippians 3:7, 'But whatever things were gain to me, those things I have counted as loss for the sake of Christ.'

Moreover, he died **to the world**. He says that the world despises him. The world wants nothing to do with him; the Jews want nothing to do with him, because he exalts Christ as the only way of salvation. When a Jew or Moslem is baptized, he becomes dead to his family; he is cut off. Similarly, Paul is cut off from the world. Paul says, 'I have died to the world and they hate me.' He was not ashamed of that. He boldly wore the scars of their persecution with a spiritual rejoicing (v. 17). Thus, Paul says the cross severs all old and sinful relationships; it changes our affinities; it changes that which attracts us; it changes the way those outside of Christ respond to us.

Second, Paul asserts in verse 15 that by the cross alone we are reconciled to God, **For neither is circumcision anything, nor**

uncircumcision, but a new creation. Notice the contrast. He says that both circumcision and uncircumcision are unimportant. Why, because they do not reconcile us to God. The really important thing is being a new creation. Through the message of the cross, sinners become new creatures. God transforms them by regeneration. In regeneration He unites them to the Lord Jesus Christ and each becomes a new creature (2 Cor. 5:17).

We may rightly infer that baptism, which replaces circumcision, does not make us new creatures. Baptism is necessary, because God has commanded us to be baptized. It marks our relation to Christ and His church, and if we are new creatures, it testifies to us of our union with Christ. Baptism, however, does not convert or regenerate.

Therefore, Paul gloried in the cross, and every true Christian must glory in the cross. Do you glory in the cross, the beauty of the scheme of redemption? Have you experienced the power of the cross? Is it the ground of your Hope? It must be if you are a Christian.

Study Questions

1. Why does Paul draw attention to his writing with large letters in verse 11?
2. How does Paul contrast himself with the false teachers?
3. What are three problems with the motivations of the false teachers?
4. What does Paul mean by the phrase 'boasting in the cross of Christ'?
5. What is the first reason Paul gives for boasting in the cross?
6. How is the world crucified to us?
7. What does it mean that we die to the world?
8. What is Paul's second reason for boasting in the cross?
9. What inference may we make from verse 15 with respect to baptism?

29

The Blessing

(Galatians 6:16-18)

It is very important that the members of a congregation understand that their minister loves them. Much good is accomplished when there is a tie of affection between a congregation and its pastor; a congregation learns and profits from the minister who they are convinced loves them. But we also realize that true love does not always appear nice and positive. If you observed a man suddenly running up and knocking his child down, your first thought might be that he is a brute to treat his child that way, and then you see a truck go speeding by and understand that it was a supreme act of love to handle the child roughly. The apostle Paul often teaches about the importance of a pastor loving his people. He has had to treat the Galatian congregation roughly. Like the father of the little boy about to step in front of the speeding truck, the apostle Paul seeks to push them out of harm's way. He must warn them of the danger of eminent apostasy and the curse that comes upon those that substitute the gospel of the Lord Jesus Christ for a false gospel.

Although Paul begins sharply, the book itself shines with love. He addresses them as his brethren and as his little children. Although he expresses himself in the shrillest tone, he cannot disguise his love for them. As he concludes the book, he makes clear his love for them. Now, he can take a deep breath; he has made his case and can conclude with these tender words of apostolic blessing, verses 16-18, **'And those who will walk by this rule, peace and mercy be upon them, and upon the Israel of God. From now on let no one cause trouble for me for I bear on my body the brand-marks of Jesus. The grace of Our Lord, Jesus Christ be with your spirit, brethren. Amen.'**

In this apostolic benediction, Paul confers genuine and lasting blessings on the Galatians.

The Declaration of the Blessing (6:16, 18)

Paul declares a threefold blessing, **'And those who will walk by this rule, peace and mercy be upon them, and upon the Israel of God.... The grace of our Lord Jesus Christ be with your spirit, brethren. Amen.'**

In verse 16, he pronounces peace and mercy and, in verse 18, grace. These three blessings are often united in Scripture; they summarize the fruit of the gospel in the lives of God's people. Paul begins his letter to the Galatians with the pronouncement of grace and peace.

The peace of the Lord Jesus Christ is a reference to the wholeness, the joy, and the contentment that are ours in the Christ Jesus. As seen above, it is a Fruit of the Spirit. This peace is threefold. First, it is an objective peace with God. He has reconciled us to Himself; He has laid down His weapons. On the basis of Christ's sacrifice and our justification, God has turned away His wrath. We are no longer at enmity with God.

Second, it is the subjective peace of conscience. To know that one is at peace with God is to enjoy peace of conscience. Conscience is quieted by the gospel (Rom. 5:1, 2).

Third, when we are at peace with God, we are enabled to live at peace with one another. We do not need to contend for our own rights; rather, we can live together with a quiet and gentle spirit. This peace is the first apostolic blessing.

Mercy is the second blessing the apostle declares. Mercy is the pity of God joined with appropriate acts as He addresses the miseries of our lives. The term is related to that rich Old Testament concept of loving-kindness. This is the covenant love of God, which is the spring of God's mercy to us. He is a Father and He loves us in the covenant as His children. Loving-kindness is the word that reminds us that He is a gentle Father, 'Just as a father has compassion on his children, so the Lord has compassion on those who fear Him. For He Himself knows our frame; He is mindful that we are but dust' (Ps. 103:13, 14). He does not deal with us according to our sins, but in His loving-kindness and compassion, He patiently bears with us and upholds us. Hence, the mercy of God is that which softens, sustains, and delivers us from the miseries and the consequences of our sins.

The third benefit is grace. Notice it is the grace of the Lord Jesus Christ; Paul uses these three main names of the Saviour in order to teach that He is the sovereign God, who became man in order to save His people from their sins. Moreover, He is God's anointed prophet, priest, and king. In Him is everything we need to be saved. He has purchased for us all the benefits of grace, the objective realities of justification, adoption, and sanctification—the power to die to sin and to be renewed in the image of Christ Jesus; the subjective realties of assurance of God's love, of boldness in prayer, of confidence, and of joy in the Holy Spirit. Christ has purchased and continues to distribute to us all these gracious benefits.

These three things together summarize the benefits of the gospel.

The Recipients of the Blessings (6:16, 17)

To whom then do these blessings belong? Paul shows us quite clearly who the recipients are. He first describes them by the nature of their faith and then by two titles. He says in verse 16, that peace and mercy belong to 'those who will walk by this rule.' The term 'walk' means to follow after or to agree with, in other words, to follow after this rule. What is this rule? This is the rule of justification by faith alone, the standard of gospel salvation and holiness that Paul has delineated in this book. He now says that all who have rejected the false gospel of the Judaizers shall enjoy God's blessing. First, he expresses the qualification positively, to those who follow the rule, and then negatively, 'From now on let no one cause trouble for me, for I bear on my body the brand-marks of Jesus' (v. 17).

With this brusque statement he sweeps aside the Judaizers. He does not want one more word from them, 'Let no one cause me trouble.' He has exposed them as cursed, false teachers.

He emphasizes this statement by pointing to his suffering for the cross of Christ, 'For I bear on my body the brand-marks of Jesus.' He says his body bears testimony that he has been persecuted; persecution is the very thing the false teachers have sought to avoid (6:12). A true believer identifies with the offence of the cross. Paul shows clearly the class of people to whom the blessings belong: those who hold to Christ by faith and identify with the offence of the cross.

Moreover, he clarifies their position by using two titles that define the recipients of God's blessing. The first is the family title, 'Brethren.' Since he has already used this title, I remind you of something that I wrote before. Paul never uses fillers. Every word, every title is chosen with care. Therefore, he is expressing by the term 'brethren' (a term that includes men and women) those who belong to God's family, God's adopted children, and the co-heirs of the Lord Jesus Christ. So this term is another way of talking about those who follow the rule or walk by the rule. If you are a Christian then you are a brother of Christ; you are a child of God.

Furthermore, because of the issues in this letter about who belongs to the people of God, he calls them, 'the Israel of God' (v. 16). This is a common way to address the covenant people, 'Redeem Israel, O God' (Ps. 25:22, cf. 130:8). Here he addresses a congregation made up mostly of converted Gentiles, Israel. The Judaizers claimed that these people had to become Jews physically (circumcision) to be part of Israel. Paul has shown that all who believe in Christ are the true seed of Abraham (3:29). Israel is the church. It matters not whether you are circumcised or uncircumcised. If, by faith, you are in union with Christ Jesus, you are God's Israel.

Hence Paul destroys the idea that God has two people, Israel and the church. No! Here he calls the church Israel. There are not two people. There is the one people of God. We are the children of Abraham; we are God's Israel. So the blessings of God, the apostolic benediction, are bestowed upon those who are in Christ Jesus.

The Reality of the Blessing

The third thing is the reality of the blessing. People oftentimes think of the apostolic blessings and the benedictions as holy prayers or divine wishes. They are nothing of the sort. The apostle says, 'Peace and mercy be upon them.' He is exercising his apostolic office in conferring blessing. He is communicating objective reality to the Galatian Christians. It remains part of the office of preaching to confer the apostolic blessing. So when an ordained minister gives the blessing it is really imparted.

Moreover, it is an experienced reality, 'The grace of Our Lord Jesus Christ be with your spirit' (v. 18). In other words this blessing is something that you are aware of in your conscience. You know that you have received this blessing.

This is the beauty of the apostolic benedictions. They really confer these things to you as an objective reality that you may experience. Therefore, when the minister gives the benediction at the end of the worship service, you are not to bow your head in prayer; rather, you ought to look up, and as one of those who walks according to the rule, say, 'Yes, Lord, I receive this blessing in Christ. I thank you for it.' You have the responsibility by faith to take hold of the blessing and to appropriate it in the same way you listen to the Word of God preached or partake of the sacraments. You are to recognize that God is conferring grace.

Study Questions

1. List the three blessings that Paul pronounces.
2. What are the three parts of peace?
3. What reality does mercy have in view? What important Old Testament concept is conveyed by the term mercy?
4. What is the grace that Paul pronounces?
5. How does Paul describe those who are the recipients of these blessings?
6. What does it mean to walk by this rule?
7. Why does Paul add the matter about false teachers no longer causing him trouble, because he bears the marks of Christ on his body (v. 17)?

8. What two titles does he use? What is the significance of the title 'Israel'?
9. How does the language teach the objective reality of the blessing conferred and the subjective experience of that reality?
10. How should we receive a benediction?

Subject Index

Scripture Index

Focus on the Bible Commentary Series

Deuteronomy: The Commands of a Covenant God – Allan Harman
ISBN 978-1-84550-268-3

Joshua: No Falling Words – Dale Ralph Davis
ISBN 978-1-84550-137-2

Judges: Such a Great Salvation – Dale Ralph Davis
ISBN 978-1-84550-138-9

Ruth & Esther: God Behind the Seen – A. Boyd Luter/Barry C. Davis
ISBN 978-1-85792-805-9

1 Samuel: Looking on the Heart – Dale Ralph Davis
ISBN 978-1-85792-516-6

2 Samuel: Out of Every Adversity – Dale Ralph Davis
ISBN 978-1-84550-270-6

1 Kings The Wisdom and the Folly – Dale Ralph Davis
ISBN 978-1-84550-251-5

2 Kings: The Power and the Glory – Dale Ralph Davis
ISBN 978-1-84550-096-2

1 Chronicles: God's Faithfulness to the People of Judah – Cyril J. Barber
ISBN 978-1-85792-935-5

2 Chronicles: God's Blessing of His Faithful People – Cyril J. Barber
ISBN 978-1-85792-936-2

Psalms 1-89: The Lord Saves – Eric Lane
ISBN 978-1-84550-180-8

Psalms 90-150: The Lord Reigns – Eric Lane
ISBN 978-1-84550-202-7

*Proverbs: Everyday Wisdom for Everyon*e – Eric Lane
ISBN 978-1-84550-267-6

Song of Songs – Richard Brooks
ISBN 978-1-85792-486-2

Isaiah: A Covenant to be Kept for the Sake of the Church – Allan Harman
ISBN 978-1-84550-053-5

Daniel: A Tale of Two Cities – Robert Fyall
ISBN 978-1-84550-194-5

Hosea – Michael Eaton
ISBN 978-1-85792-277-6

Jonah, Michah, Nahum, Nahum & Zephaniah – John L. Mackay
ISBN 978-1-85792-392-6

Haggai, Zechariah & Malachi: God's Restored People – John L. Mackay
ISBN 978-1-85792-067-3

Matthew: Can Anything Good Come Out of Nazareth – Charles Price
ISBN 978-1-85792-285-1

Mark: Good News from Jerusalem – Geoffrey Grogan
ISBN 978-1-85792-905-8

Acts: Witnesses to Him – Bruce Milne
ISBN 978-1-84550-507-3

Romans: The Revelation of God's Righteousness – Paul Barnett
ISBN 978-1-84550-269-0

1 Corinthians: Holiness and Hope of a Rescued People – Paul Barnett
ISBN 978-1-85792-598-2

*2 Corinthians: The Glories & Responsibilities of Christian Servic*e – Geoffrey Grogan
ISBN 978-1-84550-252-2

*Ephesians: Encouragement and Joy in Chris*t – Paul Gardner
ISBN 978-1-84550-264-5

1 & 2 Thessalonians: Triumphs and Trials of a Consecrated Church – Richard Mayhue
ISBN 978-1-85792-452-7

James: Wisdom for the Community – Christopher Morgan/Dale Ellenburg
ISBN 978-1-84550-335-2

1 Peter – Derek Cleave
ISBN 978-1-85792-337-7

2 Peter & Jude – Paul Gardner
ISBN 978-1-85792-338-4

1, 2 & 3 John – Michael Eaton
ISBN 978-1-85792-152-6

Revelation: The Compassion and Protection of Christ – Paul Gardner
ISBN 978-1-85792-329-2

FOCUS • ON • THE • BIBLE
ACTS
WITNESSES TO HIM
BRUCE MILNE

Acts

Witnesses to Him

Bruce Milne

Acts is an exciting story of church growth despite inner problems and outward conflict. The Book of Acts describes the spread of the gospel throughout the known world of the first century and the establishment of Christian churches in many different places. As the gospel entered new places, its preachers often faced opposition from followers of other religions, and sometimes this opposition extended to include political persecution. Nevertheless, within a generation the gospel had spread from Jerusalem to Rome and beyond. While Luke, the writer of Acts was a historian, Acts is not merely historical but also provide principles and lessons for contemporary churches to imitate as they continue to spread the apostolic gospel today.

Bruce Milne is a well-respected pastor and theologian who pastored First Baptist Church, Vancouver, Canada, for eighteen years.

ISBN: 978-1-84550-507-3

FOCUS • ON • THE • BIBLE
2 KINGS
THE POWER AND THE FURY
'Excellent, crisp, lively exposition.'
Bibliotheca Sacra'
DALE RALPH DAVIS

2 Kings

The Power and the Fury

Dale Ralph Davis

2 Kings provides a fast-paced narrative of insight into the history of Israel under its monarchy. This book is a continuation of the narrative begun in 1 Samuel, and continued through 2 Samuel and 1 Kings. Ralph finishes it off with a captivating and rewarding journey through 2 Kings.

Written between 561 BC and 538 BC, 2 Kings gives us a warning about the consequences of sin, especially the catastrophic repercussions of Israel's love affair with idolatry. Despite struggling with other problems, we see that the Jewish people learned from their experience, They never made a mistake of this enormity again.

Through prophets such as Elisha and Elijah we see God's compassion for his people and the opportunity for repentance. An opportunity spoilt by Judah, climaxing with the subjugation of the kingdom by the Babylonians.

Illuminating, accessible and laced with his unique sense of humour, Davis' practical devotional expository applies events to the contemporary reader providing parallels to alert us in the 21st century.

Dale Ralph Davis lives in rural Tennessee with his wife. Prior to that he was pastor of Woodland Presbyterian Church, Hattiesburg, Mississippi and Professor of Old Testament at Reformed Theological Seminary, Jackson, Mississippi.

ISBN: 978-1-84550-096-2

ALSO INCLUDES
The Westminster Confession Of Faith
The Larger Catechism
The Shorter Catechism
The Belgic Confession
The Heidelberg Catechism
The Canons Of Dordt
THE WESTMINSTER CONFESSION OF FAITH STUDY BOOK
A STUDY GUIDE FOR CHURCHES
JOSEPH A. PIPA, JR.

The Westminster Confession of Faith Study Book

A Study Guide for Churches

Joseph A. Pipa, Jr.

The Westminster Confession is a foundational document for countless churches worldwide. Churches of all sizes claim it as their confession, and hold to it with varying degrees of closeness. However, how many people actually have any real knowledge of the Confession or feel it is only of relevance to their church leaders?

Joseph Pipa's study book is the ideal tool for all Christians who seek to gain a better understanding of their faith through exploring an integral cornerstone of Reformed Christianity. Pipa has produced an accessible, user-friendly study aid, which illuminates the Westminster Confession for all Christians, showing it is not just a document for intellectual theologians, but is as relevant in our own lives today, as when it was written.

Also includes The Westminster Confession of Faith, The Larger Catechism, The Shorter Catechism, The Belgic Confession, The Heidelberg Catechism and the Canons of Dordt.

ISBN: 978-1-84550-030-6

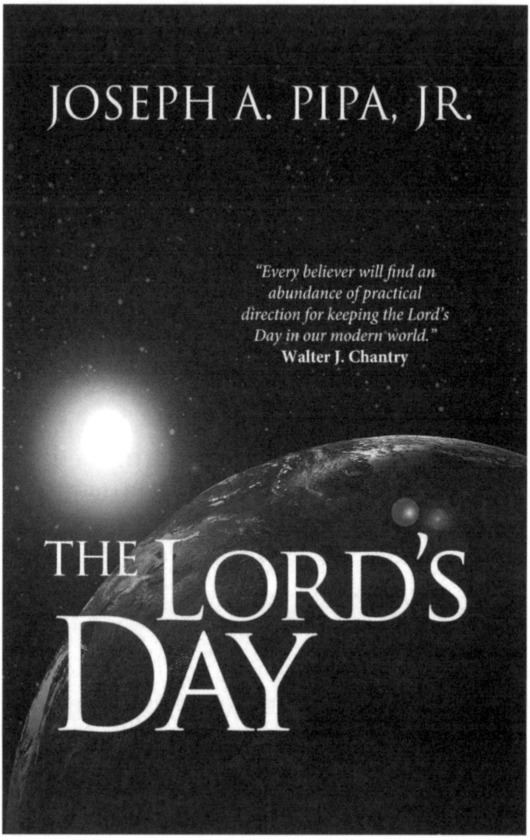
JOSEPH A. PIPA, JR.
"Every believer will find an abundance of practical direction for keeping the Lord's Day in our modern world."
Walter J. Chantry
THE LORD'S DAY

The Lord's Day

Joseph A. Pipa, Jr.

Joey Pipa is known for his warm pastoral application of tough scriptural principles. Here, he takes an authoritative look at the 'first day' – the one set aside by the church for worship. This is an area of Church practice in which we find liberal interpretations practiced by evangelical churches and vice versa – often without too much thought involved and an emphasis upon what 'feels' right.

Many of these issues are considered unclear, optional, divisive – with the unhealthy result that we tend to avoid the subject altogether.

Are we missing out on God's blessing by the way we celebrate the Lord's Day – are we too legalistic, too lax? Is the Spirit grieved by our disrespect to God or frustrated by our thralldom to unnecessary restrictions? These and other questions are answered in *The Lord's Day*.

A splendid book ... shows the delightful character of God's provision of a day of worship and rest for his people. The church has needed this book. Use your Sunday afternoons to read it!

W. Robert Godfrey,
President, Westminster Seminary in California, Escondido, California

Written with the plainness and warmth of pastoral experience which will benefit the youngest Christian. Every believer will find an abundance of practical direction for keeping the Lord's Day in our modern world.

Walter J. Chantry,
Grace Baptist Church, Carlisle, Pennsylvania

ISBN: 978-1-85792-201-1

MENTOR
Galatians
A MENTOR COMMENTARY
David McWilliams

Galatians

A Mentor Commentary

David McWilliams

Galatians was probably the first letter written by the apostle Paul. The concern with which he deals – the relationship of Christian believers to the Mosaic law – was a major problem in the apostolic church, and remains so today. As then, this issue affects our understanding of the doctrines of justification; becoming right with God and sanctification; developing a holy life. A misunderstanding and a wrong application of this relationship can result in many pastoral concerns including the nature of assurance; the basis of salvation and the unity of the church; what is required for membership. David McWilliam brings to us an awareness of Paul's teaching on these doctrines which will help us understand and refute the errors of the "new perspective" on his writings.

> Timely, lucid, and reliable, this is an excellent commentary for preachers, Bible study leaders and others. David McWilliams admirably succeeds in his aim for brevitas and claritas, the two qualities in commentators that Calvin most commended. He distils a great deal of scholarship into uncluttered and readable prose. Paul's message in Galatians has rarely been so urgently needed as today, when justification only by faith is under attack from many sides. McWilliams explains it with judicious care.
>
> *Robert Letham,*
> *Senior Tutor in Systematic and Historical Theology,*
> *Wales Evangelical School of Theology*

David McWilliams has been the senior pastor at Covenant Presbyterian Church, Lakeland, Florida for 20 years. He has a passion for Christ-centred preaching and wished to apply the theology of the life of the church.

ISBN: 978-1-84550-452-6

Christian Focus Publications

publishes books for all ages

Our mission statement –

STAYING FAITHFUL

In dependence upon God we seek to impact the world through literature faithful to His infallible Word, the Bible. Our aim is to ensure that the Lord Jesus Christ is presented as the only hope to obtain forgiveness of sin, live a useful life and look forward to heaven with Him.

REACHING OUT

Christ's last command requires us to reach out to our world with His gospel. We seek to help fulfil that by publishing books that point people towards Jesus and help them develop a Christ-like maturity. We aim to equip all levels of readers for life, work, ministry and mission.

Books in our adult range are published in three imprints.

Christian Focus contains popular works including biographies, commentaries, basic doctrine and Christian living. Our children's books are also published in this imprint.

Mentor focuses on books written at a level suitable for Bible College and seminary students, pastors, and other serious readers. The imprint includes commentaries, doctrinal studies, examination of current issues and church history.

Christian Heritage contains classic writings from the past.

Christian Focus Publications, Ltd
Geanies House, Fearn, Ross-shire,
IV20 1TW, Scotland, United Kingdom
info@christianfocus.com

www.christianfocus.com